A TEXT-BOOK OF SOCIOLOGY

WITH DETAILED TABLE OF CONTENTS

LESTER F. WARD
JAMES Q. DEALEY

ALICIA EDITIONS

DETAILED TABLE OF CONTENTS

PREFACE	1
BIBLIOGRAPHY	3

INTRODUCTION

1. THE SCIENCE OF SOCIOLOGY	11
1. Man unsocial by nature.	11
2. Human and animal societies contrasted.	11
3. Pure and applied Sociology.	12
4. Mathematical sociology.	13
5. Meaning of the term *science*.	13
6. Sociology a science.	13
7. The progress of science.	14
8. Progress of sociology.	14
2. CLASSIFICATION OF THE SCIENCES	16
9. Serial classification.	16
10. Comte's classification.	17
11. The true order of study.	17
12. Synoptical classification.	18
13. Filiation.	18
14. Basal sciences for sociology.	19
15. Sympodial development.	19
16. In botany.	19
17. In evolution.	20
18. In human history.	21
19. Anthropologic sympodes.	21
20. National decadence.	22
3. DATA OF SOCIOLOGY	23
21. Classification of data.	23
22. The general sciences.	24
23. The requirement of a general education.	24
24. The special social sciences.	25
25. Sociology and economics.	25
26. Relations to other sciences.	26

27. Purpose of sociological study.	26
28. Importance of sociology.	27

4. METHODOLOGY 29
- 29. Importance of method. 29
- 30. Logical sequence of ideas. 30
- 31. Science as a domain of laws. 30
- 32. Generalization. 31
- 33. In anthropology. 31
- 34. In great primary wants and passions. 31
- 35. Law in history. 32
- 36. The law of parsimony. 33
- 37. Shown in the pursuit of interests. 33

5. THE SUBJECT-MATTER OF SOCIOLOGY 35
- 38. Human achievement. 36
- 39. The natural history of man. 36
- 40. History of culture. 36
- 41. Distinction between organic and social evolution. 37
- 42. What is civilization? 37
- 43. Utilization of force and matter. 38
- 44. Material wealth. 38
- 45. Inventions as achievements. 39
- 46. Tools of the mind. 39
- 47. The industrial arts. 40
- 48. Protective achievements. 40
- 49. Human institutions as achievements. 41
- 50. Social continuity. 41
- 51. In historic races only. 42
- 52. Achievement through knowledge. 43
- 53. Genius. 43
- 54. Pessimism. 44
- 55. The love of achievement. 44
- 56. The immortality of deeds. 45

Part I

ORIGIN AND CLASSIFICATION OF THE
SOCIAL FORCES

6. CREATIVE SYNTHESIS 49
- 57. Definition. 49
- 58. Creation. 50

59. Social ideals.	50
60. The poetic idea.	51
61. Poesis.	52
62. Genesis.	53
63. Each science a creative synthesis.	53
64. Sociology also.	53
65. The social mind a synthesis.	54
66. Synthetic creations of nature.	54
67. Cosmic creations.	55
68. Products and properties.	56
69. Development sympodial.	56
70. The filiation of the sciences.	57
7. THE DYNAMIC AGENT	58
I. The Feelings	59
71. Two prime agents in society.	59
72. Cosmic forces.	59
73. Social force.	60
74. Psychic forces.	60
75. Psychological basis of sociology.	61
76. The feelings subjective.	61
77. Appetition.	61
78. Desire.	62
79. Philosophy of desire.	62
80. Original desires.	63
81. Derivative desires.	63
82. Biological origin of the subjective faculties.	64
II. The Conative Faculty	65
83. Energy of nature.	65
84. Mind force.	65
85. Desire a force.	65
86. The emotions as forces.	66
III. The Soul	66
87. Meaning of the term.	66
88. Its function.	67
IV. The Will	67
89. Meaning of the term.	67
90. Optimism and pessimism.	68
91. Meliorism.	68

8. CLASSIFICATION OF THE SOCIAL FORCES 70
  92. Basis of classification. 70
  93. Choice of terms. 71
  94. Classification. 72
  95. Meaning of terms. 72
  96. Relationships among the social forces. 73
  97. Paradoxes. 73
  98. Relative value of feeling and function. 74
  99. Enjoyment as an end. 75
  100. Fear of natural phenomena. 75
  101. Utilization of social forces. 76

Part II
NATURE OF THE SOCIAL FORCES

9. THE ONTOGENETIC FORCES 81
  102. The struggle for subsistence. 82
  I. Exploitation 82
  103. Cannibalism. 82
  104. Slavery. 83
  105. Labor. 84
  106. Forced Labor. 84
  107. Labor under the lash. 85
  108. The ruling classes. 85
  II. Property 86
  109. Communal. 86
  110. Origin of individual property. 86
  111. Rights in property. 87
  112. Property as wealth. 87
  113. Pursuit of wealth the mainspring of activity. 87
  III. Production 88
  114. Slave production. 88
  115. Machinofacture. 89
  116. Importance of production. 89
  IV. Social Distribution 90
  117. The surplus. 90
  118. The Ricardian law. 90
  119. Causes of social distribution. 90
  V. Consumption 91
  120. Animal consumption. 91
  121. Palatableness of food. 92

122. Protective wants.	92
123. Influence of comfort on development.	93
124. Physical importance of ample nutrition.	93
125. Nutrition essential to mental superiority.	94

10. THE PHYLOGENETIC FORCES 96

126. Two theories of sex relationship.	97
127. I. The Androcentric Theory.	97
II. The Gynæcocentric Theory	98
128. Female sex primary.	98
129. Biological development of the male.	98
130. Gynæcocracy.	99
131. Androcracy.	99
132. Andreclexis.	100
133. Subjection of woman.	101
134. Classification.	101
III. Classification of the Phylogenetic Forces	101
(1) Natural Love.	102
135. Definition.	102
136. Purity of natural love.	102
137. Regulation.	103
138. Celibacy.	103
139. Natural love a social necessity.	103
(2) Romantic Love	104
140. Worth of social feelings.	104
141. Development of emotional centers.	104
142. Beginnings of romantic love.	105
143. Ampheclexis.	106
144. Natura naturans.	106
145. Function of romantic love.	107
146. Its influence on social organization.	107
(3) Conjugal Love	109
147. Essential quality of conjugal love.	109
148. Monogamy necessary.	109
149. Equality of the sexes essential.	110
150. Morality of monogamy.	110
151. Social influence of conjugal love.	111
(4) Maternal Love	111
152. Meaning of the term.	111
153. Maternal love a conservative principle.	112
154. Its coming importance.	113

(5) Consanguineal Love	113
155. Love of kindred.	113
156. Its social influence.	113
11. THE SOCIOGENETIC FORCES	115
157. Classification.	116
I. The Moral Forces	117
158. Two kinds.	117
(1) Race Morality	117
159. Based on race preservation.	117
160. Race morality as custom.	117
161. Essential nature of race morality.	118
(2) Individual Morality	118
162. Altruism.	118
163. Sympathy.	119
164. Distinction between altruism and sympathy.	119
(3) Ethical Dualism	120
165. Altruism a relative term.	120
166. Broadening of altruism.	120
167. Humanitarianism.	121
168. Philozoism.	121
169. Love of nature.	122
170. Ethical monism.	122
II. The aesthetic Forces	123
171. Three stages of development.	123
172. Imitation and imagination.	123
173. Art.	124
174. Symmetry in art.	124
175. Modern idea of art.	125
176. Art a socializing agency.	125
177. Art as an end in itself.	126
178. Social value of art.	126
III. The Intellectual Forces	127
179. Intellectual feeling.	127
180. (1) Acquirement of knowledge.	127
181. (2) Discovery of truth.	128
182. Interest in the discovery of truth.	128
183. Generalization.	129
184. (3) Impartation of information.	129
185. The savage mind.	130
186. The leisure class.	130

187. Democracy.	131
188. Place of religion in intellectual development.	132
189. Kidd's *Social evolution*.	133
190. Religion and science.	133

Part III
ACTION OF THE SOCIAL FORCES IN THE SPONTANEOUS DEVELOPMENT OF SOCIETY

12. SOCIAL STATICS	137
191. Social mechanics.	138
192. Classification.	138
193. The dynamic agent.	139
I. The Principle of Synergy	139
194. Definition.	139
195. Cosmic dualism.	139
196. Effects of cosmic dualism in the social world.	140
197. True nature of synergy.	140
198. Illustrated by artificial structures.	141
199. Synergy in the formation of organic structures.	141
200. Structure and function contrasted.	142
201. Structure and function statical.	142
202. Social structures.	143
203. Struggle for structure.	144
II. The Social Order	144
204. Definition.	144
205. Human institutions.	145
206. Primary and secondary institutions.	145
207. Marriage.	146
208. Religion.	146
209. Law.	146
210. Morality.	146
211. Political institutions.	147
212. Language.	147
213. The nature of social structures.	148
13. SOCIAL STATICS (CONTINUED)	150
III. Social Assimilation.	151
214. Original heterogeneity.	151
215. Causes of heterogeneity.	151
216. Imitation and invention.	152

217. Expansion.	152
218. Social differentiation.	153
219. The horde.	154
220. The golden age.	154
221. Its duration.	155
222. Social integration.	155
223. Process of integration.	156
224. The struggle of races.	156
225. Conquest and subjugation.	156
IV. Social Karyokinesis	157
226. The stages in amalgamation.	157
227. (1) Caste.	157
228. (2) Inequality.	158
229. (3) Law.	158
230. (4) The juridical state.	159
231. (5) Formation of a people.	159
232. Interest unites.	160
233. Other influences.	160
234. Social chemistry.	161
235. (6) The nation.	162
V. Compound Assimilation	162
236. Compound races.	162
237. The lower races.	164
VI. 238. Pacific Assimilation	164
14. SOCIAL DYNAMICS.	166
239. Definition.	167
240. Dynamic movements.	167
241. Social progress.	168
242. Social stagnation.	168
243. Social degeneration.	170
244. Social instability.	171
Dynamic Principles	172
245. Definition of these principles.	172
I. Difference of Potential	173
246. Definition.	173
247. The principle of sex.	173
248. Asexual reproduction.	173
249. Crossing of strains.	174
250. Effect of uniform environment.	174
251. Mingling of cultures.	175

252. Progress as the result.	175
253. "Dynamic density"	176
254. Influence of war on human progress.	176
255. Western civilization.	176
256. Theory of dominant races.	177
15. DYNAMIC PRINCIPLES (CONTINUED)	179
II. Innovation	180
257. Fortuitous variation.	180
258. Social innovation.	180
259. Innovation through the leisure class.	181
260. "Instinct of workmanship".	181
261. Final criterion of a dynamic action.	182
III. Conation	183
262. Explanation of the term.	183
263. Transformation of the environment.	184
264. Social progress not desired.	184
265. Effort the dynamic principle.	185
266. Dynamic efforts are social.	185
267. Matter dynamic.	186

Part IV

ORIGIN AND NATURE OF THE TELIC
AGENT

16. THE DIRECTIVE AGENT	189
Introduction	190
268. Social progress.	190
269. The pessimistic attitude.	190
270. The error of pessimism.	190
I. The Objective Faculties	191
271. Classification of sensations.	191
272. Indifferent sensation.	191
273. Sensation.	192
274. Steps in the mental process.	192
II. Control of the Dynamic Agent	193
275. The two agencies of society.	193
276. The genetic and the telic methods contrasted.	194
277. The two classes of social phenomena.	194
III. The Final Cause	195
278. The efficient cause.	195
279. The final cause.	195

280. Telesis.	195
281. Thought utilizing force.	196
IV. The Method of Mind	196
282. Prodigality of nature.	196
283. Telic economy.	197
284. Importance of the directive agent.	197
17. THE GENESIS OF MIND	199
285. The intellect.	199
286. (1) Indifferent Sensation	200
287. (2) Tentation and Intuition.	200
288. (3) Intuitive Perception (4) Intuitive Reason	201
289. What is meant by animal reason.	201
290. Illustrations of intuitive reasoning. (5) Indirection.	202
291. Meaning of the term.	202
292. The ruse. (6) Moral Indirection	203
293. Principal forms of deception:	204
294. Against animals.	204
295. Against inferior human beings.	205
296. In various kinds of occupations.	205
297. In national and social life.	206
298. The intent and the end.	206
18. THE GENESIS OF MIND (CONTINUED)	208
(7) Material Indirection	208
299. Ingenuity.	209
300. Invention. (8) Inventive Genius	210
301. The characteristic of genius.	210
302. Instruction in invention.	211
303. (9) Creative Genius	211
(10) Philosophic Genius	212
304. In origin advantageous.	212
305. The emancipation of the intellect.	213
306. Beginnings of philosophy.	213
307. Phenomena of mind.	213
308. The study of the cosmos.	214
309. Its results.	214
310. Observation.	215
311. The scientific spirit.	215
312. The philosophic spirit.	216
313. Scientific genius.	216
314. The non-advantageous faculties.	216

Part V
ACTION OF THE TELIC AGENT IN SOCIAL ACHIEVEMENT

19. SOCIAL ACHIEVEMENT THROUGH THE CONQUEST OF NATURE	221
Introduction	222
315. Individual telesis.	222
316. The intermediate step.	222
317. Social or collective telesis.	223
318. The study of society made scientific.	223
I. Human Invention	224
319. Empirical art.	224
320. Primitive invention.	224
321. Man's capacity for conquest.	225
322. Modification of the natural.	225
323. Pre-Hellenic and Greek art.	226
324. Westward movement of thought.	227
325. In mediæval period.	227
326. The modern era.	228
327. Eighteenth and nineteenth centuries.	228
328. Power of invention.	229
II. Scientific Discovery	230
329. Invention and discovery.	230
330. The mission of science.	230
331. The stage of empiricism.	230
332. The Greek period.	231
333. Mediæval period.	232
334. Discoveries of the eighteenth century.	232
335. The problem of life.	233
336. The truth of biology.	233
337. "Origin of species."	234
338. The law of evolution.	235
20. SOCIALIZATION OF ACHIEVEMENT	236
339. Human achievement.	237
340. Socialization.	237
I. Social Regulation	238
341. Classification.	238
342. Development of social regulation.	238
343. Legal regulation.	239
344. The juridical state.	239

345. Importance of the state.	240
II. Collective Achievement	241
346. Conquest of man by society.	241
347. Necessity of collective regulation.	242
348. Growth of collectivism.	243
349. Collectivism and individualism.	243
III. Social Invention.	244
350. Backwardness of social science.	244
351. Analysis of an invention.	245
352. Social invention defined.	245
353. "Attractive legislation."	246
354. Social distribution.	246
355. The social increment.	247
IV. Social Appropriation	247
356. Knowledge as achievement.	247
357. Social hereditary.	247
358. Duty of society.	248
359. The most useful knowledge.	248
360. Need of a scientific system.	249
361. The fundamental principle.	249
362. Hindrances to civilization.	250
363. Public education.	250
364. Socialization of education.	251

PREFACE

This work is the outcome of a demand for a short text-book that would contain in essence a clear and concise statement of the field of sociology, its scientific basis, its principles as far as these are at present known, and its purposes.

In the preparation of this book emphasis has been placed on three points: first, on the social forces as the dynamic agent working unconsciously toward natural individual ends and consciously toward collective achievement under the direction of the intellect; second, on the importance of material achievement as the basis of psychical development, and on the necessity of systematic general instruction in the fundamental principles of knowledge as a basis for right social life; and third, on the arrangement of the material so as to facilitate its use for purposes of reading clubs and classes.

The work is based fundamentally on *Pure sociology*, but is in no respect a mere condensation of it. Using the material of this larger and more complete work as a basis, and supplementing it by numerous references to Dr. Ward's other sociological writings, an attempt has been made to prepare a sort of handbook containing in epitome the essential elements of a system of sociology.

It is, of course, fully admitted that other writers looking at the subject from a different standpoint may reach conclusions somewhat unlike those here advanced, but each contribution toward sociological theorizing has its own special value, and adds to the sum total of scientific knowledge.

Obviously the real justification for such elementary text-books in sociology must be found in the desire to present, in simple and popular form, those scientific principles that must ultimately be used as guides for collective activity. Action based on accurate knowledge is the keystone to social attainment.

Special acknowledgment is made to Professor George Grafton Wilson of Brown University for many kindly and valuable suggestions.

JAMES QUAYLE DEALEY, PH.D.
PROFESSOR OF SOCIAL AND POLITICAL SCIENCE IN BROWN UNIVERSITY
AND
LESTER FRANK WARD, LL.D.
OF THE SMITHSONIAN INSTITUTION AT WASHINGTON, D.C.
FEBRUARY 15, 1905.

BIBLIOGRAPHY

(References to these works in the following pages will be by titles only.)

The entire field of sociology is so vast that every bibliography must for practical purposes confine itself to a definite area. The following list includes works that especially supplement the subject-matter of this book. The list is by no means complete, but it is hoped that the selection made will prove suggestive to librarians and useful to the student for purposes of reference. A few titles of well-nigh indispensable foreign works are given, but these as far as possible in translation. An excellent classified bibliography of similar books and articles may be found in Giddings's *Principles of sociology*, pp. 423-442.

A list of Dr. Ward's more important articles on sociological subjects is added.

- *American journal of sociology*. Published bimonthly, first number July, 1895. University of Chicago.
- *The annals of the American academy of political and social science*. Published bimonthly, first number July, 1890. Philadelphia.

These both contain many thoughtful and helpful discussions of current social theory and practice.

- *Adams, Brooks.* The law of civilization and decay. 1895. New York.
- *Bachofen, Johann Jacob.* Das Mutterrecht. 1861. Stuttgart.
- *Bagehot, Walter.* Physics and politics. New edition. 1902. Appleton. New York.
- *Balfour, Arthur J.* The foundations of belief. 1895. London and New York.
- *Bluntschli, Johann Caspar.* The theory of the state. 1892. Macmillan. New York.
- *Comte, Auguste.* Cours de philosophie positive. Six volumes. Troisième édition. 1869. Paris. The positive philosophy of Auguste Comte. Translated and condensed by Harriet Martineau. Two volumes, 1853. Three volumes, 1896. Macmillan. New York and London. Système de politique positive. Four volumes. 1851-1854. Paris. Positive polity. Translated by Professor E. S. Beesley, London. Four volumes. 1875-1877. Longmans.
- *Cooley, Charles Horton.* Human nature and the social order. 1902. Scribner.
- *Cornish, Francis Warre.* Chivalry. 1901. Macmillan.
- *Crozier, John Beattie.* Civilization and progress. Third edition. 1892. London. History of intellectual development; on the lines of modem evolution. Vols. I and III. 1897. 1901. London.
- *Durkheim, Émile.* De la division du travail social. 1893, Paris. Les règles de la méthode sociologique. 1895. Paris.
- *Ellis, Havelock.* Man and woman. Third edition. 1902. London.
- *Ely, Richard T.* Evolution of industrial society. 1903. Macmillan.
- *Espinas, Alfred.* Des sociétés animales. Deuxième édition. 1878. Paris.
- *Fairbanks, Arthur.* Introduction to sociology. Third edition. 1903. Scribner.
- *Fouillée, Alfred.* La science sociale contemporaine. Deuxième édition. 1895. Paris.
- *Fustel de Coulanges.* The ancient city. Translated by Willard Small. 1896. Lee and Shepard. London.
- *Galton, Francis.* Hereditary genius. New edition. 1892. London.
- *Geddes and Thomson.* Evolution of sex. Revised edition. 1901. Scribner.
- *Giddings, Franklin H.* Principles Of sociology. Third edition. 1896. Macmillan. Elements of sociology. 1898. Macmillan. Inductive

sociology. 1901. Macmillan. Article on modern sociology. *International Monthly*. Vol. II. November, 1900. Pages 536-554.
- *Gilman, Mrs. Charlotte Stetson.* Women and economics. Second edition. 1899. Small.
- *Greef, Guillaume de.* Les lois sociologiques. Deuxième édition. 1896. Paris. Introduction à la sociologie. Two volumes. 1886-1889. Bruxelles et Paris. This is being continued in a series of articles in the *American journal of sociology*, which began January, 1903.
- *Gumplowicz, Ludwig.* Der Rassenkampf. 1883. Innsbruck. Grundriss der Sociologie. 1905. 2 Aufl. Wien. English translation by F. W. Moore. 1899. Annals. Philadelphia. See also article, An Austrian appreciation of Lester F. Ward. *American journal of sociology*. March, 1905.
- *Haeckel, Ernst.* Anthropogenie. 1874. Leipzig. And review of the same by Lester F. Ward, undertitle of Haeckel's Genesis of man. Pages 64. 1879. Stern and Co. Philadelphia.
- *Headley, F. W.* Problems of evolution. 1901. Crowell.
- *Howard, George E.* A history of matrimonial institutions. Three volumes. 1904. Chicago.
- *James, William.* The principles of psychology. Two volumes. 1890. Holt. New York.
- *Keller, Albert Galloway.* Homeric society. A sociological study of the Illiad and Odyssey. 1902. New York.
- *Kidd, Benjamin.* Social evolution. New edition. 1898. Macmillan.
- *Le Bon, Gustave.* The crowd; a study of the popular mind. New edition. 1903. Macmillan. The psychology of peoples. 1898. New York.
- *Letourneau, Charles.* La sociologie d'après l'ethnographie. Troisième édition. 1892. Paris. Sociology based on ethnology. Translated by H. M. Trollope. 1881. London. Property; its origin and development. New edition. 1901. Scribner.
- *Lilienfeld, Paul von.* Zur Vertheidigung der organischen Methode in der Sociologie. 1898. Berlin.
- *Loria, Achille.*The economic foundations of society. Translated by Lindley M. Keasbey. 1899. Scribner.
- *Mackenzie, John Stuart.* Introduction to social philosophy. Second revised edition. 1895. Macmillan.
- *Mason, Otis Tufton.* Woman's share in primitive culture. 1894. Appleton. New York.

- *Morgan, Lewis Henry.* Ancient society. 1877. New York.
- *Morrison, G. S.* The new epoch, as developed by the manufacture of power. 1903. Houghton.
- *Nietzsche, Frederick.* A genealogy of morals. 1896. Philadelphia.
- *Novicow, Jacques.* Les luttes entre sociétés humaines. 1893. Paris.
- *Patten, Simon Nelson.* The theory of social forces. Supplement to the Annals. January, 1896. Philadelphia.
- *Ratzenhofer, Gustav.* Die sociologische Erkenntnis. 1898. Leipzig.
- *Ross, Edward Alsworth.* Social control; a survey of the foundations of order. 1901. Macmillan. Moot points in sociology. A series of eight articles. *American journal of sociology.* May, 1903-September, 1904.
- *Schäffle, Albert Eberhard Friedrich.* Bau und Leben des socialen Körpers. Two volumes. New edition. 1896. Tübingen.
- *Schopenhauer, Arthur.* Die Welt als Wille und Vorstellung. Fourth edition. 1873. Two volumes. Leipzig. The world as will and idea. Translated by R. B. Haldane and J. Kemp. 1891. Three volumes. London.
- *Simmel, G.* Über sociale Differenzierung. 1890. Leipzig. The sociology of conflict: series of three articles. *American journal of sociology.* January-May, 1904.
- *Simons, Sarah E.* Social decadence. Annals. Vol. XVIII. September, 1901. Pages 251-274. Social assimilation: series of five articles. *American journal of sociology.* May, 1901-January, 1902. (Last article includes a lengthy bibliography.)
- *Small, Albion W.* The significance of sociology for ethics. 1902. University of Chicago. The methodology of the social problem. 1898. University of Chicago. The scope of sociology: series of nine articles. *American journal of sociology.* January, 1900-July, 1904. Comments in criticism of Pure sociology. See under Ward, Lester F.
- *Spencer, Herbert.* Social statics and The man *versus* the state. In one volume. The study of sociology. The principles of sociology. Three volumes. Education; intellectual, moral, and physical. All by Appleton. New York. Review of Spencer's Autobiography by Lester F. Ward. *Science.* June 10, 1904. Pages 873-879.
- *Stuckenberg, John H, W.* Sociology. Two volumes. 1903. Putnam. Introduction to the study of sociology. 1898. Armstrong.
- *Tarde, Gabriel.* Laws of imitation. Translated by E. C. Parsons. 1903. Holt. Social laws. Translated by H. C. Warren. 1899.

Macmillan. L'opposition universelle. 1897, Paris. Le logique sociale. 1894. Paris. Les transformations du droit. Quatrième édition. 1903, Paris
- *Veblen, Thorstein B.* Theory of the leisure class; an economic study in the evolution of institutions. 1899. Macmillan. And review by Lester F. Ward. *American journal of sociology.* Vol. V. May, 1900. The theory of business enterprise. 1904. Scribner. New York.
- *Wallace, Alfred Russel.* Progress of the century. 1901. Harper. The wonderful century; its successes and its failures. 1898. New York.
- *Ward, Lester F.* Dynamic sociology. Two volumes. 1883. Appleton. Psychic factors of civilization. 1893. Ginn. Outlines of sociology. 1898. Macmillan. Pure sociology. 1903. Macmillan. And Comments in criticism by Albion W. Small. *American journal of sociology.* Vol. VIII. March, 1903. Vol. IX. November, 1903, and January-March, 1904.
- *Westermarck, Edward.* The history of human marriage. 1891. London; New York.
- *White, Andrew D.* A history of the warfare of science with theology in christendom. Two volumes. 1896. New York.
- *Willoughby, W. W.* The nature of the state. New edition. 1903. Macmillan. Social justice; a critical essay. 1900. Macmillan.
- *Wilson, George G.* The place of social philosophy. *Journal of social science.* No. XXXII. November, 1894. Pages 139-143.
- *Winship, Albert Edward.* Jukes-Edwards; a study in education and heredity. 1900. Harrisburg, Pennsylvania.

SELECTED ARTICLES ON SOCIOLOGICAL TOPICS By LESTER F. WARD

- Our better halves. *The forum.* Vol. VI. November, 1888. Pages 266-275.
- Genius and woman's intuition. *The forum,* Vol. IX. June, 1890. Pages 401-408.
- The exemption of women from labor. *The monist.* Vol. IV. April, 1894. Pages 385-395.

- What shall the public schools teach? *The forum.* Vol. V. July, 1888. Pages 574-583.
- The essential nature of religion. *International journal of ethics.* Vol. VIII. January 1898. Pages 169-192.
- Ethical aspects of social science. *International journal of ethics.* Vol. VI. July, 1896. Pages 441-456.
- Broadening the way to success. *The forum.* Vol. II. December, 1886. Pages 340-350.
- Some social and economic paradoxes. *American anthropologist.* Vol. II. April, 1889. Pages 119-132.
- The psychologic basis of social economics. *Proc. A. A. A. S.* XLI. 1892. Pages 301-321. Condensed in *Annals American academy of political and social science.* Vol. III. January, 1893. Pages 464-482.
- Static and dynamic sociology. *Political science quarterly.* Vol. X. No. 2. June, 1895. Pages 203-220.
- Moral and material progress contrasted. Trans. Anthropological Society. Vol. III. 1885. Washington. Pages 121-136.
- Utilitarian economics. *American journal of sociology.* Vol. III. January, 1898. Pages 520-536.
- The transmission of culture. *The forum.* Vol. XI. May, 1891. Pages 312-319.
- Weismann's concessions. *Popular science monthly.* Vol. XLV. June, 1894. Pages 175-184.
- The natural storage of energy. *The monist.* Vol. V. January, 1895. Pages 247-263.
- Status of the mind problem. Special Papers, No. 1, Anthropological Society. 1894. Washington. Pages 18.
- Social differentiation and social integration. *American journal of sociology.* Vol. VIII. May, 1903. Pages 721-745.
- Sociology at the Paris Exposition of 1900. *Report commissioner of education.* Chapter XXVIII. 1899-1900.
- Contemporary sociology. *American journal of sociology.* Vol. VII. January, March, May, 1902. Reprinted as brochure. Chicago. Pages 70.
- Herbert Spencer's Sociology. *Independent.* March 31, 1904. Pages 730-734.
- Evolution of social structures. *American journal of sociology.* Vol. X. March, 1905. Pages 589-605.

INTRODUCTION

1

THE SCIENCE OF SOCIOLOGY

- 1. Man unsocial by nature.
- 2. Human and animal societies contrasted.
- 3. Pure and applied Sociology.
- 4. Mathematical sociology.
- 5. Meaning of the term science.
- 6. Sociology a science.
- 7. The progress of science.
- 8. Progress of sociology.

1. MAN UNSOCIAL BY NATURE.

Man is not *naturally* a social being; human society is purely a product of his reason and arose by insensible degrees, *pari passu* with the development of his brain. In other words, human association is the result of the perceived advantage which it yields, and came into existence only in proportion as that advantage was perceived by the only faculty capable of perceiving it, the intellect.

2. HUMAN AND ANIMAL SOCIETIES CONTRASTED.

For these reasons, human society is generically distinct from all animal societies.* It is essentially rational and artificial, while animal association is essentially instinctive and natural. The adaptation in the former is incomplete, while in the latter it is practically complete. Hence, the same principles do not apply to human and animal sociology. The latter is essentially a biological study; and while psychological considerations are potent in both, those that belong to animal sociology relate exclusively to feeling, while those that belong to human sociology relate chiefly to the intellect. The science of sociology, therefore, is the study of human association, including whatever conduces to it or modifies it. In calling sociology a science it is not claimed that it has as yet been established as a science. But it is maintained that it is in process of establishment, and this by the same method by which all other sciences are established.

3. PURE AND APPLIED SOCIOLOGY.

It is but natural that those who regard sociology as a science should divide the science, as other sciences are divided, into the two natural departments, pure and applied. The terms *pure* and *applied* may be used in sociology in the same sense as in other sciences. Pure science is theoretical; applied science, practical. The first seeks to establish the principles of the science; the second points out their actual or possible applications, and deals with artificial means of accelerating the natural and spontaneous processes of nature. The method of pure science is research, and its object is knowledge. In pure sociology, the essential nature of society is the object pursued. But nothing can be said to be known until the antecedent conditions are known, out of which it has sprung. By pure sociology, then, is meant a treatment of the phenomena and laws of society as it is, an explanation of the processes by which social phenomena take place, a search for the antecedent conditions by which the observed facts have been brought into existence, reaching back as far as the state of human knowledge will permit into the psychologic, biologic, and cosmic causes of the existing social state of man. Pure sociology has no concern with what society *ought* to be, or with any social ideals. It confines itself strictly with the present and the past, allowing the future to take care of itself. It totally ignores the purpose of the science, and aims at truth wholly for its own sake.

---

* Espinas, *Des sociétés animales*.

4. MATHEMATICAL SOCIOLOGY.

Sociology regarded as an exact science is sometimes called pure sociology. In this sense it is usually attempted to reduce its laws to mathematical principles, to deduce equations and draw curves expressing those laws. The application of mathematics to sociology is at best precarious, not because the laws of social phenomena are not exact, but because of the multitude and complicated interrelations of the facts. Except for certain minds that are mathematically constituted there is very little advantage in mathematical treatment. It instantly repels the non-mathematical, and, moreover, the proportion of mathematical minds is very small. Usually, a rigidly logical treatment of a subject is quite sufficient even where mathematics might have been used, and when the latter adds nothing to the conception, its use is simply pedantic.

5. MEANING OF THE TERM *SCIENCE*.

The word *science* has been variously defined. Etymologically it signifies, of course, simply knowledge. But it is admitted that there may be knowledge that is not science, and the most common definition of science is "methodized knowledge." More exactly, science is properly confined to a study of the laws of phenomena, using that expression in the broadest sense. All phenomena take place according to invariable laws whose manifestations are numerous and manifold. A mere knowledge of these manifestations is not science. Knowledge only becomes scientific when the uniform principle becomes known which will explain all the manifestations. This principle is the law. But we can go a step farther back. A law is only a generalization from facts, *i.e.*, from phenomena, but these do not take place without a cause. The uniformity which makes such a generalization possible is in the cause. But a cause can be nothing else than a force acting upon the material basis of phenomena. As all force is persistent, the phenomena it causes will necessarily be uniform under the same conditions, and will change in the same way under like changes in the conditions.

6. SOCIOLOGY A SCIENCE.

Every science, in order to be such, must be a domain of force. Until a group of facts and phenomena reaches the stage at which these can be generalized into laws, which, in turn, are merely the expressions of the

14 | A TEXT-BOOK OF SOCIOLOGY

uniform working of its underlying forces, it cannot be appropriately denominated a science. The mere accumulation of facts, therefore, does not constitute a science, but a successful classification of the facts recognizes the law underlying them and is, in so far, scientific. If, then, sociology is a science, it must agree with all others in this respect, and all knowledge that is not systematized according to this principle must be ruled out of the science of society.

7. THE PROGRESS OF SCIENCE.

The progress of science is forward march. It is in the highest degree irregular and fitful. And yet there is a certain method in it. It is the work of a vast army of workers, each working more or less independently. Whatever the field may be, the general method of all earnest scientific research is the same. Every investigator chooses some special line and pushes his researches forward along that line as far as his facilities and his powers will permit. If he is a master, he soon exhausts the resources and appliances of the libraries and laboratories and proceeds to construct a technique of his own for his special purposes. He observes and experiments and records the results. Whenever important results are reached, he publishes them. He not only publishes the results, but he describes his methods. He tells the world not only what he has found, but how he found it. If the results thus announced are at all novel or startling, others working along similar lines immediately take them up, criticise them, and make every effort to disprove them. Part of the results claimed by the first investigator will be disproved or shown to bear a different interpretation from that given them. Part of them will probably stand the fire and after repeated verification be admitted by all. These represent the permanent advance made in that particular science. But nothing is established until it has passed through this ordeal of general criticism and repeated verification from the most adverse points of view.*

8. PROGRESS OF SOCIOLOGY.

Such is the apparently desultory and haphazard, but really methodical, way in which all science advances. True, it is not at all economical, but extremely wasteful in energy and effort. It is a typical method of nature as

---

* Note in Bibliography such names as De Greef, Fouillée, Lilienfeld, Schäffle etc., and see article by Giddings.

distinguished from the telic method, or method of foresight and intelligence, but it accomplishes its purpose and has given us all the established truth we possess. The progress of discovery, of science, and of knowledge and truth in the world generally, follows this same method, whatever department we may examine. The effect of it is to give the impression during the early stages in the history of any science, that all is chaos, and that no real progress is being made. Everyone is making claims for his own results and denying those of all others, so that the mere looker-on and the public at large are led to doubt that anything is being accomplished. Just at present sociology is in that initial stage in which a great army of really honest and earnest workers is wholly without organization. Nearly everyone has a single thought which he believes to embrace, when seen as he sees it, the whole field of sociology and he is elaborating that idea to the utmost. Now it is clear that he will make much more of that idea than anyone else could make. He will get all the truth out of it that it contains. It is true that he will carry it too far and weight it down with implications that it will not bear; but these are, like the errors of all scientific investigators, subject to criticism and ultimate rejection, the real truth taking their place.

REFERENCES TO WARD'S OTHER WORKS

- *Dynamic sociology*. Introduction to volume I. Topics in Index, volume II: Animals; Anti-social tendencies; Association; Science; Sociability; Sociology.
- *Psychic factors*. Index: Sociology.
- *Pure sociology*. Preface and chapters I, II.
- *Articles*. "Contemporary sociology." "Sociology at the Paris Exposition."

2

CLASSIFICATION OF THE SCIENCES

- 9. Serial classification.
- 10. Comte's classification.
- 11. The true order of study.
- 12. Synoptical classification.
- 13. Filiation.
- 14. Basal sciences for sociology.
- 15. Sympodial development.
- 16. In botany.
- 17. In evolution.
- 18. In human history.
- 19. Anthropologic sympodes.
- 20. National decadence.

9. SERIAL CLASSIFICATION.

Philosophers of all ages have been at work upon the problem of a logical and natural classification of the sciences. In selecting from among them all that of Comte as best adapted to the subject of social science, there is no thought of condemning all others or even making odious comparisons. There is always more than one entirely correct way of classifying the phenomena of any great field. But from the sociological standpoint the most important thing to determine is the natural or serial order in which the sciences stand—not how they can be made to stand, but how they must stand, irrespective of the wishes of anyone. But any classification of the sciences must recognize the necessity of the broadest generalization, and must not attempt to work into the general plan any of the sciences of the lower orders. The generalization must go on until all the strictly coordinate groups of the highest order are found, and then these must be arranged in their true and only natural order. This Comte accomplished by taking as the criterion of the position of each the degree of what he called *positivity*, which is simply the degree to which the phenomena can be exactly determined. This, as may be readily seen, is also a measure of their relative complexity, since the exactness of a science is in inverse proportion to its complexity. The degree of exactness or positivity is, moreover, that to which it can be subjected to mathematical demonstration, and therefore mathematics, which is not itself a concrete science, is the general gauge by which the position of every science is to be determined.

10. COMTE'S CLASSIFICATION.

Generalizing thus, Comte found that there were five great groups of phenomena of equal classificatory value but of successively decreasing positivity. To these he gave the names astronomy, physics, chemistry, biology, and sociology. A glance at these suffices to show that they conform to the conditions outlined and that they must stand in this order. When carefully scanned, nearly every proper science can be assigned its natural place in this scheme. Psychology, perhaps, should be added to the number of these great coordinate sciences and placed, as Spencer has done, between biology and sociology. Not that Comte ignored it, but in the mighty sweep of his logic he made it a part of biology, calling it "transcendental biology,"* This system is a natural system, in the sense that the order is the order of nature and that the several sciences are genetically affiliated upon one another in this order. That is, each of the five great natural groups rests upon the one immediately below it and grows out of it, as it were.

11. THE TRUE ORDER OF STUDY.

From this it necessarily results that this is the true order in which the should be studied, since the study of each furnishes the mind with the proper data for understanding the next higher. In fact, none of the more

---

* See Comte and Spencer in Bibliography.

complex and less exact sciences can be properly understood until after all the simpler and more exact ones below it have first been acquired. The student, therefore, who advances in this order is approaching the goal of his ambition by two distinct routes which converge at the desired stage. He is laying the foundation for the understanding of the more complex sciences by acquainting himself with the simpler ones upon which they successively rest, and he is at the same time mounting upward in the scale of generalization from the specific and generic to the ordinal or higher groups in a systematic classification. The natural arrangement of the great coordinate groups is serial and genetic. The term *hierarchy*, applied to it by Comte, is inappropriate, since there is no subordination, but simply degrees of generality and complexity. There is genetic affiliation without subordination. The more complex and less exact sciences may be regarded as the children of the more simple and exact ones, but between parent and offspring, there is no difference of rank.

12. SYNOPTICAL CLASSIFICATION.

In contrast with this, the other classification, which may be called logical or synoptical, is a true hierarchy. It will be easier to comprehend if we liken it to the system of ranking that prevails in an army. The two kinds of classification are entirely different in principle, and the last-named occurs independently in each of the great serial groups.

13. FILIATION.

Now what concerns the sociologist is primarily the serial order of phenomena. The several groups of phenomena constituting a natural "hierarchy" of the sciences, not only stand in the relation of diminishing generality with increasing complexity, but they stand in the relation of parent to offspring, *i.e.*, of *filiation*. The more complex sciences grow out of the simpler ones by a process of differentiation. The more general phenomena of the simpler sciences are elaborated into more complex forms. They are the raw material which is worked up into more finished products, much as pig iron is worked up into tools, machinery, cutlery, and watch-springs. The simpler sciences contain all that is in the more complex, but it is more homogeneous; and the process of evolution, as we know, is a passage from the homogeneous to the heterogeneous. A serial classification is based on this principle of natural differentiation and the resulting filiation. It might be called *tocological*.* This filiation of the sciences is also an order of mutual dependence. This dependence is specially marked between any one science in the series and the one immediately below it, but in a broader sense all the higher sciences are dependent upon all the lower ones. For the sociologist it is specially important to recognize the dependence of social science on physical science, using these terms in their commonly accepted senses.

14. BASAL SCIENCES FOR SOCIOLOGY.

Social science becomes much more thorough, intelligible, interesting, and useful when based on physical science. There is no one of the more general sciences that does not throw light on sociology. Anyone who looks for them can find "analogies" all through. There are almost as many parallels between social and chemical processes as there are between social and biological. By extended comparisons in all fields we find that the operations of nature are the same in all departments. We not only discover one great law of evolution applicable to all the fields covered by the several sciences of the series, but we can learn something more about the true method of evolution by observing how it takes place in each of these fields.

15. SYMPODIAL DEVELOPMENT.

As an example of the aid that the higher sciences and the philosophy of science in general may derive from some of the more special fields of research, the branch known as paleobotany may be cited. For, an acquaintance with the extinct plant life of the globe throws much light on the conception of the development of life in all its forms and also on the nature of evolution itself, cosmic, organic, and social.

16. IN BOTANY.

The science of botany in its wide and proper sense—the natural history of plants, including their geological history—teaches that the prevailing conception of organic evolution is radically incorrect in one of its essential aspects. It shows that plant development at least, and inferentially animal development also, is *sympodial*. In explanation, it may be said that the

---

* Greek, τόκος, son.

vegetable kingdom presents two clearly marked modes of branching, known respectively as *monopodial* and *sympodial*. In monopodial branching the stem or main trunk gives off at intervals subordinate stems called branches, containing a comparatively small number of the fibrovascular bundles of the main stem, which thus continues to diminish in size by the loss of its bundles until all are thus given off and the stem terminates in a slender twig. In sympodial branching, on the other hand, the main stem or trunk rises to a certain height and then gives off a branch into which the majority of the fibrovascular bundles enter, so that the branch virtually becomes the trunk, and the real trunk or ascending portion is reduced to a mere twig, or may ultimately fail of support altogether and disappear through atrophy. This large branch at length in turn gives off a secondary branch, containing as before the bulk of the bundles, and the first branch is sacrificed in the same manner as was the original stem or trunk; and this process is repeated throughout the life of the tree or plant. As might be naturally expected, the resulting series of branches of different orders is zigzag, and in most sympodial herbs this is manifest in the plant. It is somewhat so in vines like the grape-vine, but in trees, like the linden, the forces of heliotropism and general upward growth serve to right up these several originally inclined sympodes, the abortive stems of antecedent stages vanish entirely, and the trunk becomes as erect and symmetrical as those of its monopodial companions of the forest. There are other distinctions which may be found set forth in the books, but these are the only ones that concern us here.

17. IN EVOLUTION.

Now the monopodial type of branching is, of course, the one that everybody is familiar with, and this is the type that is alone considered when we speak of the arborescent character of organic development. Its inadequacy in explaining the actual phenomena presented by organic nature has been strongly felt, and a more satisfactory explanation demanded. This demand is satisfied by the theory that evolution is sympodial.

Everywhere and always, the course of evolution in the plant world has been the same; the original phylum has at some point reached its maximum development and given off a sympode that has carried the process of evolution on until it should in turn give birth to a new sympode, which repeats the same history, and so on indefinitely. Each successive sympode possesses attributes which enable it better to resist the environment; it therefore constitutes a form of development or structural advance. Thus the entire process is one of true evolution, and has culminated in the great class of dicotyledonous exogenous plants which now dominate the vegetable kingdom.

18. IN HUMAN HISTORY.

If we rise to the plane of human history, we shall find a similar parallel here. We may look upon human races as so many trunks and branches of what may be called the sociological tree. The vast and bewildering multiplicity in the races of men is the result of ages of race development, and it has taken place in a manner very similar to that in which the races of plants and animals have developed. Its origin is lost in the obscurity of ages of unrecorded history; but when at last the light of tradition and written annals opens upon the human races, we find them engaged in a great struggle. Out of this struggle new races have sprung. These in turn have struggled with other races, and out of these still other races have slowly emerged, until at last, down toward our own times and within the general line of the historic races, the great leading nationalities—French, English, German, Slavic—have been evolved.

19. ANTHROPOLOGIC SYMPODES.

Now every one of these races of men, from the advanced nationalities last named back to the barbaric tribes that arose from the blending of hostile hordes, is simply an anthropologic sympode, strictly analogous to the biologic sympodes already described. When we concentrate our attention upon those latter aspects of this movement which we are fairly well acquainted with, we find a most remarkable parallelism between the phenomena which we popularly characterize as the rise and fall of nations or empires, and the rise and fall of the great types of life during the progress of geologic history. As we look back in imagination over the vast stretches of the past, we can see the earth peopled, as it were, by these vegetable forms, different in every epoch; and an image presents itself to the mind of the gradual rise, ultimate mastery or hegemony, and final culmination of each of the great types of vegetation, followed by its decline contemporaneously with the rise of the type that is to succeed it. This rhythmic march of evolution has been going on throughout the entire history of the planet, and the path of geologic history is strewn with the ruins of fallen vegetable empires, just as that of human history is strewn with the wrecks of political empires and decadent races.

20. NATIONAL DECADENCE.

Races and nations become overgrown and disappear.* Peoples become overspecialized and fall an easy prey to the more vigorous surrounding ones, and a high state of civilization is always precarious. Races and peoples are always giving off their most highly vitalized elements and being transplanted to new soil, leaving the parent country to decline or be swallowed up. The plot of the *Æneid*, though it be a myth, at least illustrates this truth. Troy was swallowed up by Greece, but not until it had been transplanted to Rome. Italy was the vanguard of civilization to the sixteenth century, when she transferred her scepter to Spain, which held it during the seventeenth, and in turn transferred it to France. It passed to England in the nineteenth, and bids fair to cross the Atlantic before the close of the twentieth. Race and national degeneration or decadence means nothing more than this pushing out of the vigorous branches or sympodes at the expense of the parent trunks. Some see in colonization the phenomenon of social reproduction. This is at least a half-truth. Colonization often means regeneration; it means race development; it means social evolution.

REFERENCES TO WARD'S OTHER WORKS

- *Dynamic sociology*. Chapters I and II, on Comte and Spencer. Topics in Index, in volume II: Classification of the sciences; Filiation of the sciences; Hierarchy; Sciences, classification of.
- *Outlines of sociology*. Chapters I-V inclusive.
- *Pure sociology*. Chapter V, pp. 65-79.

---

* Brooks Adams, *The law of civilization and decay.*

3

DATA OF SOCIOLOGY

- 21. Classification of data.*
- 22. The general sciences.
- 23. The requirement of a general education.
- 24. The special social sciences.
- 25. Sociology and economics.
- 26. Relations to other sciences.
- 27. Purpose of sociological study.
- 28. Importance of sociology.

21. CLASSIFICATION OF DATA.

We now turn to the last and highest of the Sciences, sociology, and what has been said is calculated to prepare us to understand the true scope of that science. The leading distinction between modern and ancient philosophy is that the former proceeds from facts, while the latter proceeded from assumptions. Every science is at the same time a philosophy. The greater part of all that is valuable in any science is the result of reasoning from facts. The more complex a science is, the greater the number of facts required to reason from, and the more difficult the task of drawing correct conclusions from the facts. When we come to sociology, the number of details is so immense that it is no wonder many declare

---

* Small, *Scope of sociology*.

them wholly unmanageable. The only prospect of success lies in a classification of the materials. This classification of sociological data amounts in the end to the classification of all the subsciences that range themselves under the general science of sociology.

22. THE GENERAL SCIENCES.

We should begin with the most general and proceed analytically toward the more and more special. In fact, it will be well to begin entirely outside of sociology proper and consider first the dependence of sociology upon the other less complex and more general sciences. These simpler sciences may themselves be regarded as constituting a part of the data of sociology. Some knowledge of them is essential to any adequate comprehension of the full scope and meaning of sociology. It may have a discouraging sound to say that in order to be properly prepared for the study of sociology one must first be acquainted with mathematics, astronomy, physics, chemistry, biology, and psychology, but when it is clearly understood what is meant by this it loses much of its formidableness. For it has never been maintained that it is necessary to become a specialist in all, or even in any of these sciences. It is only essential to have a firm grasp of the leading principles of all of them and of their relations one to another. It would be far better to devote time to this aspect of each of them than to mastering the details, as is so largely done in the present system of education. A certain amount of detail is of course necessary to furnish a full conception of what any science is and means, but it need go no farther than this.

23. THE REQUIREMENT OF A GENERAL EDUCATION.

This extraordinary tax upon the sociologist is therefore, after all, little more than the requirement that the sociological student shall first of all acquire a good general education. It does not so much prescribe the quantity of his learning as the direction it should be made to take. It says that his education should be mainly scientific, that his study of the sciences should be so ordered as to give him a clear idea of their natural relations and dependencies, that they should be taken up so far as possible in the order of their decreasing generality and increasing complexity, and that they be pursued in this direction so as to include at least the science upon which the chosen specialty directly rests. In the case of sociology, this is of course to cover the entire range of the sciences, but in reality, this is nothing more than any well-organized curriculum necessarily involves.

24. THE SPECIAL SOCIAL SCIENCES.

The primary data of sociology, then, are seen to consist of this general preliminary scientific education, this firm grasp of the broad cosmical principles that underlie and govern all departments of natural phenomena. The more specific data of sociology consist in the facts contributed by the various branches or sciences that fall directly under it, in the relation already described in the second chapter, of true hierarchical subordination.

Much has been said of late about the so-called "special social sciences" and their relation to sociology. Some regard sociology as consisting entirely of these sciences and as having no existence apart from them. Others distinguish sociology from the special social sciences, but in different ways. The latter are sometimes identified with "social science," and this is treated as distinct from sociology. There is less variety of opinion relative to the nature of the special social sciences than there is relative to what these. The special social sciences are numerous, and, in many cases, there is room for differences of opinion as to what constitutes such sciences, but the following are the principal ones about which there is little dispute: ethnography, ethnology, technology, archaeology, demography; history, economics, jurisprudence, politics, ethics—all taken in a scientific sense, and each with its natural subdivisions. No one of these, nor all of them together, can be said to form sociology, but sociology is the synthesis of them all. It is impossible to perform this synthesis without a clear conception of the elements entering into it. These, therefore, constitute the data for the process. The special social sciences, then, are not themselves the science of sociology, but they constitute data of sociology.*

25. SOCIOLOGY AND ECONOMICS.

In marking out clearly the sphere of sociology, the greatest difficulty is that of distinguishing it from political economy or economics. Although modern economics is broad in its scope and rests to a great extent upon the observed facts of human life and action, it yet concerns itself chiefly with the problems arising in connection with the production of wealth. Comte's conception of sociology is of course widely different, as he makes it one of the great coordinate groups of his so-called hierarchy, and as such to

---

* Wilson, *The place of social philosophy*.

embrace everything that pertains to man as a social being. Economics therefore belongs within the great field of sociology, and care should be taken that there be no confusion or overlapping, and that nothing that clearly belongs to economics should be treated as sociology.

26. RELATIONS TO OTHER SCIENCES.

In distinguishing sociology from the special social sciences, economics has been taken as an example because it seems to be most prone to overflow into the broader field. But there are many other sciences or branches of learning that occupy practically the same relative position. It is here that history stands, while ethnology, ethnography, and demography, with other attendant branches of anthropology, bear so strongly upon the great science of man in the social state that it is difficult to prevent them from forcing their way into it.* We may regard sociology as one of the great natural families of cosmical phenomena, under which we may range the next most general departments as so many genera, each with its appropriate species. That is, the classification of the social sciences may be made strictly synoptical. Thus understood, sociology is freed from the unnecessary embarrassment of having hanging, about it in more or less disorder a burden of complicated details which make it next to impossible to secure due attention to the fundamental principles of so vast a science. These details are classified and assigned each to its proper place (genus or species), and the field is cleared for the calm contemplation of the central problem of determining the facts, the law, and the principles of human association.

27. PURPOSE OF SOCIOLOGICAL STUDY.

Now all this vast array of phenomena manifested by man in his manifold relations with the material world constitutes the data of sociology, and something must be known about it before any one is capable of entering into the consideration of those higher laws involved in human association, which, on final analysis, are simply generalizations from the facts of lower orders. It is true that in the course of acquiring a sound general education everyone necessarily learns something about most of these things, but this is insufficient to constitute an adequate preparation for the study of sociology. This knowledge needs to be systematized and specialized, and

---

* Letourneau, *Sociology based on ethnography.*

directed to the definite end. The student needs to know just what he is pursuing it for. There is no more vicious educational practice, and scarcely any more common one, than that of keeping the student in the dark as to the end and purpose of his work. It breeds indifference, discouragement, and despair. Therefore, while it might be fruitless to attempt to teach the principles of sociology before the student were put in possession of the facts from which those principles are derived, it is of the utmost importance to inform him, as early as he is likely to understand, that there is a great general science of society toward which all this is leading, and constantly to keep him imbued with the idea of an ultimate utility beyond the mere satisfaction of the desire to know facts.

28. IMPORTANCE OF SOCIOLOGY.

It is safe then to assert that there are elements for a science of society, and that when these elements are detected, collated, and reduced to law, such a science will be established; and it is further beyond question that, when the true science of society shall be established and accepted as other sciences are accepted, its influence on the interests of man and the destiny of the race will be as much greater than that of the simpler sciences as sociology is nearer to man and more intimately bound up with all that concerns his welfare. Sociology therefore should be studied first for the sake of information relating to the laws of human association and cooperative action, and finally for the purpose of determining in what ways and to what extent social phenomena may, with a knowledge of their laws, be modified and directed toward social ideals. The supreme purpose is the betterment of society. If knowledge be had, action will take care of itself, though an important part of the knowledge is that action is its object.*

The sociological student, clearly perceiving the chaotic condition of both the industrial and the political world, and recognizing that most of the evils of society result from a lack of scientific knowledge on the part of so-called practical men, claims the right and feels the obligation to state the facts, to define social laws and principles, and to indicate their significance and their necessary bearing upon social affairs and movements. The study of sociology, therefore, is calculated to enlighten the individual purposes of men and to harmonize them with the good of society. It will tend to

---

* Mackenzie, *Introduction to social philosophy.*

unify action, to combine the innumerable streams of individual effort, and to pour their contents into one great river of social welfare.

We see, then, the high place which sociology, properly defined, should hold among the sciences, and how clear and incisive are the boundaries which mark it off from all other branches of learning. It is the cap-sheaf and crown of any true system of classification of the sciences, and it is also the last and highest landing on the great staircase of education.

REFERENCES TO WARD'S OTHER WORKS

- *Dynamic sociology*. Topics in Index, volume II: Phenomena, classification of; Sociologists.
- *Outlines of sociology*. Chapters VI and IX.

4

METHODOLOGY

- 29. Importance of method.*
- 30. Logical sequence of ideas.
- 31. Science as a domain of laws.
- 32. Generalization.
- 33. In anthropology.
- 34. In great primary wants and passions.
- 35. Law in history.
- 36. The law of parsimony.
- 37. Shown in the pursuit of interests.

29. IMPORTANCE OF METHOD.

It is the function of methodology in social science to classify social phenomena in such a manner that the groups may be brought under uniform laws and treated by exact methods. Sociology then becomes an exact science. Human history presents a chaos. The only science that can convert this chaos into a definite social universe is sociology, and this can only be done by the use of an appropriate method, by using the data furnished by all the special social sciences, including the great scientific trunks of psychology, biology, and cosmology, and by generalizing and coordinating facts and groups of facts until unity is attained.

---

* Small, *Methodology*. Durkheim, *Les règles de la méthode sociologique*.

30. LOGICAL SEQUENCE OF IDEAS.

The basis of method is logic, and the basis of logic is the law of causation. The object of method is clearness, and what is logical is usually clear. At least, the same subject, however abstruse or inherently difficult, will be clearer of comprehension if logically presented than if incoherently presented. This principle lies at the foundation of style. That which renders a style easy is the strict logical sequence of ideas. What is true of style is true of other things. It is especially true of education, and it is probable that something like double the progress could be made by pupils and students of all grades, if an exact logical method could be adopted in the order of studies, so that every new study would naturally grow out of the one that had preceded it. For every large subject is complex and embraces a great number of component subjects, and most of these can be arranged in a series of logically connected ideas or facts. A treatise on any science is easy or hard in proportion as this is done. The need of method increases with the complexity of a science. Sociology, as the most complex of all the sciences, has the greatest need of it.

31. SCIENCE AS A DOMAIN OF LAWS.

A true science is a field of phenomena occurring in regular order as the effects of natural cause, such that a knowledge of the causes renders it possible to predict the effects. The causes are always the natural forces. The order in which the phenomena occur constitutes the laws that govern the science. These laws must be studied until they are understood the same as the laws of gravitation, heat, and light in physics have been studied. In sociology there is a disposition to deny that there are any such laws, forces, or causes. The favorite standpoint of all who dispute the title of sociology to rank as a science is that of mathematics. The laws of astronomy, of physics, and to a large extent of chemistry can be reduced to mathematical notation. The assumption is that anything that cannot be so reduced cannot be a science. It does not always follow that because the phenomena embraced by a science are subject to uniform laws they can always be reduced to mathematical formulas. Only a comparatively small part of physics is of a character to require mathematical treatment. It is still less so in chemistry. Uniform laws or processes are the essentials of a science. Their mathematical expression is not essential. The sociologist, therefore, need only inquire whether society is a domain of uniform laws. That it should not seem to be is natural enough to superficial observers.*

32. GENERALIZATION.

The principle which underlies the proposition that sociology is a true science is that *in the complex sciences the quality of exactness is only perceptible in their higher generalizations*. The method in sociology is generalization. Precisely what is meant by this may require some illustration. It is essentially the process of grouping phenomena and using the groups as units. The phenomena of society are omnipresent. They obtrude upon the view at every turn. The facts that the sociologist must use are spontaneously supplied to him every moment and everywhere. He need not go in search of them. The ones that are thus hourly thrust upon him are the most important of all. If he travel through all lands, he will find the same facts. What he will find additional is only auxiliary and valuable for comparative study. Yet as a rule only the sociologist or true student of society comprehends these facts.

33. IN ANTHROPOLOGY.

In the domain of anthropology we find this truth exemplified at every point. What Tylor has called *ethnographic parallels*, viz., the occurrence of the same or similar customs, practices, ceremonies, arts, beliefs, and even games, symbols, and patterns in peoples of nearly the same culture at widely separated regions of the globe, proves, except in a few cases of known derivation through migration, that there is a uniform law in the psychic and social development of mankind at all times and under all circumstances. The details will vary with the climate and other physical differences in the environment, but if we continue to rise in the process of generalization, we will ultimately reach a plane on which all mankind are alike.

34. IN GREAT PRIMARY WANTS AND PASSIONS.

Even in civilized races there are certain things absolutely common to all. The great primary feelings and wants are the same the world over. Political organizations seem to differ immensely, but there is much more

---

* See *Pure sociology*; Kant, p. 152, Quetelet, p. 149.

agreement than difference. Creeds, cults, and sects multiply and seem to present the utmost heterogeneity, but there is a common basis even of belief, and on certain occasions all sometimes unite in a common cause. Not only are the common wants of men the same, but their passions are also the same, and those acts growing out of them which are regarded as destructive of the social order and condemned by law and public opinion are committed in the face of these restraining influences with astonishing regularity. This is not seen by the ordinary observer, but when accurate statistics are brought to bear upon this class of social phenomena, they prove to be quite as uniform, though not quite so frequent, as the normal operations of life.*

35. LAW IN HISTORY.

This then is what is meant by generalization. We have only to carry it far enough in order to arrive at unity. Society is a domain of law, and sociology is an abstract science in the sense that it does not attend to details except as aids in arriving at the law that underlies them all.

This has been called the *historical perspective*. It is the discovery of law in history, whether it be the history of the past or the present, and including under history social as well as political phenomena. There is nothing very new in this. It is really the oldest of all sociological conceptions. The earliest gropings after a social science consisted in a recognition of law in human affairs. The so-called precursors of sociology have been those who have perceived more or less distinctly a method or order in human events. All who have done this, however dimly, have been set down as the heralds of the new science. Such adumbrations of the idea of law in society were frequent in antiquity. In mediaeval times they were more rare; but before Comte had given name and form to sociology. Saint-Simon, Bastiat, Carey, and John Stuart Mill had more or less clearly formulated the general doctrine of historical determinism, and the philosophy of history had received wide recognition. The theologically inclined, when this truth was brought home to them, characterized it by the phrase "God in history," and saw in the order of events the divine hand guiding the acts of men toward some predestined goal. This is perhaps the most common view today, and the general optimism of mankind furnishes all the faith necessary to harmonize the doctrine with the scientific law of human evolution. But science deals with phenomena

---

* Cooley, *Human nature and the social order*.

and can only deal with phenomena. Sociology, therefore, becomes a science only when human events are recognized as phenomena, and as phenomena of the same general character as other natural phenomena, only more complex and difficult to study on account of the subtle psychic causes that so largely produce them.

36. THE LAW OF PARSIMONY.

Careful observation reveals the fact that all social phenomena are the results of laws. But the fundamental law of everything psychic, and especially of everything that is affected by intelligence, is the *law of parsimony*. This law was first clearly grasped by the political economists, and by many it is regarded as only an economic law. Here it is usually called the law of *greatest gain for least effort*, and is the basis of scientific economics. But it is much broader than this, and not only plays an important rôle in psychology, but becomes, in that collective psychology which constitutes so nearly the whole of sociology, the scientific corner-stone of that science also. We have seen that the quality of scientific exactness in sociology can only be clearly perceived in its higher generalizations, where we can plainly see the relations and can be sure of their absolute uniformity and reliability. When we reach the law of parsimony, we seem to have attained the maximum stage of generalization, and have a law as exact as any in physics or astronomy. It is, for example, perfectly safe to assume that under any and all conceivable circumstances a sentient, and especially a rational being, will always seek the greatest gain, or the maximum resultant of gain—his "marginal" advantage. Those who are shocked by such a proposition take too narrow a view of the subject. They think that they do not always seek their greatest gain, and give illustrations of actions performed that result in a loss instead of a gain. This is because they understand by gain only pecuniary gain, or only gain in temporary enjoyment, or immediate satisfaction. If they could analyze their feelings, they would see that they were merely sacrificing a present to a future advantage, or a lower to a higher satisfaction.

37. SHOWN IN THE PURSUIT OF INTERESTS.

But this is by no means the whole meaning of the law. It deals solely with motives, and worthy motives are as potent as unworthy ones. It is based, it is true, on interests, but interest is much more frequently good than bad. It was necessarily good, at least for the individual, in the beginning, since it had the mission to impel activities for the preservation of life and race. Men feel an interest in doing good, and moral interest is as real as any other. Ratzenhofer* shows that men have been profoundly moved by what he calls *transcendental interests*, which he defines as a striving after the infinite, and to this he attributes the great religious movements in society. If therefore we take into account all these different kinds of interest, physical, racial (*Gattungsinteresse*), moral, social, and transcendental, it becomes clear that all action is based on supposed gain of one or another of these orders. Still, the world has never reached a stage where the physical and temporary interests have not been largely in the ascendant, and it is these upon which the economists have established their science. Self-preservation has always been the first law of nature, and that which best insures this is the greatest gain. So unerring is this law that it is easy to create a class of paupers or mendicants by simply letting it be known that food or alms will be given to those who ask. In this respect men are like animals. In fact, this is precisely the principle that underlies the domestication of animals and the taming of wild beasts. So soon as the creature learns that it will not be molested and that its wants will be supplied, it submits to the will of man and becomes a parasite. Parasitism, indeed, throughout the organic world is only an application of the law of parsimony.

While therefore no law can be laid down as to how any individual will act under a given set of circumstances, in consequence of the enormous number and variety of causes that combine to determine any single act, we have a law which determines with absolute certainty how all men may be depended upon to act. If there is any apparent exception to this law, we may be sure that some element has been overlooked in the calculation.

REFERENCES TO WARD'S OTHER WORKS

- *Dynamic sociology.* Topics in Index, volume II: Generality; Generalization; Observation; Scientific method; Synthesis.
- *Pure sociology.* Chapters IV and IX, pp. 161-163.

---

* *Die sociologische Erkenntnis.*

THE SUBJECT-MATTER OF SOCIOLOGY

- 38. Human achievement.
- 39. The natural history of man.
- 40. History of culture.
- 41. Distinction between organic and social evolution.
- 42. What is civilization?
- 43. Utilization of force and matter.
- 44. Material wealth.
- 45. Inventions as achievements.
- 46. Tools of the mind.
- 47. The industrial arts.
- 48. Protective achievements.
- 49. Human institutions as achievements.
- 50. Social continuity.
- 51. In historic races only.
- 52. Achievement through knowledge.
- 53. Genius.
- 54. Pessimism.
- 55. The love of achievement.
- 56. The immortality of deeds.

38. HUMAN ACHIEVEMENT.

The subject-matter of sociology is human achievement. It is not what men are, but what they do. The animal world, properly speaking, achieves nothing. It may work changes, more or less extensive, in the face of nature, but this is merely the incidental result of activities which do not have any such effect for their object. Nothing in the nature of art exists below the human stage. Now the facts that make up the data of sociology are the manifestations of the qualities or properties of the multitudinous units of society or individual men. These differ at different times and places and constitute a complex manifold or multiple. The study of such a varying manifold, however viewed, is essentially in the nature of history, and therefore the approaches to sociological study are all primarily historical.

39. THE NATURAL HISTORY OF MAN.

This history of society readily subdivides into two groups, according to whether we study man himself in his natural aspect, or his achievements. The first of these groups is anthropology in its proper sense, and would, rigidly applied, exclude technology and archaeology. It might be extended to embrace the ruder forms of art, but it has chiefly to do with race characteristics, including everything that serves to differentiate the groups of human beings found inhabiting the earth. In short, it is *par excellence* the *natural history of man*.

40. HISTORY OF CULTURE.

The second subdivision of the subject, which relates to human achievement, considers everything which can, in the broadest acceptation of the term, be classed under the head of human institutions. This branch deals essentially with what ethnologists denominate *culture*, and constitutes *history* proper. The several stages of culture—savagery, barbarism, civilization, enlightenment—are so many steps in the general progress of what is called civilization in the broader and more popular sense. In the *history of culture*, as distinguished from the natural history of man, he is considered as primarily a producer of what did not exist before. While we are unacquainted with any stage of human history in which these two states do not coexist, it is a highly logical mode of studying the subject to treat them apart. Sociology is, therefore, concerned with social *activities*. It is a study of action, *i.e.*, of *phenomena*. It is a study of how the various social products have been created. These products once formed become permanent. They may be slowly modified and perfected, but they constitute the basis for new products, and so on indefinitely.

41. DISTINCTION BETWEEN ORGANIC AND SOCIAL EVOLUTION.

It is this fact of permanent human achievement that makes the broad distinction between animal and human societies. The formula that expresses this distinction the most clearly is that *the environment transforms the animal, while man transforms the environment.* Now it is exactly this transformation of the environment that constitutes achievement. The animal achieves nothing. The organic world is passive. It is acted upon by the environment and adapted to it. Man, on the contrary, as a psychically developed being, and in increasing degrees in proportion to his psychic development, is active and assumes the initiative, molding nature to his own use. There has been no important organic change in man during the historic period. Yet his power of vision has been enormously increased by all the applications of the lens, his power of locomotion has been multiplied by the invention of propelling machines, and his strength has become almost unlimited by calling the forces of nature to his assistance. Tools are vastly more effective than teeth or claws. In the electric transmission of thought across continents and seas he has developed an organ of which no animal possesses a rudiment. Still better he has enormously increased production through a long series of inventions. It is all the result of man's power to transform the environment. The artificial modification of natural phenomena is the great characteristic fact in human activity. It is what constitutes achievement.

42. WHAT IS CIVILIZATION?

What then in reality constitutes civilization? *Material civilization consists in the utilization of the materials and forces of nature.* The spiritual part of civilization is at least conditioned upon material civilization. It does not derogate from its worth to admit that without a material basis it cannot exist. The moment such a basis is supplied, it comes forth in all, ages and races of men. It may, therefore, be regarded as innate in man and potential everywhere, but a flower so delicate that it can only bloom in the rich soil of material prosperity. No amount of care devoted to it alone could make it flourish in the absence of suitable conditions; with such conditions it requires no special attention. It may, therefore, be dismissed from our consideration, and our interest henceforth centered in the question of material civilization, and this will be understood without the use of the adjective.*

43. UTILIZATION OF FORCE AND MATTER.

As examples of the forces that are utilized in civilization, stated in something like the historical order of their use, may be mentioned heat, light, gravitation, wind, water, steam, and electricity. The value of water as a power is in its weight, so that this is only one of the many applications of gravitation. Perhaps earlier than any other is the power of inertia in ponderable matter by which, even in the club, it is made to increase the efficiency of the unaided hands. Still more subtle, but immensely effective, is the use of the principle of the lever and fulcrum, by which effects are rendered vastly greater than the muscular force exerted. These are only a few of the most obvious of nature's powers which man learned to profit by. Of materials or substances, the simplest were wood, clay, stone, and the metals as fast as means were discovered of separating them from their ores. The reason why bronze (copper) antedates iron is that it more frequently occurs in a pure state, for it is much less abundant. Aluminum, perhaps the most abundant of all metals, was among the last to be utilized, solely because so difficult to obtain in a pure state. After these came the multitudinous chemical substances, elementary and composite, that are now applied to innumerable uses.

44. MATERIAL WEALTH.

Let us now inquire more specially what are the products of achievement. The chief failure to understand them is due to the false and superficial view that they consist in material goods, or wealth. Because welfare is so largely dependent on wealth, it is natural to suppose that wealth is the main condition to progress. Material goods, as, for example, food, clothing, and shelter, are, it is true, the ends; but the real products of achievement are means. They are the means to these ends, and not the ends themselves. Involved in the idea of achievement is that of permanence. Nothing that is not permanent can be said to have been achieved, at least in the sense in which that term is here employed. Now, material goods are all perishable.

---

* Loria, *Economic foundations of society.*

Most goods of course are consumed at once. For the real end is consumption, and goods have no value except in consumption.

45. INVENTIONS AS ACHIEVEMENTS.

Achievement does not consist in wealth. Wealth is fleeting and ephemeral. Achievement is permanent and eternal. Wealth, the transient, is material; achievement, the enduring, is immaterial. The products of achievement are not material things at all. As said before, they are not ends, but means. They are methods, ways, principles, devices, arts, systems, institutions. In a word, they are *inventions*. Every such increment to civilization is a permanent gain, because it is imitated, repeated, perpetuated, and never lost. It is chiefly mental or psychical, but it may be physical in the sense of skill. Mere muscular strength soon yields to cunning and skill. These do not achieve until they begin to create. Language itself was an achievement of stupendous import, and every one of the steps it has taken—gesture, oral, written, printed forms of language—has marked an epoch in the progress of man. Literature has become one of the great achievements. Art, too, is an achievement upon which we need not dwell. Philosophy and science must be ranked as achievements, vast and far-reaching in their consequences. The invention of tools, instruments, utensils, missiles, traps, snares, and weapons comes under this head, crowned by the era of machinofacture, artificial locomotion, and electric intercommunication.

46. TOOLS OF THE MIND.

All these are too obvious and important to have escaped the observation of anyone. But there is another class of products of achievement that are at once typical, important, and little thought of in this connection. They may be called the tools of the mind. An arithmetical notation, or mode of expressing numbers by symbols of any kind, is such a tool of the mind, and all leading races have devised something of the kind. Greece had hers, and Rome hers. We still make some use of the latter. But these systems vary greatly in value and usefulness, according to their simplicity and flexibility. The system that is now universally employed by civilized races is called the Arabic system, but it is probable that the Arabs only somewhat improved it after receiving it from the East. Its peculiar merit consists in what is called the value of position, and this it is which gives it its wonderful adaptability to business uses. It is a typical permanent human achievement. The three great arts of reading, writing, and calculating, viewed from a philosophical standpoint, have raised that part of mankind who possess them high above all those races in which they are unknown, or only rudimentary. The unreflecting have little idea of the importance of these factors in giving superiority to the advanced races. The natural superiority of civilized races as compared with uncivilized ones is greatly exaggerated, and it is almost wholly due to this vast mechanical equipment of acquired aptitudes, built up along one advancing line of social development, increment upon increment.

47. THE INDUSTRIAL ARTS.

The industrial arts form a much more obvious, though perhaps not more important, class of human achievements. They are greatly dependent at every step on the tools of the mind, and, properly viewed, they are almost as completely psychic in their nature. For all art is due to invention, and invention is a mental operation. Every tool or implement of industry, however primitive and rude, has cost a large amount, in the aggregate, of thought, although it may be the product of a long series of slight improvements, distributing the mental energy through many different minds acting in different generations. Thought is thus dynamic when applied to matter. The new and better article, if used, will wear out, but the materialized idea lives on in the reproduction of the article as long as it serves its purpose. What the inventor does is to discover the principle by which he can cause the forces of nature, including the properties of the substances that he is acquainted with, to do the work that he wishes to have done and cannot do with his unaided hands. The discovery of this principle and the mode of applying it is what constitutes the achievement. This discovery, and not the resulting material product, is the lasting element in the operation. It can be used thenceforth for all time. It never wears out and is never lost.

48. PROTECTIVE ACHIEVEMENTS.

These two great classes of products of achievement, means of handling quantities and means of utilizing forces, are perhaps the most important, and they have chiefly rendered civilization possible. But others might be enumerated which are essentially social in their character, and relate to men in a collective capacity. To mention them in something like the probable order of their development, we may enumerate military systems, political systems, juridical systems, and industrial systems. The earliest of the whole series of means for organizing the social forces were military systems, and all others grew out of them. The transition from military t& political control was natural and gradual, and the state was the normal and legitimate outcome, first military, then political. Law, too, began as an economic method of escape from the necessity of constantly exercising military and civil power, and systems of jurisprudence were a natural outgrowth of social conditions. Lastly, the industrial system, as such, could only arise under the protection of army, state, and law. These may therefore be called protective or conservative systems or achievements, and neither industry, art, nor science could thrive except under the protection of law and government having a final appeal to the military power.

49. HUMAN INSTITUTIONS AS ACHIEVEMENTS.

Finally, it may be said in general that all human institutions are achievements. Even those that we now consider bad were useful in the wider sense in their day and age. The fact that they were developed and actually came into existence proves to the sociologist that they must have served a purpose. The term *institution* is capable of such expansion as to embrace all human achievement, and in this enlarged sense institutions become the chief study of the sociologist. All achievements are institutions, and there is a decided gain to the mind in seeking to determine the true subject-matter of sociology, to regard human institutions and human achievement as synonymous terms, and as constituting, in the broadest sense of both, the field of research of a great science.

50. SOCIAL CONTINUITY.

These products of achievement that we have been considering have one fundamental condition, without which they would have been impossible. They absolutely require *social continuity*. Social continuity is an important factor, but it does not apply to all the populations of the globe. It is a purely sociological fact that all the human races do not belong to one and the same series of cultural development. Many of them are so primitive that even when brought into contact with the historic races, they have nothing to contribute to the general stream of culture, and become simply subjects for natural history study, like the flora and fauna of the regions they inhabit. But there are others, such, as most of the Asiatic races, who have followed lines of their own, and must have a certain culture history,

42 | A TEXT-BOOK OF SOCIOLOGY

which, however, is so unlike that of the European races that there is very little in common between them. Oriental civilization seems to have consisted chiefly in what may be called spiritual culture, largely ignoring material culture. But as matter alone is dynamic, they have acquired very little social energy, or social efficiency. They have not called nature to their assistance, and consequently they are practically powerless when brought into competition with Western civilization. They lack in great measure the industrial efficiency of the West. They lack chiefly the mechanic arts, and have developed but little machinofacture, being confined in the main to manufacture in the literal sense. They have not employed the two great agencies, steam and electricity. Even if their civilization represents a longer line than that of the Occident, it is certainly immensely behind it in these respects, which we regard as the most important ones.

51. IN HISTORIC RACES ONLY.

Sociology, as distinguished from anthropology, deals mainly with historic races, because here alone is social continuity, the *sine qua non* of achievement. Such races may properly be called, in analogy to the use of the term in biology, the *favored races*. These alone have built up a civilization. They have achieved and handed down the products from generation to generation, and from age to age. The study of uncivilized races, therefore, is, and must remain, anthropology and not sociology. This is true even for the Asiatic civilizations. They can be used by the sociologist to furnish valuable illustrations and comparisons, but beyond this they form no part of sociology proper. Should they ever adopt Western methods, acquire the Western spirit, and fall entirely into line with the Western world, the case would be changed. The widest chasm that separates the East from the West is the lack of individuality in the former contrasted with the exuberant individualism of the latter. The spirit of resignation, the prevailing philosophy of quietism, the denial or complete subordination of the will to live, that prevail under Buddhism, Brahminism, Shintoism, and other Orientalisms, are fatal to that vigorous push which has wrought Western civilization. Desire is the social force, and where there is no desire, no will, there is no force, no social energy. Civilization is the product of active social energy. It is this that makes men fight and conquer and struggle, and undertake voyages of discovery in search of golden fleeces, or El Dorados, or Northwest Passages. It impels mankind to explore, to migrate, to invent, to labor, to produce wealth, to seek knowledge, to discover truth, to create objects both of use and beauty, —in a word, to achieve.

52. ACHIEVEMENT THROUGH KNOWLEDGE.

It must be clear from all that has been said that the essential characteristic of all achievement is some form of *knowledge*. But knowledge, unlike capacity, cannot be transmitted through heredity. It has to be acquired anew by every member of society, and handed down to later generations. A few rare minds have dimly seen that civilization consists in the cumulative light of knowledge. But this conception is only an approach toward the truth. No one man, however wise, and though immortal, could have accomplished what all men have accomplished. This brings us in full view of one of the most important and at the same time most neglected factors of social evolution, viz., that of individuality in achievement. Civilization advances in much the same way that science advances. It is not the work of anyone man, but of thousands of men. Each one of these thousands does a somewhat different work from any other. This is due to the natural inequalities of men, chiefly to varied intellectual capacities and attainments which cause them to follow different and almost infinitely varied lines and produce correspondingly varied results. Different schools of art are represented by great masters; each has added something to the work of all the rest. There are schools of architecture, of sculpture, of painting, of music; types of poetry and prose literature; systems of philosophy; world views and religious systems; qualitative and quantitative powers of perceiving utilities, resulting in innumerable inventions and arts—all due to natural inequalities in men. It is thus that civilization acquires its volume and that it becomes that infinitely complex and varied field of study which the sociologist finds before him.

53. GENIUS.

Here arises the question of the nature of genius in general. It is necessary to use the word *genius*, if we use it at all, in a very broad sense. Genius is a sort of focalization of psychic power. While there is an immense range to the human mind in general, and enormous differences in the aggregate capacity of different minds, this difference is still further increased by a sort of unconscious or natural concentration of psychic power in special ways in the same mind. That is to say, a mind of only average aggregate capacity may draw off from all but one of its faculties and add on to that one, until it becomes wonderfully keen or able or efficient in that one direction. This is the case with most typical geniuses in any particular form of achievement. It is proverbial that artists are very mediocre in all but their art. It is the same with poets and usually with philosophers. It is a sort of psychic division of labor that society creates, whereby with a large number of workers it can accomplish the maximum results, just as by the industrial division of labor much greater results are accomplished than could be done if all were doing all kinds of work and only doing them moderately well.

54. PESSIMISM.

It cannot be denied that the paucity of true men in the world tends to make a thoughtful person pessimistic, unless he has learned to study man objectively as a naturalist studies animals. The point of view of this chapter furnishes a remedy for this form of pessimism. It does not really study men or the human race at all. That belongs to other sciences than sociology; chiefly to anthropology. It studies activities, results, products, in a word, achievement. Viewed in this light the contemptible side of humanity vanishes from view, and only what is worthy or grand is presented to the gaze. Even the relatively trifling character of the contribution of most individuals need not absorb attention, but only aggregates. Just as the geologist, although no one knows as well as he that the great ledges and cañon walls were built up by minute accretions through eons of time, need not dwell upon these aspects, but may study as a whole the miles of stratified rock, so the sociologist may forget the paltry littleness of each increment to civilization and the still more paltry motives that inspired it, and study the monument that the race has thus erected, classifying each stratum, as does the geologist, and working out the stages of human culture. But the sociologist has an advantage over the geologist. The latter finds the world completed, so far as need concern him. But the sociologist deals with a fresh young world. He can see it grow, and he has a perfect right not only to speculate as to the future of society, but also to try to accelerate its growth.

55. THE LOVE OF ACHIEVEMENT.

We see, then, that the results of human effort in bringing about civilization may all be comprehended under the single word *achievement*, for it is the sum-total of human achievement that we call civilization. While achievement is exclusively the work of individual men, it can only take place in a social state of cooperation on a grand scale. The chief ambition of all vigorous minds and enlightened spirits becomes that of contributing something to the great stream of civilization. It is for this today and not for pelf that the student burns the midnight oil, that the genius sweeps the skies of fancy, that the philosopher probes the depths of nature, that the inventor tests the properties of substances and the actions of forces, that the specialist in any branch of science delves deeper than any of his predecessors. It is said that the love of approbation is the principal motive, and this may be admitted to be a less worthy motive than the love of achievement. But when we look over the history of achievement, we shall find that love of approbation plays a less prominent rôle than would seem from an observation of contemporary workers. Mere love of activity and pleasure in mental exertion are powerful motives and have caused the most sustained labor often in immensely fertile directions. While therefore the love of approbation enters into the motives of men, it is usually mingled with the love of achievement, which often includes the idea of doing some good, and of benefiting mankind. The desire to be remembered after death, or in remote future ages, must be very strong in many. This seems exactly intermediate between the love of approbation and the love of achievement. It is the love of approbation in the form of ambition to be enrolled after death on the scroll of immortal fame as one of the contributors to the monument erected to the work of the world. And it cannot be doubted that the feeling of being in the great current of intellectual progress is the highest and most powerful of all incentives.

56. THE IMMORTALITY OF DEEDS.

Thus far only a few have contributed to this stream, but the percentage is probably increasing, and might under improved social conditions be greatly increased; the time may come when all may at least aspire to the honor of laying some small offering on the altar of civilization. As the ages go by and history records the results of human action, it becomes clear to larger numbers that this is the true goal of life, and larger numbers seek it. It is seen that only those who have achieved are remembered, that the memory of such grows brighter instead of dimmer with time, and that these names are likely to be kept fresh in the minds of men forever. Achievement, therefore, comes to constitute a form of immortality, and has an exceedingly attractive side. This hope of immortality has doubtless formed one of the important motives in all ages, and in the future there is likely to be a still stronger tendency in this direction. Whatever other forms of immortality may be taught and believed in the immortality of deeds is not an article of faith, but a demonstrated fact. Social immortality is the immortality of achievement.

REFERENCES TO WARD'S OTHER WORKS

- *Dynamic sociology*. Topics in Index, volume II: Civilization; Future existence; Genius; Immortality; Invention.
- *Psychic factors*. Chapter XVI. Index: Action; Civilization; Immortality; Transformations.
- *Pure sociology*. Chapter III.

PART I

ORIGIN AND CLASSIFICATION OF THE SOCIAL FORCES

6

CREATIVE SYNTHESIS

- 57. Definition.
- 58. Creation.
- 59. Social Ideals.
- 60. The poetic idea.
- 61. Poesis.
- 62. Genesis.
- 63. Each science a creative synthesis.
- 64. Sociology also.
- 65. The social mind a synthesis.
- 66. Synthetic creations of nature.
- 67. Cosmic creations.
- 68. Products and properties.
- 69. Development sympodial.
- 70. Filiation of the sciences.

57. DEFINITION.

There is a fertile truth taught most clearly by chemistry, that a compound of two substances is something more than the sum of those substances, and is in a proper sense a third and different substance. That its properties are in some way derived from and due to those of its components is not denied, but the relation is one that no human insight can fully comprehend. This chemical synthesis has long been believed to typify a large number of other phenomena in all departments of nature. The moment we recognize that this universal chemism, or intimate blending of elements with complete loss of individuality and reappearance in new forms, as distinguished from mere mechanical mixture or amalgamation, is *creative*, a flood of light is shed on the entire process, and we then see how it can be that an infinite variety may spring from relatively few elements, or, indeed, from an assumed unitary substratum of the universe.

58. CREATION.

The popular conception of creation is vague and confused. The old view, and the theological view generally, is the making of something without materials—creation out of nothing. But the mind cannot conceive this, and in the face of mediaeval theologism the maxim *ex nihilo nihil fit* has always been constantly repeated and never seriously gain-said. The only rational or thinkable idea of creation has always been that of putting previously existing things into new forms. It is common to speak of the perfection of nature and to hear it said that art imitates nature. These are both false conceptions. Nature is everywhere imperfect, and art always aims to improve upon nature. The mind at a certain stage of development, or with a certain amount of cultivation and training, becomes capable of forming ideals of perfection. It acquires the power of seeing the defects in nature and of supplying them in imagination. This is the creative imagination which precedes all art. Creative genius is the next step, which is the capacity for supplying these defects in nature outside of the imagination in some concrete objective way. The fine arts are the ways in which it does this.

59. SOCIAL IDEALS.

We have seen that the essential condition of all art is the psychic power of forming ideals. Their execution is certain to follow their creation. It has often been remarked that persons of an artistic turn of mind often become, especially in later life, social reformers, and the examples of Ruskin, William Morris, Howells, Bellamy, and others are brought forward. An artist or art critic, like Ruskin, possesses a mind specially constituted for seeing ideals in nature. Such a mind instantly detects the defects in everything observed and unconsciously supplies the missing parts. After a life engaged in the search of ideals in the world of material things, the mind often grows more serious and is more and more sympathetic. It lays more stress on moral defects, and in the most natural way conceivable it proceeds to form ethical and social ideals by the same process that it has always formed aesthetic ideals. The defectiveness of the social state in permitting so much suffering is vividly represented, and the image of an ideal society in which this would be prevented spontaneously arises in the mind. Instinctively, too, the born artist, now become a social artist, proceeds to construct such an ideal society, and we have a great array of Utopias, and Arcadias, and Altrurias, in which imagination drives out all the hard, stern realities of life, and leaves only Edens and Paradises. The highest flights of artistic ingenuity and creative power are attained, and by looking forward and backward every shadow that is cast on society is banished, leaving only sunlit Elysian fields.

In other words the moral and social reformer exercises the same faculty as the poet, the sculptor, and the painter, and out of all these fields of art there have been recruited, in this perfectly natural and legitimate way, philanthropists, humanitarians, socialists, idealists, religious, economic, and social reformers.

60. THE POETIC IDEA.

The train of thought that we have been following out naturally leads us to consider the nature of the poetic idea. The close relation or practical identity of poetry and prophecy has been frequently recognized, and a comprehension of the truths of organic development may supply the materials for a clear conception of so different a phenomenon as the unfolding of a poetic or prophetic formula. A true poet, especially one whose mind is stored with the wisdom of the world, is in very truth a prophet, and is the subject of veritable inspirations, which he occasionally formulates as it were unconsciously. He is a seer, *i.e.*, he sees truth that others do not see. He sees it only vaguely and utters it vaguely in forms that may seem meaningless to his contemporaries, but after time has wrought its changes and separated out the elements that were in his mind the meaning of his phrases emerges, and the truth vaguely expressed becomes definite and clear. The faculty is, like imagination, a purely creative one. The truth expressed was never presented to the senses, but only its elements, which he puts together and constructs a new truth which time will ultimately reveal.

Now the objective evolution of nature is parallel to the subjective evolution of mind, and a study of evolution throws light on mental processes. In the organic world we know that the course of evolution is from the homogeneous to the heterogeneous through systematic differentiation. Similarly in the mental world *a poetic idea is a homogeneous, undifferentiated truth* embodying the germs of many distinct truths which, in the process of time and of the general development of ideas, are destined to take clear and definite forms. As such, its vagueness of both conception and expression belongs to its essential character.

61. POESIS.

This term is used in the primary sense of the Greek word*, and not in the later derivative sense of poesy or poetry. In this sense it is the exact opposite of genesis. Most of what has been said of what is called fine art is true also of practical art. Whichever should stand first, and they were doubtless developed *pari passu*, inventive genius, as well as creative genius, is a faculty for putting together raw materials so as to form new combinations. The product is something different from that which existed before. It is a creation. Poesis is a form of creative synthesis. In aesthetic creation the thing made is an ideal freed from the crudities of nature and beautiful to contemplate. In inventive creation the thing made is useful and serves a practical purpose. Here the defects of nature that are specially attended to are the obstructions to existence. Nature is wasteful and extravagant, and inventive genius works for economy. The special quality to which inventive genius applies itself is *utility*. Here is a new or fourth category to be added to the conventional three—truth, beauty, goodness. The useful is not the same as the good, as used in this formula, but it is even more important because of universal application, while the field of ethics is a restricted one which is constantly contracting. The completed formula should then be: the true, the beautiful, the good, and the useful, in which the useful is not put last because least, but only because the last to be recognized.

But poesis is more than invention and more than art. It is both. It embodies a form of imagination as well as a form of creation. Or rather, as in aesthetic art, it first creates an ideal and then creates an object which materializes that ideal. The chief difference is in the nature of that ideal. Instead of an ideal beauty it is an ideal utility. Not enough has yet been said of this wonderful faculty of imagination. The popular conception of it is far too narrow. We sometimes hear of scientific imagination. There certainly is such. It is that faculty which coordinates the disordered

---

* ποίησις, a making.

impressions received through the senses and out of them constructs a truth. For truth is also an ideal, and thought is a form of creative synthesis. Experience never furnishes truth. Nothing but a creative faculty can bring truth from fact.

62. GENESIS.

Thus far only the psychological aspect of creative synthesis has been considered. Its cosmological aspect is still more important, but can be better understood in the light of these studies in mind. The truth now to be enforced is that nature also creates. Something is made to exist which did not exist before. It is made of preexisting materials, but it is different from any of those materials. What we miss is the ideal, for the creations of nature, being genetic, do not proceed from ideals. They are none the less creations. Wherever there is combination, as distinguished from mixture, something new results, and there is creative synthesis.

63. EACH SCIENCE A CREATIVE SYNTHESIS.

The order of the dependence of the sciences may now be seen to be something more than the inverse order of generality and complexity. There is a still deeper truth, viz., that each of the higher sciences is a product of the creative synthesis of all the sciences below it in the scale. Each science is thus distinct, though not independent. It is a new and different field of phenomena. Chemistry is not physics, but a science apart. Biology is not chemistry, nor is psychology, as Comte maintained, biology. Sociology is not psychology, still less biology. It is a science, new in the sense that it is newly created and newly discovered. It is the product of the recompounding of the simpler sciences.

64. SOCIOLOGY ALSO.

This principle also explains the relation of sociology to the special social sciences. It is not quite enough to say that it is a synthesis of them all. It is the new compound which their synthesis creates. It is not any of them, and it is not all of them. It is that science which they spontaneously generate. The special social sciences are the units of aggregation that organically combine to create sociology, but they lose their individuality as completely as do chemical units, and the resultant product is wholly unlike any of them and is of a higher order. All this is true of any of the complex sciences, but sociology, standing at the head of the entire series, is enriched by all the truths of nature and embraces all truth. It is the *scientia scientiarum*.

65. THE SOCIAL MIND A SYNTHESIS.

Still another vexed question finds its solution here, to wit, the question of the social consciousness or collective mind. It receives the same answer as the rest. The social mind is a product of spontaneous creative synthesis of all individual minds. In this sense it is real. It differs widely from any individual mind, and sometimes seems to be embryonic, *i.e.*, to take the form of the more primitive mind of man as we observe it in uncivilized races. This is due to the fact that in manifestations of the social mind the artificial restraints of civilized life are removed. The period of the evolution of civility is very short compared with the pre-civilized period, and the coat of civility is thin. The process of becoming civilized has been one of restraint. The civilized man puts his best foot forward. Civilized life helps to do this. Living in houses, everyone concealed from his fellows, favors the process. Now in the crowd, the restraints of civilized life are removed. The thin veneering that covers men's acts in society peels off, and the true character of the civilized man as an enlightened savage comes to light. The veneering consists of about half culture and half hypocrisy. The social mind partly lays off both these garbs and represents men more nearly as they are. The acts which would be objectionable in private life are shifted to the broad shoulders of all the rest, and no individual holds himself responsible for them.*

66. SYNTHETIC CREATIONS OF NATURE.

Nature is creative as well as man, and we may now briefly review a few of the most important of these synthetic creations. The fact to be insisted upon is that evolution is through and through creative. As change after change goes on from the nebular chaos toward universal cosmos, from cosmos to bios, and from bios to logos, long stretches intervene between these several great stadia, during which the creative products have not as yet assumed such definite forms as to constitute turning-points or crises in the march of the world's progress. But ever and anon such a stage is reached, and a new creative product is brought forth, so unlike anything

---

* Le Bon, *The crowd; Psychology of peoples*; Ross, *Social control*, pp. 45, 46.

that has hitherto existed, and so cardinal in its nature as to give, as it were, a new point of departure to all future evolution. At every such stage the universe seems to change front and thenceforward to march in a new direction. There have been many such cosmical crises, after each of which there has been a virtually new universe.

67. COSMIC CREATIONS.

Every world system is a cosmic creation. The material history of our planet has doubtless been repeated thousands of times in all the countless star systems within the limits of our universe, but in the course of this history there have been specially evolved three of the epoch-making properties that we are considering, viz., life, feeling, and thought. But these properties belong to certain material products that have first been evolved, each of which was a new creation. They have appeared at long intervals, and each successive product, while possessing all the properties of the one that immediately preceded it, possesses the one additional property by which it is specially distinguished. Each product is at once the

effect of antecedent causes and the cause of further effects, and the kinds of causes to which these latter belong may also be classified. Placing these products in a column in the ascending order of their development, and the properties they possess, the quality of their activities, the phenomena they manifest, and the nature of the causes through which they work, in parallel columns, we shall have the following table:—

SYNTHETIC CREATIONS OF NATURE

Products	Differential Attributes			
	Properties	Activities	Phenomena	Causes
Society	Achievement		Social	Telic
Man	Intellect		Psychic	
Animals	Feeling	Molar		Conative
Plants	Life		Vital	
Protoplasm	Motility			
Organic Compounds				Efficient
Inorganic Compounds	Chemism	Molecular		
Chemical Elements			Physical	
Universal Ether	Vibration	Radiant		

68. PRODUCTS AND PROPERTIES.

Each of these steps in evolution, or synthetic creations of nature, may be regarded as something new, *i.e.,* as something that had no existence before. Although their primary elements always existed, the combinations resulting in the several products constitute so many distinct things. Each new plane of existence thus attained is a fresh base of operations. The successive products and properties are so many discrete degrees in the history of the universe. Protoplasm is unlike any other product of chemism, and is, as Huxley says, the physical basis of life. Out of it sprang the plant world and the animal world. The chief differential attribute of the animal, however, is feeling—the property of self-awareness. The highest animals, it is true, possess the germs of intelligence, but for convenience of tabular representation, and for all practical purposes, intellect may be made to begin with man. The will belongs to animals and is the kind of force or causation that they employ. At bottom it is a form of the efficient cause, but it is deserving of a special designation. We will call such causes conative. The phenomena presented by protoplasm and by plants are vital. The differential (additional) phenomena presented by animals, including man, are psychic. But intellect is essentially a final cause. Man, with all the attributes of all the lower products and intellect added, generates another and highest product, society. That which chiefly distinguishes it from all other cosmic creations is its capacity for achievement. Social phenomena thus inaugurate another, and thus far the last, new departure in the history of evolution, viz., the movement toward civilization.

69. DEVELOPMENT SYMPODIAL.

It will not have escaped attention that at every one of the culminating points a new direction is given to the whole scheme by the appearance of a new product with its added attributes. The march of cosmic, as of organic, evolution is thus zigzag. It is perfectly homologous to the stem of a sympodial plant, which consists of a series of branches each of which has appropriated practically all the energy of the plant.

For the differential attribute which each cosmic product possesses in addition to those of all before it immediately becomes paramount, and the antecedent ones sink into relative insignificance. Each product with its concomitant attributes is thus a true sympode, and cosmic evolution is also sympodial.

70. THE FILIATION OF THE SCIENCES.

Finally it is to be noted that the series is parallel to that of the sciences of the "hierarchy." We saw that the sciences could be arranged in a natural succession, and that when so arranged they grow out of one another in such a manner that the term *filiation* could be properly applied to it. But this is because there is a corresponding relation among the phenomena themselves. This corresponding relation is the genetic succession of cosmic products with their differential attributes that we have been considering. The higher are generated by the lower through creative synthesis, and are thus affiliated upon them. The filiation of the sciences is the simple correlate of the filiation of the products and attributes of evolution.

REFERENCES TO WARD'S OTHER WORKS

- *Dynamic sociology*. Chapters Ill-VII inclusive, volume I. Topics in Index, volume II: Evolution; Force; Genesis; Ideas; Life.
- *Psychic factors*. Psychic; Psychology.
- *Outlines of sociology*. Chapters X and Xl.
- *Pure sociology*. Chapter V, pp. 79-96.
- *Article*. Natural storage of energy.

THE DYNAMIC AGENT

- **I. The Feelings.** —
- 71. Two prime agents in society.
- 72. Cosmic forces.
- 73. Social force.
- 74. Psychic forces.
- 75. Psychological basis of Sociology.
- 76. The feelings subjective.
- 77. Appetition.
- 78. Desire.
- 79. Philosophy of desire.
- 80. Original desires.
- 81. Derivative desires.
- 82. Biological origin of the subjective faculties.

- **II. The Conative Faculty.**—
- 83. Energy of nature.
- 84. Mind force.
- 85. Desire a force.
- 86. The emotions as forces.

- **III. The Soul.**—
- 87. Meaning of the term.
- 88. Its function.

- **IV. The Will.—**
  - 89. Meaning of the term.
  - 90. Optimism and pessimism.
  - 91. Meliorism.

I. THE FEELINGS

71. TWO PRIME AGENTS IN SOCIETY.

By glancing again at the table of synthetic creations of nature it may be observed that the mode of producing effects, called the *cause* in the last column of the table, is in feeling conative, and in intellect telic. This distinction is fundamental, and upon it depends the primary subdivision of sociology. A conative cause is a form of the efficient cause, but it is psychic instead of physical; this distinction is fundamental, and calls for a wholly different method of treatment. The telic or final cause is not a force, as is every form of efficient cause, but it utilizes efficient causes and thus produces effects. It will be both convenient and correct to regard both the conative and the telic cause as agencies in sociology, or, still more definitely, as the two prime *agents* in society. The conative cause, being a true force, is the *dynamic agent*, the word *dynamic* being here used in its primary sense denoting force. The final cause is the *directive agent* of society, the nature of which will be set forth in Part IV.

72. COSMIC FORCES.

The synthetic creations of nature have their characteristic properties or modes of acting, and it is through these that they produce effects. Taken together these active properties constitute the forces of nature. These separate and apparently different forces are, however, only so many aspects of the one universal force, but it is convenient to treat them as distinct. Each of these products, moreover, may be said to form the basis or subject-matter of a science, and these sciences also are distinct. They are creations, and represent successively new aspects of cosmic history. Every true science is a domain of forces, and the nature of the forces differs with the science. As man possesses feeling in common with the lower animals, it is important to note that feeling constitutes the dynamic agent, and is therefore the highest attribute that we have to consider so long as we are dealing with the dynamic agent.

73. SOCIAL FORCE.

Now feeling is a true cosmic force, and constitutes the propelling agent in animals and in man. In the associated state of man it is the social force, and with it the sociologist must deal. Under this agency social phenomena take place according to uniform laws which may be studied in the same way that the laws of any other domain of phenomena are studied. Sociology is thus a true science, answering to the definition of a science, viz., a field of phenomena produced by true natural forces and conforming to uniform laws. But feeling as the dynamic agent manifests itself in a variety of ways, and just as it is convenient and practically correct to speak of a plurality of natural forces, so it is convenient and practically correct to speak of a plurality of social forces.

74. PSYCHIC FORCES.

The conservation of energy and correlation of forces are as applicable to psychic and social forces as to physical forces. This truth has been perceived by sociologists, but failure to understand the principle of creative synthesis has led to grave misconceptions. Some of them, for example, talk as though these higher forces were eternal and could never be added to or subtracted from, but were unchangeable in quantity. The truth is that they are comparatively recent developments. There can be no psychic force where there is no mind, no vital force where there is no life. There can be no mind where there are no brain or nerve ganglia, no life where there is no animal, plant, or protoplasm. The products must first be created in which the forces inhere, but of course the properties appear *pari passu* with the products, and both conform to the process of genesis, or becoming, through infinitesimal increments. Before life and mind can exist they must first be constructed. To say that they exist in some diffused state in the universe is as false as to say that houses exist in a bank of clay out of which bricks may be made. Vital and psychic forces are new creations, and they can only be brought into existence through the delicate instrumentalities of organic development. Physiological dynamos must be established at convenient points, and from these ganglionic power-houses the currents of life and sensibility must be sent round through the animal tissues. Motor and sensor apparatus must be perfectly adjusted. Finally a great central storage battery, the brain, must be devised and put in charge of the whole system. All this must be accomplished before any great development of vital and psychic force can take place. From this point on greater and greater quantities of mind power can be stored for use, until the phenomena of intelligence shall at length dimly appear and thenceforward increase, until mind reaches the stage at which it can contemplate its own history and development.

75. PSYCHOLOGICAL BASIS OF SOCIOLOGY.

The social forces are therefore psychic, and hence sociology must have a psychologic basis. It cannot be based directly upon biology, which only manifests the phenomena of the vital forces. It may be said that animals possess feeling although coming within the domain of biology. This is true, and psychology begins with the animal. It is psychology that rests on biology. Here there is direct filiation, and mind is of biologic origin. The popular conception of "mind" is wholly inadequate for the sociologist. The word *mind* certainly must include the feelings, the emotions, the passions, the will. This is of course recognized by scientific psychologists, who usually divide psychology into two departments, the one consisting of the senses and the intellect, and the other of the emotions and the will. A clear distinction between these two departments of mind is fundamental to the sociologist. He must discover the forces that govern social phenomena, and the thinking faculty is not a force. Feeling is a true force, and its various manifestations constitute the social forces.

76. THE FEELINGS SUBJECTIVE.

The feelings had, moreover, a much earlier origin than the intellect, so that during a prolonged period they constituted the only psychic manifestations, and do so still throughout practically the entire animal world. This great primordial half of mind is sometimes appropriately said to constitute the *affective* side of mind, since it embraces all the *affections* in the broadest sense of that word. It is also, with equal propriety, called the subjective department of mind, the phenomena being wholly subjective or relating to the organism, and never objective or relating to the external world.

77. APPETITION.

It is essential to our present purpose to point out that one of the inherent qualities of feeling is that of seeking an end. That is to say, it is appetitive, and this is popularly recognized by the word *appetite*. All appetites belong to the subjective department of mind. A general term for this quality is *appetition*. Appetition is a motive and impels to action. It is this that constitutes it a force. It is an efficient cause, not a final cause. In a word, it is conative. It is the psychic motive to action. Action is certain to follow the motive unless prevented by some physical obstacle or by other motives that antagonize it and produce a state of psychic equilibrium. It is further true that no psychically endowed being can move without a motive. Such a thing would be an effect without a cause.

78. DESIRE.

In common parlance, appetition, or psychic motive, is simply desire, and desire of whatever kind is a true natural force. The collective desires of associated men are the social forces. This use of the word *desire* is, however, very broad. It embraces all wants, volitions, and aspirations. From this point of view feeling is identical with desire. Primarily all feeling is intensive. It not only consists in an awareness of self, but in an awareness of some need. Wasting tissues constantly need to be renewed, and feeling consists in a sense of this need. With increased complexity of structure other needs arise, until in man and society the wants are unlimited in number and variety. Man's whole affective nature is composed of them. All emotions and all passions consist, on final analysis, of appetitions. All cravings, yearnings, and longings, all hopes, anticipations, aspirations, and ambitions are such. But they may be negative, or forces of repulsion instead of attraction. Such are fear, hate, envy, jealousy. When the desire is beyond all hope of satisfaction, they take the form of grief, sorrow, disappointment, and despair. Man is thus a theater of desires, positive, negative, or suppressed, all of which cause some form of action, and which together constitute the dynamic agent.

79. PHILOSOPHY OF DESIRE.

It is therefore well worth our while to consider for a moment the philosophy of desire. Desire is a sensation, and it must be regarded as an unpleasant sensation. The activity it causes is always expended in removing the restraint. Until this is accomplished the sensation must be a disagreeable one. If it were agreeable, the effort would be in the direction of continuing it, not of terminating it. Desire is therefore in the nature of pain. But supposing that the desire is fresh and healthy, its satisfaction is a pleasure, and when we consider the great number and variety of desires to which man is subject and the fact that most of them are actually satisfied sooner or later, we may form some idea of the volume of pleasure that is thus yielded. It constitutes the bulk of all that makes existence tolerable. It is possible to make a rough calculation of the relative amount of satisfied and unsatisfied desire. If the latter prevail over the former, we have a social state which Dr. Simon N. Patten has happily characterized as a "pain economy," and if the reverse is the case, we have his "pleasure economy."* All social progress, in the proper sense of the phrase, is a movement from a pain economy toward a pleasure economy, or at least a movement in the direction of the satisfaction of a greater and greater proportion of the desires of men.

80. ORIGINAL DESIRES.

Of the stronger, conscious, and often violent desires those of hunger and love of course hold the first place. These are original, *i.e.*, not in any sense derivative, and belong to all creatures. They are both perfectly typical desires, and all that has been said of desire in general applies to them. They are the chief mainsprings to action, and it may almost be said that all other desires are directly or remotely derived from them. This statement, however, would require qualification. But these forces have not diminished with higher organization and the appearance of the other desires. They are quite as strong in man as in animals, and in the higher types of men as in the lower types. In society they become the principal social forces and the foundations of sociology. They impel mankind to the performance of the great bulk of all the operations of society. They are strong and reliable forces and capable of working out spontaneously most of the problems that physical life presents.

81. DERIVATIVE DESIRES.

Political economists early seized upon this truth, and it may be regarded as the basis of all economics. The failure of mathematical economics to meet the modern problems of life and business was not due to any flaw in positing the reliability of human impulses. It correctly grasped the fundamental forces of society, but it grounded on the failure to recognize the importance of the higher forces. These, as we shall see, were a factor before the era of machinery, and have steadily advanced in importance

---

* *The theory of social forces*, pp. 59, 60, 75.

with civilization, until they have become second only to the primary motives that we are considering. With the development of mankind the derivative forces come more and more into the foreground until a point is at length reached at which they seem at least to be more potent agencies than the original forces. These are also true natural forces, and simply swell the volume of social energy. Sociology takes account of them all, and is the science which treats of what the social forces have done and are doing, and of how they accomplish results.

82. BIOLOGICAL ORIGIN OF THE SUBJECTIVE FACULTIES.

The supreme importance to sociology of the dynamic agent justified in a previous work* a lengthy explanation of the biologic origin of the subjective faculties. The substance of this argument may here be briefly indicated. The object of nature seems to be to convert as large an amount as possible of inorganic into organic and organized matter. As an aid to this object there developed in certain of its creations an interest, an intensive feeling, a capacity for pain and pleasure. This agency, intended as an aid to function, became ail end in itself, in that sentient beings sought pleasure for its own sake irrespective of function, and this threatened the success of the organic experiment as a whole. Then followed *the elimination of the wayward,* which Darwin called *natural selection,* and Spencer, *the survival of the fittest.* To check this growing destructive tendency two devices were developed; instinct for the animal world in general, and reason for man alone. Reason took the form of counteracting the pursuit of dangerous pleasures by the fear of greater pains. It also elaborated a system of social control provided with coercive machinery so as to hold the refractory in check. This social instinct, or group sentiment of safety, developed into religion, law, and government. Further intellectual development, and wider knowledge and wisdom, may ultimately enable men to dispense with all social restraints to unsafe conduct, but the world is still far from this ideal.

---

* *Pure sociology,* chapter VII.

II. THE CONATIVE FACULTY

83. ENERGY OF NATURE.

Nature is not only a becoming, it is a striving. The universal energy never ceases to act, and its ceaseless activity constantly creates. The quantity of matter, mass, and motion in the universe is unchangeable; everything else changes—position, direction, velocity, path, combination, form.—To say with Schopenhauer that matter is causality involves an ellipsis. It is not matter but *collision* that constitutes the only *cause*. This eternal pelting of atoms, this driving of the elements, this pressure at every point, this struggle of all created things, this universal nisus of nature, pushing into existence all material forms and storing itself up in them as properties, as life, as feeling, as thought, this is the hylozoism of the philosophers, the self-activity of Hegel, the will of Schopenhauer, the atom-soul of Haeckel; it is the soul of the universe, the spirit of nature, the "First Cause" of both religion and science—it is God.

84. MIND FORCE.

We saw that feeling, at first so completely at the service of function, soon became the *end* of the creature and threatened to defeat the very purpose for which it was created, rendering necessary the further creation of powerful checks to this tendency. So long as the functional ends of life were not put in jeopardy these new activities of the mind were harmless, and, indeed, since they represented a great increase of life power, they were useful in accelerating the consummation of nature's ends. The addition of mind force greatly increased the quantity of force that had been withdrawn from the physical world and converted into organic energy. The conative form of causation now at work was far more potent than the purely mechanical form that had hitherto prevailed.

85. DESIRE A FORCE.

It can now be better seen how desire came to constitute the real psychic force. Desire presupposes memory, which must therefore be one of the earliest aspects of mind. In fact, memory is nothing but the persistent representation of feeling, continued sense vibrations after the stimulus is withdrawn, and involves no mystery. In case of an agreeable sensation, as the pleasure fades on the withdrawal of the stimulus, a desire arises to renew or continue the pleasure, and this is all that constitutes desire. But though simple in its explanation, it is powerful and far-reaching in its effects. But for this interruption in the agreeable states with faint intermediate mnemonic vibrations, there would be no activity directed to the renewal or repetition of those intenser states. The withdrawal of the stimulus is in the nature of a deprivation or want, and this is the true character of all desire.

86. THE EMOTIONS AS FORCES.

As the activities thus produced normally led to function and secured the preservation, perpetuation, and increase of life, it was to the interest of these ends that this conative power be increased to the utmost, and consequently we find that in the higher organisms special centers exist in connection with the leading functions for the accumulation of this energy, and the performance of such functions is attended with intense satisfaction, while inability to perform them creates an almost irresistible desire. This is of course best exemplified in the two great primordial functions, nutrition and reproduction, with the corresponding physical imperatives, hunger and love, which are typical desires. But in the higher mammals, and especially in man, many other centers have been developed —storage batteries of psychic energy—which, though in the main more or less connected with the primary ones, are practically distinct. Hence arise emotions, painful as well as pleasurable, and these are chiefly in the nature of desires. They all represent the deprivation of something once enjoyed. If there is the least chance of regaining the lost object, there is scarcely any limit to the amount of exertion that will be put forth for the attainment of that end. This renders them the most powerful forces in society, and next to the efforts put forth for the supply of the primary wants above mentioned, the emotions constitute the chief social stimuli or social forces.

III. THE SOUL

87. MEANING OF THE TERM.

What is the soul?* Our own English word soul is so far given over to religious usage, under the influence of the doctrine of immortality, that it is

---

* G. Stanley Hall, *Adolescence*, volume II, chapter X.

difficult to separate it from that world view and look upon it as a real scientific fact. The German word *Seele* seems not to be so trammelled, and expresses the phenomenon of *animation* or conscious spontaneous activity. This is the central idea in the conception of the soul, and it was possessed by the first and lowest animate beings. The moment an interest to move in a definite way for a definite purpose was planted in them the soul was born, and their continued conscious activities under the spur of that interest is that which has produced the varied forms of animal life.

88. ITS FUNCTION.

The soul is well described in Genesis as "the Spirit of God" that "moved upon the face of the waters," for the sea must have been the cradle of life in which consciousness first dawned. From the standpoint of hylozoism this spirit may be said to "sleep in the stone, dream in the animal, and awake in man," for its elements lay dormant in the inorganic world, and it was only in man, and in a higher type of man, that self-consciousness arose, viz., a consciousness of consciousness. But as more and more inorganic matter was converted into living forms, larger and larger quantities of physical and vital energy were converted into psychic energy, and the soul grew and acquired greater power. It became a transforming agency and a potent influence in the transmutation of species and the development of higher and more multiform types of life. It was the chief cause of variation and hence the prime factor in organic evolution. On the human plane the soul has become enriched by the introduction of all the derivative affections, the passions and emotions of which we have spoken, until it has carried its transforming influence beyond the individual organism into the social organism and into the environment, and has become the agent of social evolution.

IV. THE WILL

89. MEANING OF THE TERM.

*When we consider all this volume of feeling as essentially a striving, we find in it all the elements of the will. It is the conative faculty, and in this lies its immense importance to sociology. Feeling, as we have seen, starts

---

* Schopenhauer, *The world as will and idea.*

with interest, and immediately becomes a desire. Using desire in its widest possible acceptation, there is a sense in which it may be identified with will. It is the wish, the vow, the prayer, the yearning, of the soul. To clothe this with all the attributes of will we have only to observe it passing into action. Will is the active expression of the soul's meaning. If it does not pass into action, it at least passes into effort, and it is effort rather than action in which the dynamic quality inheres. The interests of life must be subserved; pains experienced or feared must be escaped; life must be preserved and continued; hopes, aspirations, ambitions, goals, must be realized. It is will that accomplishes all this. Without it all is lost. This is the meaning of optimism as a principle of nature rather than a world view or tenet of philosophy. There is no balancing of the gains and losses of existence. There is no faltering or hesitation. Existence must be preserved, and nature has pointed the way. The will gives the command and the body obeys. The effort is put forth, and the result is limited only by the amount of physical power and the amount of resistance encountered.

90. OPTIMISM AND PESSIMISM.

Optimism is the normal attitude of all sentient beings. No other attitude is possible in the animal world or in any type of mankind that has not reached a high degree of intellectual development. Only such a developed intellect when deprived of an adequate knowledge of nature is capable of inventing a quietistic philosophy. The doctrine of the denial of the will, if it could be rigidly enforced, would quickly terminate the course of any race that should practice it. Natural, spontaneous, or impulsive optimism is true, and is a healthy social influence. It means self-preservation, race continuance, and social progress. But rational optimism is both false and shallow. The moment the light of reason is turned upon it, it withers and decays. A little reason corrupts and neutralizes the optimistic impulses and produces that false and mongrel optimism that teaches the folding of the arms and the gospel of inaction. More reason penetrates to the dark reality and ends in pessimism or the gospel of despair and nirvana.

91. MELIORISM.

But it is possible to probe still deeper and to find again the hope that characterizes the first blind sub-rational or ultra-rational struggle for existence. Rational optimism and pessimism are products of the naked reason, than which no guide is more unsafe. The true guide, the Moses that is to lead man out of the wilderness, is *science*. The naked reason must be clothed. Man must learn to *know*. He must learn how and why he is subjected to all these woes, and then he may see a way of escaping them. The only science that can teach this is social science. This science does teach it, and it gives forth no uncertain sound. The mental and social state to which social science Points is neither optimism nor pessimism, but *meliorism*. Meliorism means the liberation of the will, so that it may assert itself as freely and as vigorously as it ever did under the rule blind impulse. It means the massing and systematic application of all the vastly increased powers of developed man to the perfected machinery of society. The avenues of action should be cleared and not choked up as at present. Different social movements should be along appointed paths and not in opposite directions in the same path so as to neutralize each other. The combined social will may thus be so adjusted as to exert its full force in one harmonious and irresistible effort toward the accomplishment of the supreme social end.

REFERENCES TO WARD'S OTHER WORKS

- *Dynamic sociology*. Topics in Index, volume II: Conative faculty; Consciousness; Desire; Emotions; Fatalism; Feelings; Meliorism; Optimism; Pessimism; Will.
- *Psychic factors*. Chapters VI-XV inclusive and Chapter XIX. Index: Consciousness; Desire; Dynamic; Emotional sense; Emotions; Feelings; Meliorism; Optimism; Pessimism; Soul; Will.
- *Pure sociology*. Chapters VI-VIII inclusive.

8

CLASSIFICATION OF THE SOCIAL FORCES

- 92. Basis of classification.
- 93. Choice of terms.
- 94. Classification.
- 95. Meaning of terms.
- 96. Relationships among the social forces.
- 97. Paradoxes.
- 98. Relative value of feeling and function.
- 99. Enjoyment as an end.
- 100. Fear of natural phenomena.
- 101. Utilization of social forces.

92. BASIS OF CLASSIFICATION.

There are many ways of classifying social phenomena.* In a certain very wide sense all force is one, but from its different modes of manifestation it is convenient to recognize a number of forces. Our point of view is that of regarding sociology as a true science, and the principal characteristic of a true science is that it is a domain of natural phenomena produced by a special class of forces. The forces producing social phenomena are the social forces, and taken together they constitute the dynamic agent. The social forces are wants seeking satisfactions through efforts, and are thus

---

* See e.g. *Stuckenberg, Sociology*, volume I; *Fairbanks, Introduction*.

social motives, or motors inspiring activities. They reside in the individual, but become social through interaction, cooperation, and cumulative effects. They are all primarily physical or physiological, even those classed as spiritual, for the organism is the only source from which they can emanate.

93. CHOICE OF TERMS.

At the outset, we encounter the obstacle presented by the choice of terms. Although the dynamic agent consists wholly in feeling, such is the poverty of the language of feeling that it would be difficult or impossible to find the requisite terms in that vocabulary. For this reason it seems best to choose most of the terms from the language of function. Here there is comparatively little difficulty. The world has always avoided as far as possible the expression of feeling. It exposes too plainly the bodily and mental states, which are naturally concealed. Under the highest states of feeling indifference is feigned. If the feeling is pleasurable, there is either an ascetic sense of its sinfulness or a sense of shame in its avowal, and it is experienced in silence. If it is painful, it involves the admission of imperfection or defectiveness, which no one wishes to admit. Everything thus conspires to the suppression of the utterance of feeling and to prevent the possibility of the development of a rich and copious language of feeling. But when it comes to function, the case is reversed. Here the language is rich and the vocabulary ample. This is because of the supposed dignity and nobility of function. It is instinctively felt that the preservation of the individual and the race, the maintenance of the social order, the furtherance of social progress, and the aesthetic, moral, and intellectual development of mankind are paramount considerations upon which any amount of effort and energy may be profitably expended. The consequence is that they have from the first been made the subjects of exhaustive treatment, and thousands of volumes have been written dealing with them from almost every conceivable point of view. It is this that has rendered the language of function so full and complete.

94. CLASSIFICATION.

The classification, then, may be given the following form:—

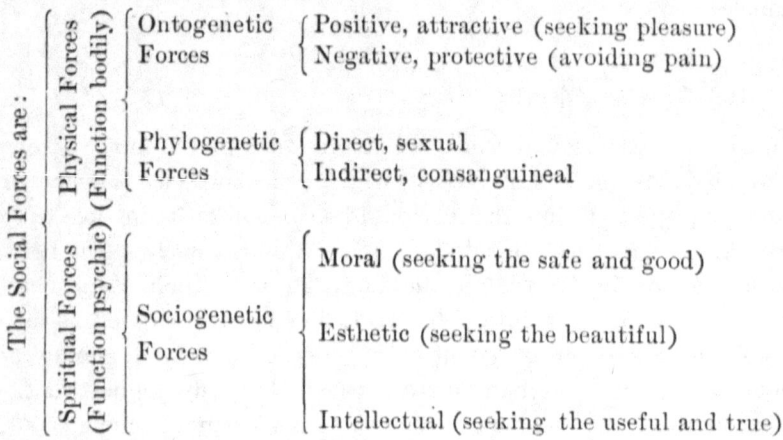

95. MEANING OF TERMS.

The Ontogenetic or the Preservative Forces may be called the Forces of Individual Preservation; the Phylogenetic or the Reproductive Forces may be called the Forces of Race Continuance; and the Sociogenetic Forces as a whole may be called the Forces of Race Elevation. Although the forces called preservative in the above table of classification are desires and wants of individuals, and serve primarily to preserve the lives of individuals, it is also true that they are the influences which work for the maintenance of the social order through the principle of social synergy,* and they are therefore the forces of social as well as individual preservation. We shall therefore use, as synonymous with the expression "preservative forces," the expression *ontogenetic forces*. In like manner the "reproductive forces" may be called the *phylogenetic forces*, as the influences that work the perpetuity and continuity of the *phylum*, hereditary stock, or race. From the standpoint of function they take no account of the individual, but in continuing the race they make the life of the individual, as it were, continuous. In thus continuing the membership of society they continue society itself. This is true social reproduction. The

---

* See chapter XII.

term *sociogenetic forces* is applied to the "spiritual forces," meaning by this that they are psychic in a somewhat different and "higher" or "nobler" sense than the physical forces, which are designated as "physical," not that they can be other than psychic, but simply that their *functions* are physical, while the functions of the spiritual forces are also psychic. As "forces of race elevation," these are the chief civilizing agencies. They are also the chief socializing agencies. But the difference between civilizing and socializing agencies is not wide. Whatever is socializing either is, or may become, civilizing. Socialization is the first step toward civilization, and all aesthetic, moral, and intellectual influences are working for civilization chiefly through socialization.

96. RELATIONSHIPS AMONG THE SOCIAL FORCES.

Many other relationships might be pointed out among the social forces. The physical forces may be regarded as original and the spiritual as derivative, and it is practically true that the latter are confined to the human race, while the former are common to both men and animals. It is also true that while the former become social by stimulating activities which unconsciously produce social effects, the latter are essentially socializing and tend to race elevation and universal culture. Again, all the physical forces may be regarded in one sense as negative, since they are directed to the prevention of pain rather than the production of pleasure. Hunger, thirst, cold, fear, want of every kind, and also love, are painful states, to escape from which men continually strive, while the satisfactions derived from successful efforts in these directions are for the most part momentary and count for next to nothing as pleasures compared to the gain of having escaped from the pains. On the other hand the spiritual forces may be classed as positive, since to a much less degree are they directed to the relief of pain, and they are almost wholly directed to securing pleasures whose absence is not felt as a pain. Sympathy, it is true, is a secondary or *representative* pain, an echo in self of the pains of others, but most moral action is performed for the pleasure it yields, and not to escape from even this form of pain. The aesthetic forces are still more positive in this sense, while the intellectual forces seem to be wholly so.

97. PARADOXES.

Among other relations of the social forces we find a class which may be characterized as *paradoxes of the social forces*. The facts last stated might be classed among these paradoxes, viz., that the physical impulses are negative, while the spiritual ones are positive. But it is also true that the physical forces are altruistic, while the spiritual forces are egoistic. The maintenance of life and of the race are highly altruistic objects, and it is these that the physical forces secure. On the other hand, the spiritual forces are egoistic. This follows from what has just been said, in that they are not modes of escape from danger to the individual and the race, but ways of pursuing pleasure for its own sake. There is great confusion in the popular ideas of high and low, coarse and refined, worthy and unworthy. The most worthy and noble of all things are those that preserve and perpetuate the race. This is function and the end of nature. The physical social forces are therefore those that represent the highest necessity, while the spiritual forces chiefly represent utility. The fundamental criterion of utility is the quantity of satisfaction yielded, and, measured by this standard, it is clear that the spiritual interests far outweigh the physical interests of developed man. Physical satisfactions have greater intensity, but spiritual satisfactions have greater duration. This gives volume to spiritual pleasures much more than sufficient to counterbalance the greater intensity of physical pleasures. The physical forces are characterized by their necessity, while the spiritual forces are characterized by their utility. The former chiefly serve function and secure the ends of nature, standing thus largely oil the biological plane, while the latter minister to feeling and secure the ends of man, and therefore stand wholly on the sociological plane. The first are ontogenetic and phylogenetic, while the second are exclusively sociogenetic.

98. RELATIVE VALUE OF FEELING AND FUNCTION.

Here may be mentioned one of the most far-reaching laws in the domain of sociology, viz., that while function is fixed in quantity, feeling increases in proportion to development. It would be easy to illustrate this in the lower orders of life where everything seems to be subordinated to function, and nature seems wholly indifferent to feeling. In biotic progress it is obvious that the capacity for both pleasure and pain increases with the advance in structure. There has been a steady rise, as it were, in the price of life. The lowest savages value life at a very low figure and throw it away on the slightest provocation. The value put upon human life is one of the safest tests of true progress. But it is not life alone that is valued; it is rather what life affords. The primitive man is not only indifferent to life, but he is also indifferent to pain, as witness the horrible mutilations to which savages so often voluntarily submit, as we are told, without manifesting the usual reflex movements which even the thought produces in us. The savage, like the animal, lives chiefly in the present, and does not suffer the acute pains which a developed imagination enables the more refined organizations to represent in advance to the mind.

99. ENJOYMENT AS AN END.

But most important of all is the growing sense of *good* which equally characterizes the progress of intelligence. Not merely does man more and more value life and shrink from pain, but he progressively enhances his estimate of enjoyment, and properly so. This is to him the only good, and having been developed as a correlate of function it is safe in the long run to trust it. It has served this purpose well thus far, and upon those who deny it this function rests the burden of proof. What specially concerns the sociologist is the fact that with the development of the race more and more attention has been devoted to attaining the satisfactions of life, until these become in the most advanced societies the real if not the avowed ends of existence. To the credit of mankind be it said, moreover, that in all peoples at all developed, the lower satisfactions come gradually to constitute only a subordinate part of the object of existence, and more and more effort is expended in attaining those satisfactions which, though not essential to self-preservation or race continuance, possess for all elevated natures a far higher value.

100. FEAR OF NATURAL PHENOMENA.

In closing this chapter it is worthy of remark that the attitude of the civilized world toward the social forces is analogous to the attitude of the savage toward the physical forces. All know that this is one of apprehension. Fear and not love of nature is the characteristic of primitive peoples. There is something peculiarly awe-inspiring about the phenomena of nature. The fear they arouse is out of all proportion to the real danger. The sensation produced by earthquake shocks has been graphically described by Humboldt and Darwin, who, although rationally assured that there was little real danger, could not suppress that instinctive terror that all men have inherited from the savage state when nature was regarded as conscious and malignant. The sense of personal helplessness gives rise to those indescribable terrors that natural phenomena inspire. The idea of the possibility of influencing natural events or controlling physical forces thus manifested is wholly foreign to the primitive man, and the feeling is that if the inscrutable powers of nature really intend his destruction, there is no remedy.

101. UTILIZATION OF SOCIAL FORCES.

Now, civilized man, although he has learned not only to avert the dangers of the physical forces, but even to subjugate and utilize them, has made no progress with the social forces, and looks upon the passions precisely as the savage looks upon the tornado. Man is only civilized in relation to the lower and simpler phenomena. Toward the higher and more complex phenomena he is still a savage. He has no more thought of controlling, much less utilizing, the social forces than the savage has of controlling or utilizing the thunderbolt. Just as pestilences were formerly regarded as scourges of God, so the so-called evil propensities of man, which are nothing but manifestations of social energy, are still looked upon as necessary inflictions which may be preached against but must be endured. This difference is wholly due to the fact that while we now have sciences of physics, chemistry, geology, and bacteriology, which teach the true nature of storms, electricity, gases, earthquakes, and disease germs, we have no science of social psychology or sociology that teaches the true nature of human motives, desires, and passions, or of social wants and needs and the psychic energy working for their satisfaction. The sociologist who has a proper conception of his science as similar in all essential respects to these other sciences, and as having, like them, a practical purpose and use for man, looks upon the social forces as everybody looks upon the physical and vital forces, and sees in them powers of nature now doing injury, or at least running to waste, and perceives that, as in the other case, they may, by being first studied and understood, be rendered harmless and ultimately converted into the servants of man, and harnessed, as the lightning has been harnessed, to the on-going chariot of civilization.

REFERENCES TO WARD'S OTHER WORKS

- *Dynamic sociology*. Topics in Index, volume II: Fear; Function *vs.* feeling; Happiness; Non-essential social forces, Paradox; Pleasure; Preservative forces; Social forces.

- *Psychic factors*. Chapter XVIII. Index: Feeling *vs.* function; Happiness; Pain; Pleasure; Social forces.
- *Outlines of sociology*. Chapter VII.
- *Pure sociology*. Chapter XII.
- *Article*. Some social and economic paradoxes.

PART II

NATURE OF THE SOCIAL FORCES

9

THE ONTOGENETIC FORCES

- 102. The struggle for subsistence.

- **I. Exploitation:**
- 103. Cannibalism.
- 104. Slavery.
- 105. Labor.
- 106. Forced Labor.
- 107. Labor under the lash.
- 108. The ruling classes.

- **II. Property:**
- 109. Communal.
- 110. Origin of individual property.
- 111. Rights in property.
- 112. Property as wealth.
- 113. Pursuit of wealth the mainspring of activity.

- **III. Production:**
- 114. Slave production.
- 115. Machinofacture.
- 116. Importance of production.

- **IV. Social Distribution:**
- 117. The surplus.
- 118. The Ricardian law.
- 119. Causes of social distribution.

- **V. Consumption:**
- 120. Animal consumption.
- 121. Palatableness of food.
- 122. Protective wants.
- 123. Influence of comfort on development.
- 124. Physical importance of ample nutrition.
- 125. Nutrition essential to mental superiority.

102. THE STRUGGLE FOR SUBSISTENCE.

In this chapter, we have to consider the influence which those human activities that have subsistence for their ends exert on the creation and transformation of social structures. The struggle for existence in the animal world did not cease with the emergence of the human species out of that into the social world, but has always continued. At a very early stage the environment raises opposition and threatens injury, and defensive activities are added to the appetitive activities. The struggle grows more intense and the group sentiment is generated and creates incipient society. The primitive group or horde is the resultant social structure. Thus far the competition is with one another and with the environment, but when the time arrives for social integration to begin, the competition is one of group with group and wholly new elements enter into the struggle. The stage of race antagonism is reached and the era of war begins. The chase for animal food is converted into a chase for human flesh, and anthropophagous races arise, spreading terror in all directions.

I. EXPLOITATION

103. CANNIBALISM.

All social processes that can be called economic have their origin in exploitation. In entirely primitive social groups each individual goes about in the way that animals do, seeking food and shelter, and consuming whatever he finds. There is no social result any more than in the case of animals, certainly no more than in the case of such animals as dig holes or build nests. The efforts thus put forth have only the biological effect of somewhat strengthening the organs thus brought into exercise. The skill acquired in securing animal food strengthens the brain and increases the power of adaptation to varied physical conditions, which was the prime requisite to social differentiation. But early in the stage of social integration, the idea of making some economic use of such proximity was not slow to rise in the minds of those groups that proved themselves superior. The use of the bodies of the weaker races for food was, of course, the simplest form of exploitation to suggest itself. But this stage was succeeded by that of social assimilation through conquest and subjugation. The profound inequality produced by subjugation was turned to account through other forms of exploitation. The women and the warriors were enslaved, and the system of caste that arose converted the conquered race into a virtually servile class, while this service and the exemptions it entailed converted the leaders of the conquering race into a leisure class.

104. SLAVERY.

Such was the origin of slavery, an economic institution which is found in the earlier stages of all the historic races. The moral prejudices of the modern advanced races naturally cause wholly false views to prevail relative to slavery, which the sociologist finds it very difficult to contend with. As a matter of fact there never was a human institution that was not called forth in response to a social demand, which, from the scientific standpoint, means a social necessity.

But many structures, both organic and social, outlive their usefulness and persist as impediments to the life and health of the organism and of society. With regard to the institution of slavery we may say that it was an advance upon the practice of extermination, and still more upon cannibalism. It prevailed throughout antiquity and persisted in Europe through the Middle Ages. The sentiment condemning it is relatively modern. It is certainly confined, with very rare exceptions, to the last two centuries, and chiefly to the nineteenth century, and has been almost exclusively confined to that form of slavery which consisted in importing inferior races from their native country, chiefly Africa, and enslaving them in civilized countries.

105. LABOR.

Economists, socialists, statesmen, and industrial reformers, however widely they may differ on other matters, are agreed that all value in the economic sense is due to labor, but most of them talk as though labor was natural to man, and as though the main question was how to give men work enough to do. However this may be in civilized societies now, nothing is more certain than that the original problem was how to make men work. It does not seem to be seen that the human race has been radically transformed in this respect, and that the modern industrious artisan or laborer is utterly unlike his primitive ancestor. The pursuit of food wherever it can be found by the members of the primitive horde can no more be called labor than can the grazing of a buffalo or the browsing of an antelope. Nor is there any true labor involved in the operations of races in the next higher stages of culture, such as the work of the women in performing the drudgery of the camp. It may be safely inferred from all that is known of actual savages and primitive peoples, that prior to the period of social integration, and at the beginning of the period of conquest, mankind, both the conquered and the conquering races, were utterly incapable of sustained labor and had no conception of it. Men of that type would be perfectly worthless in the industrial world today. Their productive power in the economic sense would be nil.

106. FORCED LABOR.

Now contrasting the disciplined laborer of modern society with the undisciplined savage, this enormous and all-important change in human character has to be accounted for. How did man learn to work? Did the needs of existence teach him self-denial, tone down his wild, unsettled nature, and discipline his mind and body to daily toil? Not at all. It is safe to say that if left wholly to these influences, man would never have learned to labor. It required some other influence far more imperative and coercive. In a word, nothing short of slavery could ever have accomplished this. The aim of the conquering race was to gain the maximum advantage from the conquest. The only thing the conquered race possessed that had any permanent or continued value was its power of serving the conqueror. This could not escape the mind of the latter, however low his stage of intelligence, and as a matter of fact and of history, so far as these are known, this has been perceived and generally acted upon. The women and the warriors at least, and as many others as were needed, were enslaved and compelled to serve the conquering race.

107. LABOR UNDER THE LASH.

The motive to labor is no longer the desire to enjoy the fruits of labor. This, as we have seen, is never sufficient to induce primitive man to perform prolonged and arduous tasks. The motive now is fear of the lash. The slave must work or suffer any punishment his savage master pleases to inflict. If flogging does not suffice, he may be tortured; and if torture fails, he will be killed. No pen will ever record the brutal history of primitive slavery through generations and even centuries of which mankind was taught to labor. The bitterest scenes of an Uncle Tom's Cabin would be an agreeable relief from the contemplation of the stern realities of this unwritten history. It will never be known how many, unable to adapt themselves to such a great change from their former free, wild, capricious life, faltered, failed, and fainted by the way, to have their places taken by stronger, more flexible, and more adaptable ones, that could bear their burdens and transmit some small increment of their new-found powers of endurance to their posterity. For the capacity to labor is a typical "acquired character" that has been transmitted in minute additions from parent to offspring and from generation to generation of slaves, until great numbers of men were at last born with a "natural" or constitutional power to apply themselves to monotonous tasks during their whole lives. This truth has been dimly perceived by certain writers, but its immense economic importance has been almost completely overlooked.

108. THE RULING CLASSES.

The number of conquering races has always been relatively small and the number of conquered races has of course been correspondingly large. This came at length to mean that the "ruling classes" constituted only a small fraction of the population of the world, while the subject classes made up the great bulk of the population. It is riot, therefore, a small number of men that have been thus kept in training all these ages, but practically all mankind. It may sound paradoxical to call slavery a civilizing agency, but if industry is civilizing, there is no escape from this conclusion, for it is probably no exaggeration to say that, but for this severe school of experience continued through thousands of generations, there could have been nothing corresponding to modern industry.

86 | A TEXT-BOOK OF SOCIOLOGY

II. PROPERTY

109. COMMUNAL.

*An animal can scarcely be said to possess anything. Primitive hordes of men may be said to possess the few things needed for their existence, but here the line is practically drawn at the artificial. Even a club is artificial. The skin of an animal used as a blanket has cost the effort and skill of skinning the animal, and this usually presupposes some kind of instrument, a sharp-edged flint, for example, and such things may be said to "belong" to their "owners." But for most of the possessions of undeveloped races communal or group ownership is the prevalent form. One may call this property, but it is at best only an embryonic form of property in an economic sense. In this respect, as in so many others, the unassimilated races are sharply marked off from the assimilated races.

110. ORIGIN OF INDIVIDUAL PROPERTY.

We have now to deal with economic phenomena from still another point of view, viz., from that of the origin of property. As already said, the earlier form of property is chiefly communal, but the later form is individual possession. As property is only valuable in so far as it satisfies desire, the first form of individual property consisted largely in slaves, *i.e.*, in something that could serve, the owner and satisfy his wants. Beginning with women, used both to gratify the lust and also to wait on the person of the military chief, it extended to men, who could surround him with all manner of luxuries and do his general bidding. The other principal form of individual property, unknown in the earlier state, was land. The lower races lay claim to certain regions of country as hunting-grounds, but no one member of the group pretends to an exclusive right to any subdivision of that region. But after the conquest of one race by another, the leading warriors of the conquering race lay claim to all the territory occupied by the subject race and proceed to divide it up among themselves, assigning boundaries to the shares of each individual. This assumes more complex forms with successive assimilations, and ultimately creates the latifundia and the feudal fiefs.

All the other forms of property grow out of these two general classes,

---

* Letourneau, *Property*.

and the ruling classes come into the possession of flocks and herds, castles, vehicles, tools, weapons, and everything that can, minister to a life of ease and domination.

111. RIGHTS IN PROPERTY.

The true economic idea of property is the possession of useful commodities in excess of immediate needs. But as has been pointed out by many writers, property in this sense is impossible except under the protection of law and under the power of the state. When, then, the régime of law begins, rights are recognized and the state protects them. Now for the first time there arises the possibility of property, and it is at this stage that property as a human institution begins. When a man can own a camel or a buffalo skin, or a spear, or a bronze axe, and be secured in its possession without having to fight for it, or conceal it, it becomes property, and next to personal safety, the first and most important function of the state is to guarantee the security of rightful possession.

112. PROPERTY AS WEALTH.

Of the many ways in which the principle of permanent possession, or property, contributed to social development, the principal one was the incentive it furnished to accumulation. When it is seen that anyone may own much more of a thing than he can immediately use, can hold it for future consumption, or can barter it for other things that he does not possess, he will begin to acquire as large an amount as possible of that which he can most easily obtain and hold it in store for these and other purposes. But property in this sense means much more than this. It was the basis of exchange, of trade, of commerce, and of business in general as well as of industry in the more restricted sense. Property, when thus guaranteed and made convertible and flexible, is made an end and is pursued as such. A new desire, a new want, is thus created, which finally develops into a most imperative want. Property assumes the character of wealth, and the pursuit of wealth, wholly irrespective of the power to use it, becomes the supreme passion of mankind.

113. PURSUIT OF WEALTH THE MAINSPRING OF ACTIVITY.

A large part of the final intensity that this passion acquired was, of course, due to the adoption of a symbol or representative of property in the form of a circulating medium. Through this device all forms of property became blended and reduced to one, and the pursuit of wealth was converted into the pursuit of money which stands for wealth. Besides the legitimate effect in giving simplicity and ease to all business transactions, the introduction of money lent an additional charm to the pursuit of wealth and greatly intensified the passion. It gave rise to a universal plutolatry, which took fantastic forms, creating both misers and spendthrifts on the opposite margins of the social beam, but which had for its main and solid effect to penetrate and illumine the darkest corners of the material world. To it the material civilization of the great historic races is chiefly due. As a factor in human achievement this super-preservative social force, "the love of money," has had no rival, and still remains the mainspring of economic and industrial activity. If to the moralist it is "the root of all evil," to the sociologist, studying the causes of social development, it is the root of all the good there is in material civilization.

III. PRODUCTION

114. SLAVE PRODUCTION.

Production is the creation of property. This, though true, is not a definition, since there are forms of property, such as land, which are not properly produced. But production is only possible through labor, and is therefore a relatively late institution. Economists give a very broad meaning to production, as anything that creates or increases value. It might naturally be supposed that under a system of slavery, where the majority of the population is compelled to labor, production would be very rapid, but this is not the case. However large the number of slaves the masters find ways of consuming all they produce. The non-working classes, though numerically small, and naturally wasteful. Mr. Veblen* has shown how the mere maintenance of caste requires gratuitous and ostentatious waste of property, and this is greatly increased by rivalry in displaying wealth on the part of the members of the leisure class. The maintenance of the military rule consumes a large share, and another large portion goes to administration. In all the early societies there exists, besides the governing class properly so called, a sacerdotal class, which is a leisure class *par excellence*. This class is habitually the recipient of large emoluments and

---

* Veblen, *Theory of the leisure class.*

costly luxuries. All these expenses are paid by slave labor and by tribute from the free industrial class. Societies thus organized produce little in excess of their supposed needs, and slaveholding nations do not acquire wealth. That modification of this condition known as feudalism also represents a minimum of production and of wealth.

115. MACHINOFACTURE.

The earlier economists laid great stress on agriculture and the production of raw materials, and did not clearly see to how great an extent the value of the latter could be increased by skilled labor expended upon them. But now it is held that the real wealth of nations consists chiefly in this refinement of the original products. Agricultural nations are never rich, and mining countries do not become rich until provided with extensive manufactories. The great wealth of the leading nations of the world at the present time is almost wholly due to *machinofacture*.

116. IMPORTANCE OF PRODUCTION.

The sociological importance of production as thus understood consists in the power of highly elaborated products to satisfy desire, contribute to ease, comfort, and the enjoyment of life, and, in general, to render existence tolerable and desirable. Anyone going out of the centers of civilization into regions where "modern conveniences" have not penetrated immediately feels this. It is a common mistake to suppose that men usually have the means of satisfying all their wants. Aside from the very rich, whose unsatisfied wants consist of things that money will not buy, everyone at all times wants unnumbered things that money would buy if he had it. And aside from the abject poor that swarm in the richest countries, there is the great toiling proletariat who not only want many things that they never dare to hope for, but also need much to prevent physical suffering. There is therefore call for a greatly increased production, and there is no danger that too many useful things will be produced.

IV. SOCIAL DISTRIBUTION

117. THE SURPLUS.

The principles of economic distribution are very simple and have been repeatedly set forth. With them we have nothing to do here. But what may be distinguished as social distribution presents a problem. Under the exact scientific laws of political economy all surplus production should go to the ruling, owning, employing class. The slave of course owns nothing, any more than does a horse. But neither should the wage-worker own anything. The wage, according to the Ricardian law, is fixed at the precise amount that enables him to live and reproduce. If he is able to possess anything beyond these requirements, the wage is correspondingly reduced. If he weakens and fails to keep up his numbers, the law will spontaneously eke out his wage till he can again keep even.

118. THE RICARDIAN LAW.

Now, the question is, has this law always operated rigidly in society? So far as slavery is concerned we may say that it has; but outside of slavery has the working-man always been obliged to be content with the means of subsistence, including that of a family large enough to insure the rearing of two children for each pair to the age of reproduction, so that the number shall not diminish? If anything beyond this has occurred, then there has been social distribution to that extent. It can now be seen what is meant by social distribution. It is the socialization of wealth. It is some transgression of the iron law. It is the existence of defects, cracks, pores, and fissures in the economic dam, by which some small part at least of the surplus production seeps through and finds its way into the hands of the wage-earner. It is some check to the economic law whereby wages in excess of those required to live and reproduce fail to cause their prompt contraction to that point. No one need of course be told that in the present state of the world, at least, this process is going on.*

119. CAUSES OF SOCIAL DISTRIBUTION.

We are content to have discovered that the social forces have

---

* Willoughby, *Social justice*.

spontaneously secured some degree of social distribution, and we may cast a glance at some of the special causes that have produced this result. It is impossible at the outset for the ruling class to obtain a complete monopoly of labor, and after the establishment of civil law and the formation of the state, whereby rights to property were recognized, the economic laws operating among individuals of all degrees of inequality of mind and character, soon generated a sort of archetypal bourgeoisie with a multiplicity of small owners of varying degrees. As all know, the exploiting class then became chiefly the bourgeoisie, and under legal and political protection, especially after the era of machinery began, wealth passed into the hands of industrial leaders, and the great economic struggle began. But industry had now become greatly diversified, the remote regions of the world bad been opened up, and there were innumerable outlets for the laborer, dissatisfied with his lot. The great differences in ability and character among workmen produced grades and stimulated ambition. Exceptionally bright hands were called to more lucrative places, compelling employers to raise wages in order to retain their best men. Those who had received the higher grades of salary for considerable time found themselves in position to withdraw and set up business for themselves, thus becoming employers and perhaps "captains of industry." Such are a few of the ways in which the iron law of wages has been gradually mitigated, and social distribution secured.* Social distribution increases with increasing production, and if for no other purpose, therefore, than to increase the social distribution, increase of production is a social desideratum. The laborer becomes an element in the market, and it is more and more the interest of the proprietor of goods to let him share in their consumption. Increased production means diminished price, and the latter at last comes within the resources of the real producer.

V. CONSUMPTION

120. ANIMAL CONSUMPTION.

If political economy has nothing to do with consumption, sociology has everything to do with it. Consumption means the satisfaction of desire, the enjoyment of life, in short, human happiness. Animals and the inferior

---

* Durkheim, *De la division the travail social*. Ely, *Evolution of industrial society*.

types of men literally "eat to live." The stomach is the main seat of the nutrient attraction. The food is put there as quickly as possible and not allowed to linger on the way to tickle the papillae of the tongue and palate. Feed a hungry dog bits of meat and watch the process of deglutition. The interval between the time when the morsel touches the animal's jaws till it is safely landed in the stomach is as short as the action of the organs can possibly make it. It is so nearly instantaneous that the eye can scarcely follow the wave that flits along the throat during the act of swallowing. It cannot be said that such an animal takes any pleasure in eating. The demand for nutrition is so imperious that it wholly excludes all other considerations. The satisfaction is no doubt intense, but the enjoyment is nil. It might almost be said that the length of time it requires for food to pass from the lips to the stomach is a measure of civilization. It typifies the transition from a complete subjection to function to a recognition of feeling as also an end, from mere negative satisfaction to positive enjoyment, from a pain economy to a pleasure economy.

121. PALATABLENESS OF FOOD.

Such a movement there has been throughout the history of human development. In connection with food alone it has consisted in a general improvement in the palatableness of food. Instead of being eaten in its natural state nearly all food is now prepared, the most important part of the preparation consisting in cooking it. This preparation of food, besides greatly increasing the number of food products, converting into food many things that previously were not edible, has chiefly tended to render all kinds of food better, more savory, more palatable and toothsome, and thus to convert the nutritive act from a mere imperative necessity into a greater and greater source of enjoyment. Along with this, and as a consequence of it, there has gone an increased inclination to masticate food, and thus to prolong the period of this enjoyment. The habit of eating slowly, of providing a variety of articles of food, of preparing them in a variety of ways, of combining them variously, and of seasoning food, and all the arts of modern cookery—all this represents the same process of seeking to derive the maximum good from the physical necessity of eating.

122. PROTECTIVE WANTS.

Not less marked has been the tendency in the same general direction in the satisfaction of the defensive and protective wants of mankind. If we leave out the means of protection from human enemies in the form of offensive and defensive weapons, these consist chiefly in clothing, shelter, and fuel. To review the progress in all these would be both tedious and unnecessary, but we have only to point to architecture as an aesthetic art to show that the movement was toward the realization of ideals, and that the needs of existence soon ceased to be the motive that caused man to build. In modern times the chief architectural motive is *comfort*, which, after all, is the same as pleasure, enjoyment, happiness. Almost the same might be said of clothing, except that here the field was more open for the extravagances of fashion, and even these are a form of enjoyment for those constituted to prefer them. Upon the whole the evolution of dress has conduced to the fulness of social life.

123. INFLUENCE OF COMFORT ON DEVELOPMENT.

The relation that the full satisfaction of men's wants bears to the physical and mental development of the race is of the highest interest to the sociologist. Many travelers have noted the superior size of the chiefs and rulers of the lower races, and the fact seems to be general. It is also often remarked that civilized men are usually superior to savages physically as well as mentally. The general physical superiority of great men in all departments, notwithstanding certain marked exceptions which have, attracted attention because anomalous, has also been occasionally noted. Galton expresses a common feeling when he says: "A collection of living magnates in various branches of intellectual achievement is always a feast to my eyes; being, as they are, such massive, vigorous, capable-looking animals."* A false notion to the contrary of all this prevails, but one has only to look around. Go into any business establishment and you will in nine cases out of ten instantly pick out the proprietor by his superior physique. It is pretty generally true not only that a sound mind requires a sound body, but that superior minds, including all the qualities of character that insure success, are associated with superior bodies, usually larger than the mean for the race, and well-formed, healthy, active, and strong.

124. PHYSICAL IMPORTANCE OF AMPLE NUTRITION.

Galton would concede all this, but his conclusion from it is that these men

---

* *Hereditary genius*, p. 321.

94 | A TEXT-BOOK OF SOCIOLOGY

are where they are because they are superior. It would probably be more nearly true to say that they are superior because they are where they are. The real truth lies between these two propositions. Galton has emphasized the first. The second should be fully recognized. Life is very flexible. It adapts itself to circumstances. Its preservation is so essential that it cannot be destroyed by reducing the amount of nutrition. In the history of life there have been wide vicissitudes in this respect, and the organism has been adapted and adjusted to these vicissitudes. If food is abundant, the organism comes up to that standard and is correspondingly robust. If the supply falls off, the standard is lowered to correspond, but life goes on. Unless too sudden, a great diminution of the supply can thus be sustained without destroying life. The creature becomes what is called *stunted*, but does not perish.

125. NUTRITION ESSENTIAL TO MENTAL SUPERIORITY.

Ample natural nutrition enjoyed by a whole people or by a large social class will cause a healthy development which will ultimately show itself through physical and mental superiority. Thus far, such has been the history of mankind that it has always been a special class that has been able to obtain the means thus fully to nourish the body. That class has always been superior physically to the much larger class that has always been inadequately nourished. Adequate protection from the elements in the way of houses, clothes, and fires tends in the same direction, while improper exposure dwarfs and deforms both body and mind. Leisure, in the proper sense of exemption from the necessity of making painful and prolonged exertion, coupled with such physical and mental exercise as the system demands, or the normal use of all the faculties, cooperates with full nutrition and adequate protection to develop the faculties and perfect the man. On the other hand compulsory exertion in the form of excessive and protracted labor, blunts and stunts all the faculties and tends to produce a more or less deformed, stiffened, and distorted race of men. When we remember that in real truth these two opposite influences have been at work in human society ever since its organization, with the intense persistence of caste conditions working to prevent the mixing of the classes, we have abundant cause for all the observed physical and mental inequalities in men. The reason why this explanation is not clearer is that during the past three centuries the original conditions have been disturbed and a great social panmixia has been going on, greatly obscuring the elements of the problem. Still, although slavery has been abolished and the feudal system overthrown, the new industrial system is largely repeating the Pristine conditions, and in the Old World especially, and more and more in the New, class distinctions prevail, and differences of nutrition, of protection, and of physical exertion are still keeping up the distinction of a superior and an inferior class. The former has come up to the limit of its possibilities; the latter is arrested on the plane at which it can exist and reproduce. And thus is exemplified the truth that *"man ist was man isst."* This, too, is the great truth that lies at the bottom of the so-called "historical materialism." Not only does civilization rest upon a material basis in the sense that it consists in the utilization of the materials and forces of nature, but the efficiency of the human race depends absolutely upon food, clothing, shelter, fuel, leisure, and liberty.

REFERENCES TO WARD'S OTHER WORKS

- *Dynamic sociology*. Topics in Index, volume II: Acquisition; Distribution of wealth; Exchange; Foods; Labor; Land; Money; Nutrition; Population; Production; Property; Slavery; Wealth.
- *Psychic factors*. Index: Acquisition; Labor; Wages.
- *Pure sociology*. Chapter XIII.
- *Articles*. Psychologic basis of social economics; Utilitarian economics.

10

THE PHYLOGENETIC FORCES

- 126. Two theories of sex relationship.

- 127. I. THE ANDROCENTRIC THEORY.

- II. THE GYNÆCOCENTRIC THEORY.—
- 128. Female Sex primary.
- 129. Biological development of the male.
- 130. Gynæcocracy.
- 131. Androcracy.
- 132. Andreclexis.
- 133. Subjection of woman.

- III. CLASSIFICATION OF THE PHYLOGENETIC FORCES.—
- 134. Classification.
- (1) Natural Love.
- 135. Definition.
- 136. Purity of natural love,
- 137. Regulation.
- 138. Celibacy.
- 139. Natural love a social necessity.
- (2) Romantic Love.
- 140. Worth of social feelings.
- 141. Development of emotional centers,

- 142. Beginnings of romantic love.
- 143. Ampheclexis.
- 144. Natura naturans.
- 145. Function of romantic love.
- 146. Its influence on social organization.
- (3) Conjugal Love.
- 147. Essential quality of conjugal love.
- 148. Monogamy necessary.
- 149. Equality of the sexes essential.
- 150. Morality of monogamy.
- 151. Social influence of conjugal love.
- (4) Maternal Love.
- 152. Meaning of the term.
- 153. Maternal love a conservative principle.
- 154. Its coming importance.
- (5) Consanguineal Love.
- 155. Love of kindred.
- 156. Its social influence.

126. TWO THEORIES OF SEX RELATIONSHIP.

The proper subject of this chapter would be the influence exerted by those forces that have reproduction for their functional end in the direction of creating and transforming social structures. Keeping in view, however, the genetic method of treatment, the subject demands that exploration be made into the remote and obscure beginnings and pre-human course of things leading up to and explaining the facts that lie on the surface of the highly artificial and conventionalized society of today. At the outset, therefore, two theories will be presented to account for the existing relations between the sexes, between which the reader can choose according to the constitution of his mind, or he can reject both. The first may be called the *androcentric theory*, the second the *gynæcocentric theory*.

127. I. THE ANDROCENTRIC THEORY.

The androcentric theory is the view that the male sex is primary and the female secondary in the organic scheme, that all things center, as it were, about the male, and that the female, though necessary in carrying out the scheme, is only the means of continuing the life of the globe, but is otherwise an unimportant accessory, an incidental factor in the general result. This is the general statement of the androcentric theory as a tenet of biological philosophy, but as a tenet of sociology or anthropology, it becomes the view that man is primary and woman secondary, that all things center, as it were, about man, and that woman, though necessary to the work of reproduction, is only a means of continuing the human race, but is otherwise an unimportant accessory, an incidental factor in the general result.

II. THE GYNÆCOCENTRIC THEORY

128. FEMALE SEX PRIMARY.

The gynæcocentric theory is the view that the female sex is primary and the male secondary in the organic scheme, that originally and normally all things center, as it were, about the female, and that the male, though not necessary in carrying out the scheme, was developed under the operation of the principle of advantage to secure organic progress through the crossing of strains. The theory further claims that the apparent male superiority in the human race and in certain of the higher animals and birds is the result of specialization in extra-normal directions, due to causes which have nothing to do with the general scheme, but which can be explained on biological and psychological principles; that it only applies to certain characters, and to a relatively small number of genera and families. It accounts for the prevalence of the androcentric theory by the superficial character of human knowledge of such subjects, chiefly influenced by the illusion of the near, but largely, in the case of man at least, by tradition, convention, and prejudice. But it so happens that while the facts depended upon to support the androcentric theory are patent to all, those that support the gynæcocentric theory are latent and known to very few. A fuller statement of the basis for this theory is therefore essential.

129. BIOLOGICAL DEVELOPMENT OF THE MALE.

In brief it may be said that the male was created at a comparatively late period in the history of organic life, but soon began to assume more or less the form and character of the primary organism, which is then called the female. Selection of the best examples and rejection of the inferior ones caused the male to rise in the scale and resemble more and more the primary organism, or female. But other qualities were also selected than those that the female possessed. This was due to the early development of the aesthetic faculty in the female, and these qualities were in the nature of embellishments. The male, therefore, while approaching the form and stature of the female, began to differ from her in these aesthetic qualities. The result was that in the two highest classes of animals, birds and mammals, the male became in many cases, but not in all, highly ornamental, and endowed with numerous peculiar organs, called secondary sexual characters. To further selection a plurality of males often occurred, and these became rivals for female favor. This led to battles among the males, which further developed the latter, especially in the direction of size, strength, weapons of offense, and general fighting capacity. These qualities were never used to force the female into submission, but always and solely to gain her favor and insure the selection of the successful rivals. In many birds and mammals these qualities thus became greatly overdeveloped, resulting in what may be called male efflorescence. To a considerable extent, but less than in many other species, the immediate ancestors of man possessed this overdevelopment of the male, and in most primates the male is larger, stronger, and more highly ornamented than the female.

130. GYNÆCOCRACY.

When the human race finally appeared through gradual emergence from the great simian stock, this difference in the sexes existed, and sexual selection was still going on. Primitive woman, though somewhat smaller, physically weaker, and aesthetically plainer than man, still possessed the power of selection, and was mistress of the kinship group. Neither sex had any more idea of the connection between fertilization and reproduction than do animals, and therefore the mother alone claimed and cared for the offspring, as is done throughout the animal kingdom below man. So long as this state of things endured the race remained in the stage called *gynæcocracy*, or female rule. That this was a very long stage is attested by a great number of facts.

131. ANDROCRACY.

As it was brain development which alone made man out of an animal by enabling him to break over faunal barriers and overspread the globe, so it was brain development that finally suggested the connection between fertilization and reproduction, and led to the recognition by man of his paternity and joint proprietorship with woman in the offspring of their loins. This produced a profound social revolution, overthrew the authority of woman, destroyed her power of selection, and finally reduced her to the condition of a mere slave of the stronger sex, although that strength had been conferred by her. The stage of gynæcocracy was succeeded by the stage of androcracy, and the subjection of woman was rendered complete.

132. ANDRECLEXIS.

Under the patriarchate, or patriarchal family, woman was reduced to a mere chattel, bought and sold, enslaved, and abused beyond any power of description. At a later stage, brought about by the collision of primitive hordes and by a general system of wars and conquests resulting in race amalgamation, forms of marriage more or less ceremonial arose, which, though all in the nature of the transfer of women for a consideration, still somewhat mitigated the horrors of earlier periods, and resulted in a general state of polygyny among the upper classes. The powerful effect of race mixture in hastening brain development, coupled with its other effect in creating a leisure class in which the physical wants, including the sexual, were fully supplied, resulted in a high aesthetic sense in man, and led to a widespread system of male sexual selection, or andreclexis,* through which the physical nature of woman began to be modified. Although this could affect only a comparatively small percentage of all women, it was sufficient to produce types of female beauty, and it is chiefly to this cause that woman has acquired the quality of a "fair sex," in so far as this term is applicable. The general effect of male sexual selection, however, was rather to diminish than to increase her real value, and to lower than to raise her general status. It increased her dependence upon man, while at the same time reducing her power to labor or in any way protect or preserve herself.

---

* The various kinds of selection play such an important rôle in modern dynamic biology that they seem to demand a special terminology. The phrases *natural selection, artificial selection, sexual selection,* etc., besides being too long for convenient use, are not all free from ambiguity. For example, sexual selection does not indicate which sex does the selecting, but it is generally understood that by it only female selection is meant. To express the opposite it is necessary to say, male sexual selection. It should be possible to designate each different kind of selection by a single word, and the following terms are therefore proposed. They are derived from the Greek word ἐκλεξις, *selection,* and an appropriate first component expressing the kind of selection:—

Geneclexis, natural selection; *teleclexis,* artificial (intentional) selection; *gyneclexis,* female sexual selection; *andreclexis,* male sexual selection; *ampheclexis,* mutual sexual selection.

133. SUBJECTION OF WOMAN.

Throughout all human history woman has been powerfully discriminated against and held down by custom, law, literature, and public opinion. All opportunity has been denied her to make any trial of her powers in any direction. In savagery she was underfed, overworked, unduly exposed, and mercilessly abused, so that in so far as these influences could be confined to one sex, they tended to stunt her physical and mental powers. During later ages her social ostracism has been so universal and complete that, whatever powers she may have had, it was impossible for her to make any use of them, and they have naturally atrophied and shriveled. Only during the last two centuries and in the most advanced nations, under the growing power of the sociogenetic energies of society, has some slight relief from her long thraldom been grudgingly and reluctantly vouchsafed. What a continued and increasing tendency in this direction will accomplish it is difficult to presage, but all signs are at present hopeful.*

134. CLASSIFICATION.

With this brief statement of the gynæcocentric theory we may now consider the

III. CLASSIFICATION OF THE PHYLOGENETIC FORCES

Just as the ontogenetic forces may be summed up in the word hunger, so the phylogenetic forces may be summed up in the word *love*. As the phylogenetic forces must consist in different modes of manifestation of the one general force, love, the classification becomes that of the different kinds of love, in so far as that sentiment, or psychic unit, has undergone differentiation. Thus viewed, there are five kinds of love that are sufficiently distinct to be separately treated, though all are genetically connected. The order adopted is rather convenient than either genetic or chronological, and the special reasons for preferring it will appear as we proceed.

---

* Fustel de Coulanges, *The ancient city*; Westermarck, *History of human marriage*; Howard, *Matrimonial institutions*; Geddes and Thomson, *Evolution of sex*; Gilman, *Women and economics*; Ellis, *Man and woman*; Bachofen, *Das Mutterrecht*.

The sociologist recognizes the five following modes of manifestation of the phylogenetic forces, or forms of love:—

(1) Natural, (2) Romantic, (3) Conjugal, (4) Maternal, and (5) Consanguineal love.

These will be treated in the above order.

(1) NATURAL LOVE.

135. DEFINITION.

Natural love is the innate interest created by the principle of advantage and implanted, primarily in the male, to secure fertilization and the crossing of strains. It is the original form of all lave, and all other forms are derivatives of it. It is still found in full strength even in those individuals, races, and peoples who possess the derivative forms in their highest development. This is because the derivative forms alone are powerless to secure the primary ends of reproduction and variation, and however much a refined sentiment may deprecate the necessity, it remains, and seems likely to remain, a necessity.

136. PURITY OF NATURAL LOVE.

The fundamental reason why natural love is deprecated by developed minds is that during the second or metaphysical stage of development of human thought matter was held to be vile, and only the spiritual, including mind, was considered pure. This conception prevailed far into the positive stage; but science, which is the essence of the positive world view, teaches the spirituality of matter, and is fast dispelling the false metaphysical attitude with regard to it. It is therefore probable that the purity of natural love will ultimately be recognized by all enlightened minds. The same metaphysical state of mind is responsible also for the general tendency to underrate and belittle sexual matters in society, to keep them perpetually in the background, and to maintain the utmost possible ignorance of them on the part of the youth of both sexes. The reason why this method fails and leads to such unhappy results as it is now known to do is that it puts forward a falsehood, viz., that such matters are unimportant, when in fact they are the most vital of all the subjects of human contemplation. The purity and nobility of natural love have been perceived by all truly great minds, but few have had the courage to speak a word in favor of its redemption from the false and hypocritical odium that a pharisaical world seeks to cast upon it. A more rational and scientific standpoint shows that the sexual passion, everywhere and always, has been the great life-tonic of the world, the sublimest and most exalted as well as the purest and noblest of impulses.

137. REGULATION.

That such a tremendous power in society should require regulation goes without saying, but what are all marriage systems but modes of regulating this power? Nature can of course be controlled, but cannot, any more than any other natural force, be destroyed or suppressed. It can only be directed. But it may be wrongly as well as rightly directed. It may be made to flow in dangerous as well as in safe channels. In general it may be said that man has succeeded fairly well in his attempts to direct the phylogenetic forces, chiefly through marriage systems, which have usually grown out of manifest necessities.

138. CELIBACY.

The phylogenetic forces are somewhat exceptional, in that they are to some extent subject to the individual will. Unlike the ontogenetic forces, their suppression in the case of any particular individual does not result in death. From this has arisen the false idea that they are capable of permanent suppression with impunity. All who are competent to speak upon this question agree that this is not the case. The most common of these abnormal forms that the permanent suppression of the phylogenetic forces assumes is that of mysticism, which is a sort of disease due to sexual cerebration. Whatever may be the power of particular individuals under the influence of religious or philosophical ideas to suppress by the exercise of the will the spontaneous demands of their nature, this must always be confined to a very small fraction of the human race, and for the great mass of mankind no such considerations can have weight, or check the perennial flow of the great stream of passion that surges through society.

139. NATURAL LOVE A SOCIAL NECESSITY.

We must therefore distinguish between individual necessity and *social necessity*. Sexual satisfaction is a social necessity. The phylogenetic forces are as irresistible as the winds or the tides. Not only is the sexual instinct the powerful social stimulus that has been described, but it is also an essentially social bond. The primary association is necessarily sexual. Society must begin with the propagating couple, and as this primary association necessarily increases the membership of the group, it is clear that the basis of society must be sexual. It is therefore obvious that the sociologist cannot ignore such vital considerations, but must deal with sexual phenomena as with other social phenomena. It is not maintained that there has been any disposition on the part of sociologists to overlook the statical phenomena of primitive group life. What has been overlooked, or even purposely avoided, is the dynamic side of the subject. Kinship groups, hordes, tribes, states, and nations are simply effects. They should not absorb all attention to the exclusion of the causes that have produced them. These causes are the social forces, and the special causes of this class of effects are the phylogenetic forces that form the subject of this chapter. There has been a systematic avoidance of this vital question, and the story of the world has consequently been left only half told. In fact, human history and sociology as they now exist are only expurgated editions, stale and lifeless from the omission of the mainsprings that have ever impelled the machinery of society.

(2) ROMANTIC LOVE

140. WORTH OF SOCIAL FEELINGS.

All social forces are psychic, and in that sense spiritual. The application to any of them of the term *physical* is therefore not strictly correct, but if it is done not to stigmatize them, but for the sake of distinguishing some from others, it maybe justified and even useful. All feeling is psychic, but feelings differ in many ways, and these differences are more or less correlated. In general those feelings which are most vague and least definitely located in the body, those that are most internal, and those that are least intense and most durable, are classed as more spiritual, more elevated, and more refined. And in fact, there can be no doubt of the general correctness of this popular view; though lower from the standpoint of necessity, since they are not essential to life, they are higher from the standpoint of *utility, i.e.*, they are *worth more—more worthy*.

141. DEVELOPMENT OF EMOTIONAL CENTERS.

But these feelings are derivative, and are the consequences of a qualitative development of the physical organization of man. For it is not the brain of man alone that has developed. The brain is only one of the many nerve plexuses of the body, and there is no reason to suppose that it is the only one that has undergone structural refinement. Primarily brain mass is the cause of intelligence, and other things equal, increase of brain mass represents increased intelligence. But brains differ in kind as well as in size. Since the period of social assimilation this has undoubtedly been the principal advance that has been made. The cross-fertilization of cultures worked directly upon these qualitative characters, rendering the most thoroughly mixed races, like the Greeks and the English, highly intelligent. Now, while there can be no doubt that this higher brain development vitally influences all the other nerve plexuses of the body, since every conscious feeling must be referred to the brain, it is altogether probable that a process of qualitative improvement has also and at the same time been taking place in the entire nervous system, and especially in the great centers of emotion, and if the serious study of these plexuses could be prosecuted, as has been that of the brain, differences would in all probability be detected capable of being described, as this has been done for the brain. In other words, the development of the human race has not consisted exclusively in brain development, but has been a general advance in all the great centers of spiritual activity.

142. BEGINNINGS OF ROMANTIC LOVE.

It is this psycho-physiological progress going on in all races that have undergone repeated social assimilation, that has laid the foundation for the appearance in the most advanced races of a derivative form of natural love which is known as romantic love. It is a comparatively modern product, and is not even general among highly assimilated races. It is practically confined to the races that represent the accumulated energies of all the past and the highest human achievement, and is limited to the last nine or ten centuries of the history of these. It began to manifest itself some time in the eleventh century of the Christian era, and was closely connected with the origin of chivalry under the feudal system.* Whatever may be said of the Middle Ages as tending to suppress the natural flow of intellectual activities, there can be no doubt that they were highly favorable to the development of emotional life. The intense religious fervor that burned in its cloisters for so many centuries served to create centers of feeling, until the men and women of the eleventh century found

---

* Cornish, *Chivalry*.

themselves endowed with far higher moral organizations than those of the ancient Greeks and Romans. They had been all this time *using* their emotional faculties as they never bad been used before, and the Lamarckian principle of increase through use is as true of those faculties as it is of external muscles and organs. Without a preparation in this latent growth of the emotional faculties neither chivalry nor romantic love could have made its appearance.

143. AMPHECLEXIS.

Romantic love was due primarily to the greater equality and independence of woman. She reacquired to some extent her Iong-lost power of selection, and began to apply to men certain tests of fitness. Romantic love therefore marks the first step toward the resumption by woman of her natural scepter which she yielded to the superior physical force of man at the beginning of the androcratic period. It involves a certain degree of female selection or gyneclexis, and no longer permitted man to seize, but compelled him to sue. But it went much farther than this. It did away with the pure male selection that prevailed throughout the androcratic régime. The great physiological superiority of the new régime cannot be too strongly emphasized. Its value to the race is incalculable. Female selection, or gyneclexis, as we saw, created a fantastic and extravagant male efflorescence. Male selection, or andreclexis, produced a female type, characterized by diminutive stature, and beauty without utility. Both these unnatural effects were due to lack of mutuality. Romantic love is mutual. The selection is done simultaneously by man and woman. It may be called *ampheclexis*. Its most striking characteristic consists in the phenomenon called *falling in love*.

144. NATURA NATURANS.

It is not commonly supposed that this so-called tender passion is capable of cold, scientific analysis. It is treated as something trivial, and any allusion to it creates a smile. Yet over and over again in the course of our studies we have encountered the mysterious but silent power that unconsciously compasses ends not dreamed of by the agents involved, the unheard voice of nature, the unseen hand, the *natura naturans*. Nowhere has there been found a more typical or more instructive example of this than that which is furnished by romantic love. The end is nothing less than perfectionment of the human race. Whatever individuals may desire, the demand of nature is unmistakable. Primarily the object is to put an end to all tendencies toward extremes and one-sided development. It tends toward the establishment of a mean, which may be regarded as an ideal. It is not an ideal in the sense of exceptional beauty, unusual size, excessive strength, or any other extraordinary quality. It is an ideal in the sense of a normal development of all qualities, a symmetrical rounding out of the whole physical organism. In this of course certain qualities that are considered most valuable fall considerably below the level attained in certain individuals, and this is why it has been supposed to aim at mediocrity. But it is certainly more important to have a symmetrical race than to have a one-sided, top-heavy race, even though some of the overdeveloped qualities are qualities of a high order.

145. FUNCTION OF ROMANTIC LOVE.

Generally speaking persons of opposite "temperaments," whatever these may be, attract each other, and the effect is a gradual crossing and mutual neutralizing of temperaments. Romantic love is therefore a great agent in perfecting and balancing up the human race. It follows as matter of simple logic that it should be given full sway as completely as comports with the safety and stability of society. All attempts to interfere with its natural operation tend to check the progress of perfecting the race. Under the androcratic régime, during which woman had no voice in the selecting process, and under the patriarchal system generally where the marrying is done by the patriarch and neither party is consulted, nature's beneficent aims were thwarted, races grew this way and that, and mankind acquired all manner of physical and mental peculiarities. There were of course counteracting influences, and natural love, especially in the middle classes, helped to maintain an equilibrium, but male selection dwarfed woman, and slavery dwarfed both sexes. Where a reasonable degree of freedom of the sexes exists and there is no scarcity of men or of women, this passion of love becomes from a biological, from an anthropological, and from a sociological, point of view, the highest of all sanctions. It is the voice of nature commanding in unmistakable tones, not only the continuance, but also the improvement and perfectionment, of the race.

146. ITS INFLUENCE ON SOCIAL ORGANIZATION.

With regard to the essential difference between romantic love and natural love, it consists chiefly in the fact that the passion is satisfied by the *presence* instead of the *possession* of the one toward whom it goes out. The great superiority of romantic love is that it endures while at the same time remaining intense. But "true love never runs smooth," and herein lies the chief interest of romantic love for sociology and its main influence on human progress. Besides its effect thus far pointed out in perfecting the physical organization of man, it has an even greater effect in perfecting his social organization. It is the special quality of romantic love to develop intense activity on the part of great numbers of the human race at the age of greatest efficiency. All this activity is expended upon the immediate environment, and every throe of the struggle transforms the environment in some degree. The greater part of this transformation is useful and contributes to its full extent to social progress. In the early days and in the upper classes the demands of woman may have been somewhat trivial. Man must do something heroic, must prove his worthiness by acts of prowess, and such acts may even be opposed to true progress. But they at least develop manhood, courage, honor, and under the code of chivalry they must have a moral element, must defend the right, protect the weak, avenge dishonor, and uphold virtue. But in the lower ranks even then, and everywhere since the fall of the feudal system, woman demanded support and the comforts of life, luxuries where possible, and more and more leisure and accomplishment. Today she demands a home, social position, ease, and economic freedom. More and more, too, she requires of men that they possess industry, thrift, virtue, honesty, and intelligence. Man must work for all this, and this struggle for excellence, as woman understands that quality, is an extraordinary stimulus, and leads to all forms of achievement.

But man also selects, for romantic love is mutual. Woman has as much to lose as man if it results in failure. Man therefore sets ideals before woman. She must be worthy of him and naturally follows the course that he gives her to understand is most pleasing to him. Thus she develops herself in the direction of his ideals, and both are elevated. She may also to some extent transform the environment, if it be no more than the inner circle of the family. The combined effect, even in an individual case, is considerable, but the volume of achievement thus wrought is made up of thousands, nay, millions of small increments in all lands and all shades and grades of life, building ever higher and broader the coral reef of civilization.

(3) CONJUGAL LOVE

147. ESSENTIAL QUALITY OF CONJUGAL LOVE.

The love of a man for his wife or of a woman for her husband is an entirely different sentiment from that last considered. In a certain way it grows out of it, but it retains none of it, and it has other elements that are wanting in romantic love. Monogamic life, to be successful, requires a certain amount of philosophy. At least it requires character. It calls for qualities of heart and head that lie deep and that come out in their natural purity and vigor as soon as the storm of passion passes away. Then, freed from the thrall of passion, the cleared-up mind can begin to relish other pursuits and gain satisfactions of other and more solid and useful kinds. But in all properly constituted minds there remains at least a memory of the tender emotion which predisposes to the appreciation of mutual companionship not hitherto enjoyed, and this sentiment, planted in natural soil, grows rapidly, and soon begins to overshadow all others. One of the happiest traits of human nature consists in the fact that, where there are no repugnant elements, the mere personal proximity of individuals leads to attachments and to a degree of appreciation and mutual valuation that is wholly disproportionate to real worth. There can of course be no doubt that conjugal love is a step more "psychical" and "spiritual" than romantic love, just as the latter is a step more so than natural love. It is more durable, possesses greater volume, greater utility, more real worth, and hence is more worthy.

148. MONOGAMY NECESSARY.

It must be obvious that conjugal love as here portrayed cannot exist under polygamy. It cannot then be older than romantic love and must be confined to the same races and peoples. The forms of monogamy that preceded that epoch were chiefly economic in their purpose. Polygamy is essentially a sort of monopoly, and as fast as the spirit of liberty gave power to more and more men in society, they revolted against that monopoly and secured as far as possible an equal distribution of property in women. Owing to the substantial numerical equality of the sexes this could only be attained by limiting every man to one wife. Although it is difficult to find any direct announcement of this principle as the basis of monogamy, still it is one of those spontaneous, self-executing laws that operate silently and perpetually until they work out the inevitable solution. The transformed society accepts the result without knowing why, and crystallizes it into an institution (monogamy), which is first generally accepted, then surrounded with a legal and religious sanction, and finally defended as something existing in the nature of things or as "ordained of God," or both.

149. EQUALITY OF THE SEXES ESSENTIAL.

As the property idea gradually disappeared and woman came to be looked upon, not as a possession, but as a human being, a new adjustment became necessary. So long as a wife was only the property of her husband there could be no conjugal infelicity. Between them there existed such a social chasm that no more friction could arise than between a man and his horse. But when woman came to be regarded as well-nigh the equal of man, all this was changed, and there arose the possibility of a conflict of wills. Both conjugal love and conjugal infelicity are products of mutuality. The recognition of a certain degree of equality is an essential condition to both. The respect and friendly feeling, growing in part out of the memories of romantic and natural love, and in part out of propinquity, work upon certain natures in the direction of forming and more closely knitting the fibers of conjugal love, thus making the parties more and more indispensable and "dear" to each other, until this bond becomes exceedingly close, even indissoluble. On the other hand, the conflict of wills may tend more and more to separate and estrange, and ultimately result either in complete repugnance and separation, or in one or other of the innumerable family jars that make up domestic infelicity.

150. MORALITY OF MONOGAMY.

The careful and impartial student will admit that, taking into account the past history and present condition of those peoples among whom romantic and conjugal love exist at all, both sentiments, but especially the latter, are on the increase, and that the human race is growing more and more monogamic. Monogamy involves an enormous moral strain. It is a severe discipline in requiring the constant habit of mutually yielding the one to the other in the exercise of the will. The race is developing in this direction, and it becomes from age to age more easy to surrender the will to another with whom everything in life is so closely bound up. There are all degrees of difference in the distance to which different individuals have advanced in this direction, and the present status of marriage simply reflects these differences. To some monogamy is still intolerable, to others it is barely endurable, to still others it is generally satisfactory as the best condition attainable, while to a considerable number it is an ideal condition whose improvement even cannot be conceived of.

151. SOCIAL INFLUENCE OF CONJUGAL LOVE.

It remains only to point out that conjugal love is a social force even more efficient than either of the forms of love thus far considered. The principal stimulus is that of providing for the family that naturally grows out of this relation. For the man this is unquestionably the most productive of all stimuli. It is sufficiently intense to cause sustained effort, and instead of being only an episode of a few months or at most years duration, it is permanent, and continues from the date of the marriage until death to impel to deeds, if not of glory and renown, at least of usefulness and social value. Instead of having only the incentive of the desire to please another, it has added to this the incentive of work for its own sake. Freed from the distractions arising out of earlier forms of love, he can work for other ends and aim at worthier ideals. In a word, the mental conditions attending conjugal love are the best possible for human achievement, and, as we have seen, this is the supreme test of social efficiency. Of all the phylogenetic forces, then, conjugal love seems to be the one that has contributed the greatest volume of human achievement, and it is therefore not to be wondered at that it is in the European race and during the past three or four centuries that the greatest achievements have been wrought by man.

(4) MATERNAL LOVE

152. MEANING OF THE TERM.

It is not parental love with which we now have to deal, but with maternal love, which is one of those attributes, like natural love, that is commonly, but erroneously, called an *instinct*. The intention in using this term is to imply that it is something organic and inherent in the physical constitution, and in so far this view is correct. Maternal love is something that differs *toto cœlo* from parental love and parental affection as distinguished from the maternal emotion. Nor is maternal love based on sympathy, or if sympathy enters into it, it is as a distinct and added element and has nothing to do with it primarily. Sympathy is the basis of man's moral nature, a product of a high rational power, capable of not only representing to self the painful states of others, but of experiencing the reflex of such representation in self as a form of pain. Maternal love is a faculty planted in the nature of woman through the laws of survival and advantage as conditions to the preservation and continuance of the race. It does not consist essentially or primarily in the love of the helpless. This latter can only be experienced by a highly rational being, while maternal love, at least, is shared alike by man and most of the animals with which most men are chiefly familiar. This last-mentioned fact does not detract from the beauty, purity, or worth of maternal love as a human attribute. It is one of the characteristic attributes of the great class of animals called *mammals* to which man belongs, and is directly connected with the leading function that distinguishes that class from all others, viz., the suckling of the young.

153. MATERNAL LOVE A CONSERVATIVE PRINCIPLE.

Maternal love is an essentially conservative principle, but such principles are as useful to society as are the active and constructive ones. Hitherto its effects have been chiefly biological in protecting and preserving the race. As a social force it has only operated in a more or less negative way. Sometimes, however, it shows its immense power, and as a human passion it has been made the theme of many tragedies. No author has portrayed this power more accurately or more forcibly than Victor Hugo, and nowhere has he done this better than in his *Quatre-vingt Treize* and the rescue of the children from the Tourgue: "Maternity raises no issue: one cannot discuss with it. What makes a mother sublime is that she is a sort of beast. The maternal instinct is divinely animal. The mother is no longer a woman, she is simply female." And it is true. The highest flights of this passion are those that most assimilate that animal stage when the female was the supreme guardian of her own. Then the female was not only the race, but did all the work of the race and chose the male besides. It was through this long discipline that not only maternal love, but maternal courage and maternal efficiency, were developed; and notwithstanding the trials to which woman was so long subjected, she is still capable of rising to the occasion, and without hesitation or deliberation, of defending her children in the face of the greatest dangers. Under this powerful spur her acts often seem almost miraculous.

154. ITS COMING IMPORTANCE.

With the advent of a stage of complete equality of the sexes this power is destined, it would seem, to play a much more important rôle than it has ever done in the past or than it plays in the present state of even the most advanced societies, and if women ultimately become the equals of men in the art of portraying events, it is from them that we must expect this passion to be embellished and brought out in the literature of the future.

(5) CONSANGUINEAL LOVE

155. LOVE OF KINDRED.

The love of kindred is probably an exclusively human attribute. It is generically distinct from maternal love, although it is felt by the mother in addition to that sentiment. It is the whole of parental love as such, and also of filial and fraternal love. In the horde there naturally exists a sentiment of attachment on the part of each member of the kinship group for all the rest. Under the matriarchate all consider themselves as brothers and sisters, since the father is unknown, and in all races where there exists uncertainty as to the father, all the members of the clan are brothers.

156. ITS SOCIAL INFLUENCE.

The social value of this sentiment consists in the fact that it comes to constitute the blood bond, or feeling of attachment that exists among all the members of an ethnic group, and this bond, as is well known, is exceedingly strong. Properly to discuss it, however, it is necessary to look specially at its negative side, since it is here that lies its dynamic quality. In fact, it would have been quite possible and proper to treat all the forms of love from their negative or correlative aspects. For to every *love* there is a correlative *hate*, and the force of repulsion is sometimes even more powerful than the force of attraction. The hate corresponding to natural love, romantic love, and conjugal love takes the form of *jealousy*. The form of hate corresponding to maternal love is quite different. It is mingled with fear, and consists in general hostility to all dangerous or threatening influences. Any person, animal, or thing that stands, or is thought to stand, in that attitude is hated and combated. When it comes to consanguineal love, especially in that generalized form constituting the blood bond, the corresponding hate becomes *race hatred*. Everybody has some idea of what race hatred means, for it is not confined to savages, but exists between the most civilized peoples. It was at the beginning and has always remained the principal cause of war. To the sociologist it is one of the prime factors of social progress, since without it there could never have been that series of social assimilations so fertile in producing modifications of structure and civilization.

REFERENCES TO WARD'S OTHER WORKS

- *Dynamic sociology.* Topics in Index, volume II: Family; Female supremacy; Love; Love-forces; Love sentiment; Male; Marriage; Modesty; Monogamy; Polygamy; Polygyny; Reproduction; Sex; Sexual; Women.
- *Psychic factors.* Index: Female superiority; Male; Woman.
- *Pure sociology.* Chapter XIV.
- *Articles.* See Bibliography; Our better halves; The exemption of women from labor; Genius and woman's intuition.

11

THE SOCIOGENETIC FORCES

- 157. Classification.

- I. The Moral Forces.—
- 158. Two kinds.
- (1) Race Morality
- 159. Based on race preservation.
- 160. Race morality as custom.
- 161. Essential nature of race morality.
- (2) Individual Morality
- 162. Altruism.
- 163. Sympathy.
- 164. Distinction between altruism and sympathy.
- (3) Ethical Dualism
- 165. Altruism a relative term.
- 166. Broadening of altruism.
- 167. Humanitarianism.
- 168. Philozoism.
- 169. Love of nature.
- 170. Ethical monism.

- II. The aesthetic Forces.—
- 171. Three stages of development.
- 172. Imitation and imagination.

- 173. Art.
- 174. Symmetry in art.
- 175. Modern idea of art.
- 176. Art a socializing agency.
- 177. Art as an end in itself.
- 178. Social value of art.

- III. The Intellectual Forces.—
- 179. Intellectual feeling.
- 180. (1) Acquirement of Knowledge.
- 181. (2) Discovery of Truth.
- 182. Interest in the discovery of truth.
- 183. Generalization.
- 184. (3) Impartation of Information.
- 185. The savage mind.
- 186. The leisure class.
- 187. Democracy.
- 188. Place of religion in intellectual development.
- 189. Kidd's Social evolution.
- 190. Religion and science.

157. CLASSIFICATION.

The sociogenetic forces are the socializing and civilizing impulses of mankind. Although derived from the others and deeply rooted in the physical nature of man, the sociogenetic forces as active agents in the world are relatively modern, and are the products of the complicated series of events brought about by the action of primary social energy. These civilizing energies are so recent and so feebly seated that even in the most advanced races they form as yet only a thin veneering over the fabric thus wrought.

The sociogenetic forces naturally fall into three large groups, moral, aesthetic, and intellectual, and perhaps, upon the whole, the best ground for an arrangement is their immediate derivation from the essential forces, and especially from the phylogenetic group, placing that class first which seems to emerge most immediately out of the latter. The order of treatment will therefore be, as already given, viz., I, the moral forces; II, the aesthetic forces; III, the intellectual forces.

I. THE MORAL FORCES

158. TWO KINDS.

Considered from the standpoint of its origin, morality is of two kinds: *race morality* and *individual morality*. The roots of both of these classes penetrate very deeply. Both of them are exclusively human attributes, but both have their strict homologues in the animal world. As the passage from animality to humanity was wholly the result of brain development and consequent dawn of intelligence, so both kinds of morality were the products of the rational faculty.

(1) RACE MORALITY

159. BASED ON RACE PRESERVATION.

In Paragraph 82 attention is called to the "group sentiment of safety" out of which were subsequently differentiated nearly all important coercive human institutions, such as religion, law, and government. It was certainly the beginning of race morality, the primary factor of which was the *mos*, from which term the word *moral* is derived. This form of morality operates entirely in the interest of function and against the claims of feeling. It seems therefore to be precisely the opposite of the currently accepted morality, which is based wholly on feeling. For however much it may be necessary to restrain feeling, the moral quality can only arise in connection with feeling creatures. But race morality is no more concerned with the feelings of the individual than nature seems to be when everything is sacrificed to the safety of the race. In fact, in race morality man simply assists nature, or becomes an integral part of the natural forces that make for race preservation. The group puts its sanction upon everything that has this tendency.

160. RACE MORALITY AS CUSTOM.

Race morality, therefore, consists essentially in custom, and if the customs of the world are all scrutinized, the majority of them will be found to consist in restraints to conduct inimical to race safety. At least such was their primitive purpose, but many have of course departed widely from that purpose, which may now be difficult to trace. Here it becomes difficult to distinguish morals from religion. The latter is little more than the addition of supernatural penalties for the violation of the laws of race safety. This is probably the basis for the widespread belief that religion is essentially moral. The current moral teaching consists essentially in a morality of restraint, and is undoubtedly a survival of primitive race morality. Most of its precepts are negative or prohibitory, and based on the deep-seated sense of the danger of overindulging the passions.

161. ESSENTIAL NATURE OF RACE MORALITY.

Race morality must be carefully distinguished from individual morality. From the standpoint of the former, the effect of an action upon individuals has nothing whatever to do with its rightness or wrongness. The bottom of it all is the effect on the safety of the human race. "Duty" is simply conduct favorable to race safety. Virtue is an attitude of life and character consistent with the preservation and continuance of man on earth. Vice is the reverse of this, and is felt as an attack upon the race. If we can get rid entirely "of the idea that "good" and "evil" have any connection whatever with benefit or injury to the individual or to any sentient being, and clearly grasp the truth that they relate exclusively to race safety and race danger, we can see that the quality of actions approved or disapproved has nothing to do with the pleasure or pain they may cause, but relates solely to their effect upon the race. The idea of the race, however, narrows as we descend in the scale of civilization, and with the savage it is limited to his own race, clan, tribe, or horde.

The view that the morality of restraint is a survival of primitive race morality is the only one consistent with its defence, for most of it tends to diminish the amount of enjoyment instead of tending to increase it, as the opposite view would require. Whether it actually does secure race safety is another question. It may be only a social vestige, and as such have a somewhat pathologic character.

(2) INDIVIDUAL MORALITY

162. ALTRUISM.

Individual morality is based on altruism. Human altruism, in so far as it is not biological, is based on sympathy, and this is also the basis of all morality except race morality. First of all then, be it said, morality is a product of brain development. But the "moral sense," the conscious altruism, the ability to feel with other feeling beings, was not an early psychic attribute, but required a relatively high degree of brain development. It consists in a power of *representing* the psychic states of others to self. It is only the *intensive* sensations that are thus represented, which consist exclusively of pleasurable and painful states. The power of representation is the distinguishing characteristic of the growing intellect, but it is twofold, or takes two different directions, producing two distinct psychic faculties, the one subjective, the other objective. The subjective faculty produced by representation is sympathy, the objective one is imagination. We have only to do with the first of these here.

163. SYMPATHY.

That sympathy is a rational faculty admits of no doubt. All developed human beings constantly experience it. It might be an idle speculation to try to ascertain the absolute beginning of sympathy. It may be the reverse of Spencer's idea that it grew out of "love of the helpless." It is, indeed, probable that this was about the earliest manifestation of sympathy. It may also be that it first appeared in woman, as a mother with her strong native love of her offspring, which, though in itself an entirely different faculty, early blended with, or helped to create, the derivative reason-born faculty of altruism. Altruism or sympathy would not be a force, it could not be a motive, if it did not reside in the agent, *i.e.*, if it were not egoistic. All motives are necessarily egoistic. To condemn a motive because egoistic is therefore to condemn all motives. But the origin of subjective reflex motives marked an epoch in the history of man. From the standpoint of sociology and of human progress generally, this was the most important of all the steps the race has taken. The egoistic reason unaided by the altruistic reason could only work such results as the subjection of woman and the aggrandizement of the strong. These, if continued long enough and not counteracted, would become highly antisocial. They might even bring about the destruction of the race.

164. DISTINCTION BETWEEN ALTRUISM AND SYMPATHY.

Altruism is therefore an essentially socializing force, *i.e.*, it is sociogenetic. Its name alone reveals its social character. Although itself egoistic it always expends itself on another. There can be no altruism without an *alter*. Altruism is not strictly synonymous with sympathy. The latter, though not necessarily negative, is usually so used. It is representative pain; scarcely representative pleasure. Altruism applies equally to both. But altruism differs from sympathy in another respect. Sympathy is not necessarily a desire. It is simply a feeling. True, it naturally suggests action. But this involves an intellectual operation, a knowledge of how to act to attain the end. There are many pains which the sufferer does not know how to relieve, and therefore does not act. Sympathy may sometimes be such a pain. Altruism is a complex conception. It is sympathy plus the desire to act. Or it may be representative enjoyment plus the desire to increase the enjoyment observed and represented. It is not merely a feeling, it is also a motive. Finally, the necessity that in all altruistic action at least two individuals be affected renders it *essentially social*. Its primary quality is *sociability*. Altruism and sociability are indissolubly connected. Sociability arises as a natural and necessary consequence of altruism, and without a certain amount of sociability there could be no proper society.

(3) ETHICAL DUALISM

165. ALTRUISM A RELATIVE TERM.

There is a well-known but long, nameless fact which Dr. Edward A. Ross has appropriately called *ethical dualism*. The fact itself is too familiar to require any elaborate treatment. When we speak of altruism today, a very different idea arises in the mind from that which it is necessary to form of the altruism of primitive man. The difference is not so much in the nature of the sentiment as in its object or range. There can be no doubt that altruism, or *other-love*, in its rudimentary form is a direct offshoot from consanguineal love. It begins with the nearest of kin and is very slow to emerge from that condition. In the horde, the tribe, and also in the clan there exists a certain attachment, amounting in the end to an affection, on the part of every member, to and for every other member of the group. This is the extent of primitive altruism, and beyond the group, as was pointed out, in place of love or affection there is hate or detestation.

166. BROADENING OF ALTRUISM.

From this point on there is an ever widening circle within which this altruistic affection goes out. Maternal love is the most intense of all affections, but it is also the most restricted. Parental love is an increase in the amplitude with a diminution of the intensity. The more general forms of consanguineal love repeat the process in the same way, and when the kinship group becomes large, the same absolute quantity of force may be regarded as distributing itself to all the members. Then the personal element is lost sight of and we have simple race attachment. At last, when the stage is reached at which a new people and a nation are formed, the altruistic principle reappears in a new form. The amalgamated mass becomes a unit, and the original blood bond has its counterpart in what is vaguely called *love of country*, in which conception the people are included along with the land and physical environment. At any stage, however, it is easy to see that man's moral nature has always been dual. The sacred books of the Hebrew race show conclusively that morality was one thing for the Jew and another for the Gentile. With the Greeks all outside of Greece were "οἱ βάρβαροι." It was not otherwise in Rome, and it has always been so for all peoples and nations. Persons who may be very sympathetic as regards others of their own race are often utterly indifferent to those of another race.

167. HUMANITARIANISM.

It is only with the highest types of men in enlightened nations that the widest circles of ethical influence are produced. Here we find a few individuals who are called philanthropists, and whose altruism is less or not at all limited by considerations of race or nationality. Sympathy here often outruns the judgment and involves inconsistencies and wasted effort. The greatest danger is in ignoring the law of parsimony and creating parasitic degenerates (Paragraph 37). A curious fact in connection with this is that the great conquering races are the most philanthropic, the most altruistic. Humanitarianism may be distinguished from philanthropy as a still further step in the same direction, in which benevolent sentiments are placed more under the control of reason and philosophy. Properly it has nothing to do with dispensing charity, but seeks rather to reorganize society so that the minimum pain and the maximum enjoyment may be insured. Its aim is *meliorism*. In its most advanced form it eschews measures and devotes itself to the propagation of ideas, and especially to the diffusion of those forms of knowledge which, universally shared, will spontaneously and automatically work all needed and all possible reform.

168. PHILOZOISM.

The love of animals, which might be called *philozoism*, may be regarded as still another step in the spread of altruistic sentiments, including now all sentient beings in its wide embrace. A true, rational, and consistent love of animals and man because they are all feeling creatures is a noble impulse and marks the highest point in purely ethical development.

169. LOVE OF NATURE.

Here we should probably stop, but there is another step that seems to be in the same direction, although it transcends the bounds of the ethical world and hence can scarcely be called a form of altruism. This step is the *love of nature*. It is not love in the sense of possible sympathy or of any conceivable benefit that can be done, and yet it still is love. It is the connecting link between the moral and the aesthetic, and yet it is not wholly a sense of pleasure in the contemplation of the beautiful or the sublime. It is the most disinterested of all sentiments, since there is no possible way in which man can contribute anything to nature. It is also wholly free from all expectation of material benefit from nature. It is not curiosity to know more of nature, although this, or at least an ardent desire to do so, necessarily accompanies it. Reduced to its simplest terms it is nothing more than an *appreciation* of nature. But when we reflect on what is implied in nature, this is seen to be a lofty sentiment. For nature is *infinite*, and the serious contemplation of nature brings the mind into relations with the infinite. It is this which gives both dignity and charm to the sentiment, and connects it with religion, which, as Ratzenhofer says, is at bottom the striving of the finite mind after the infinite.

170. ETHICAL MONISM.

Such is ethical dualism, but the point to which we have traced it lies beyond the limits that are embraced by that expression. It is no longer a dualism, it is a monism. In *ethical monism*, while there is no longer any love in the proper sense, so also there is no hate. If it could become universal, there would be no need of any altruism. Human beings and animals would no more need sympathy than do mountains and clouds. If all producible happiness were actually produced, and all preventable suffering were actually prevented, there would not only be no "science" of ethics, but there would be no ethics, no moral conduct, no conduct at all as distinguished from natural activity. The world would become "amoral" or anethical. Ethics, which Spencer erects into a great science coordinate with and higher than sociology, would be eliminated from the world through the normal operation of its own laws.*

II. THE AESTHETIC FORCES

171. THREE STAGES OF DEVELOPMENT.

The aesthetic faculty does not seem to be traceable quite as far back as is animal altruism. All sexual selection (gyneclexis) is based on it, and we saw how early this began to transform the male element, to mold it into forms and to adorn it with hues that charmed the female. This faculty has passed through three stages, each a step higher than the preceding. These may be called respectively the receptive, the imaginative, and the creative. The first of these is passive, while the other two are active in different ways. Between the passive stage and the imaginative stage there intervenes another psychic faculty which is not generally connected with the aesthetic, but which can be shown to be the natural and necessary prelude and condition to imagination. This latter is a comparatively high stage in aesthetic development and does not probably appear as an animal attribute at all, but only as an exclusively human attribute. The animal faculty corresponding to it and directly leading into it is *imitation*. Imitation is itself a very high animal attribute. It probably has its germs in some of the lower vertebrates, possibly in insects, but makes its first marked appearance in birds, notably in parrots, mocking-birds, and birds related to these. It is faint or wanting in many mammals, but comes forth in its fullest developments in the apes.

172. IMITATION AND IMAGINATION.

But the bird, the ape, the animal, gets no farther than this. If any animal has the rudiments of imagination, it does not and cannot express them so that man can recognize that faculty. The ape imitates that which it sees. It never puts two things together to form a third thing which has no objective existence. This would be imagination. Imagination is essentially creative, and by calling the third stage creative it was not intended to deny this. Imagination can only work with the materials in consciousness, but it can dispose these at will and is not restricted to dealing with them in the

---

* Nietzsche, *Genealogy of morals*; Small, *Significance of sociology for ethics*.

form in which it finds them. It makes ideals out of these reals by a grouping of its own. It thus creates

173. ART.

The creative stage in the development of the aesthetic faculty is that in which ideals are embodied in visible form so as to be cognizable by others besides the one who imagines them. It is art. This is a much later stage, but until it is reached the aesthetic faculty as a transforming agent is chiefly a biotic force and works through selection and heredity. Now it becomes a social force and begins to exert its influence upon social structures. Ideals are realized and become aesthetic creations. Such creations are among the most important of human achievements. We have seen that imitation preceded imagination, and imagination preceded creation. Now the earliest art was the most creative and the least imitative, and progress in art has, in a certain sense, been in the direction of a return to imitation. In the beginning the artificial creations of man differed *in toto* from anything real. There was only the rudest attempt to imitate nature. Egyptian and Assyrian art and the old Chinese and Japanese art are all conventionalized, and do not closely resemble the objects they are intended to represent. They only symbolize them. There must, however, necessarily be a limit to this slavish imitation of the artificial, and this was accompanied by a corresponding tendency toward the imitation of the natural, until at last in Grecian art we have works of art that are, although still ideals, nevertheless "true to nature," in the sense that every part brought together to form a whole has its counterpart in nature, was, indeed, in most cases, copied from nature. The whole, however, was unlike any whole in nature, and consisted of the *best* parts of many wholes combined to form an ideal whole.

174. SYMMETRY IN ART.

But there was still another step, or series of steps, chiefly in the same direction. The sense of the beautiful seems at first to have been limited to what may in general be called symmetrical forms. The more geometrically perfect they were the more they attracted the primitive aesthetic sense. Hence we find that savages are most attracted by artificial objects, such as beads, buttons, canes, umbrellas, and other mechanically wrought products. The natural objects first to appeal to man's aesthetic faculties were such as the rainbow, and the sun and moon, which present a shining circular disk. A very distant and symmetrical mountain might also appeal to them. Next to these objects came animals, trees, and flowers; finally the rounded human body, especially the female form, came to be counted beautiful. Art had scarcely gone farther than this with the ancient Greeks, and little advance was made down to the renaissance. Landscape painting was scarcely known, and there is no evidence that nature at large was even admired by man. The present love of "scenery" is very modern, and it is not probable that even the Greeks could have appreciated Switzerland. As Humboldt says, early man did not love, he only feared, nature.

175. MODERN IDEA OF ART.

Now the modern idea of the beautiful, as most fully expressed in the heterogeneous reduced to order by perspective and rational synthesis, was an added faculty, not possessed by early man nor by existing savages, and the development of this faculty produced a complete revolution in art, immensely increasing its power to produce human enjoyment and stimulate activity. It also tended toward the imitation of nature, somewhat at the expense of the creative faculty, although this latter still has a wide field for its exercise. But nature in the large—scenery, landscape, wood, meadow, stream, hill, mountain, lake, sky, cloud, and sea—is so intrinsically beautiful that it is the highest aim of the artist to represent it exactly as it presents itself.

176. ART A SOCIALIZING AGENCY.

It has been said that art is non-progressive, that it serves no useful purpose in the world, that it does not raise the moral tone of society, that it adds no new truth to man's stock of knowledge, that it makes man no more comfortable, no better, and no wiser. This might almost be true without constituting an argument against the cultivation of the aesthetic faculty. Love of the beautiful and its pursuit do not claim to constitute either an ontogenetic or a phylogenetic force in society. They constitute a typical sociogenetic force. Art is a socializing agency. It is an agency of civilization as distinguished from preservation and perpetuation. It is not a necessity. Shall we call it a luxury? It is much more. In a pain economy it may be a luxury, but above that it becomes a utility. It finally becomes a *spiritual necessity*. As soon as the class of wants which may be distinguished as *needs* are satisfied, this spiritual want, which, as we have seen is planted deep in the animal nature, at once asserts itself, and the satisfaction of a spiritual want is as important as that of a material want. It serves to swell the volume of life. Men have aesthetic interests as well as economic interests, and their claims are as legitimate.

177. ART AS AN END IN ITSELF.

In a word, the aesthetic sentiment is an end in itself. Its satisfaction becomes one of the ends of the feeling being. The very word *aesthetic* means feeling. The enjoyment of life consists in satisfying feelings. So long as feelings can be satisfied, the more and the stronger they are, the greater the volume of enjoyment. So long as desires are innocent, *i.e.*, do no injury to the individual or to others, it is a gain even to create them. The peculiarity of art is that it *creates desire in order to satisfy it*. This is as true of other arts as it is of music, but it is so obviously true of music that Schopenhauer* made that an art entirely distinct from all the rest, the purpose of which, he claimed, is to typify and represent all the passions of the soul. It represents the will, which is ever striving, and when its end is attained, striving anew, and so on forever.

178. SOCIAL VALUE OF ART.

When we reflect how much richer human life is for this one art, we can form some idea of the sociogenetic value of art as a whole. But a glance through the great galleries of the world is calculated to impress one even more deeply with the quantity of achievement in those far older arts, notably sculpture, while for architecture one needs only to remain outside and admire the monumental piles that adorn all the great capitals of the world and are copied again and again even in the New World and in Australia. The older buildings may sometime crumble and decay, but the different styles of architecture are imperishable and constitute the real achievements. Literature is properly to be regarded as an art. It was action before it was words, poetry before it was prose, rhythm before it was rhyme, and aesthetic before it was practical. In fact it is only during the nineteenth century that its function as an aesthetic end was to any considerable extent subordinated to its function as a means of conveying thought.

---

* *Die Welt als Wille und Vorstellung*, 3. Aufl., Leipzig, 1859, volume I, p. 307.

III. THE INTELLECTUAL FORCES

179. INTELLECTUAL FEELING.

*Throughout the long series of psychic phenomena that are produced by the dynamic agent, we have thus far been dealing, only with those psychic faculties which may be classed under the head of emotions or affections, although in the aesthetic faculty we saw that imagination partakes decidedly of the nature of an intellectual faculty, and also that sympathy was only possible through the exercise of true reason. Still sympathy itself is wholly feeling, and the love of the beautiful is also a feeling. We now rise a step higher toward a true intellectual operation and have to deal with an affection that resides in the organ of thought itself. The intellectual affection, emotion, or appetite must be distinguished from thought itself. The truth is that the mind, or, if anyone prefers, the brain, has an *interest* in its own operations, and the exercise of the intellectual faculty is attended with a satisfaction or pleasure, as definite and real as the satisfaction or pleasure attending the exercise of any other faculty. We are therefore still dealing with feeling, and there is no generic distinction between intellectual feeling and other forms of feeling. The mind enjoys the work it does, and often undertakes work that it can only do imperfectly, merely because it is "hard," and requires greater effort, being impelled by the satisfaction yielded by this effort.

180. (1) ACQUIREMENT OF KNOWLEDGE.

The mind has an interest chiefly in three things: 1, to acquire knowledge; 2, to discover truth; 3, to impart information. The interest in the acquisition of knowledge is perhaps the most intense, and partakes more exactly of the nature of a true appetite than either of the others. It is most prominent in the young, but may continue through life. Many young persons at a certain stage in their mental and physical development, usually for some years after the age of puberty, become literally hungry for knowledge, and devour everything that comes in their way. At first they are almost omnivorous, and are bent on storing their minds with everything that they did not know before. They will learn anything, and have small powers of discrimination. Later on they begin to discriminate for themselves, and

---

* Crozier, *History of intellectual development*, volume I.

many almost self-educated men have succeeded in organizing their knowledge to good advantage. But this is exceptional, and systematic guidance is almost essential to any real success.

181. (2) DISCOVERY OF TRUTH.

After the mind has become thus stored with knowledge the time at length arrives when it begins to work upon its own materials. The psychologists tell us how this is done.* This is a strictly creative process. By ransacking, as it were, every corner of the brain certain likenesses are discovered between images impressed upon different areas, or cells, or what not, and these are confronted and scrutinized, and their relations discovered. Something new results, something different from any of the separate items of intelligence that had been acquired during the receptive period. It may have no resemblance to any of them, yet it results from them. It is a *relation* subsisting between two or more of them, but it is real and definite, and constitutes a *tertium quid*, created by the brain's own activities. The mind *knows* it, so that it is an additional item of knowledge, but it did not come directly from the external senses; only its elements thus came. If the original knowledge acquired directly through the senses, including that kind of indirect acquisition that comes from reading and listening to others, be called *fact*, the new kind of knowledge created out of this by the mind itself in the manner described, may be called *truth*.

182. INTEREST IN THE DISCOVERY OF TRUTH.

The creative process of the mind is attended, like the receptive process, with a strong interest and an intense satisfaction, and constitutes the second step in the act of generating intellectual energy. It bears less resemblance to a true appetite than does the first process, but the interest, zeal, and enjoyment are scarcely less. Indeed, there is a certain depth and volume to the satisfaction attending the discovery of truth that has no parallel in the mere acquisition of knowledge. Knowledge that is acquired is simply taken from the common stock and appropriated by the individual. It was already possessed by others, perhaps by thousands or millions of men. But a truth excogitated out of the knowledge thus acquired may not be known to anyone else. In the majority of cases, of course, the same truth has been evolved by other minds from similar

---

* James, *The principles of sociology*, Volume I, pp. 284 ff.

materials, but the discoverer does not usually know this, and at least imagines that he is creating something wholly new. This interest in the priority of discovery is exceedingly strong and fascinating and becomes the chief spur to original thought.

183. GENERALIZATION.

The mind of a well-informed person contains a large store of facts and an equally large store of truths, *i.e.*, logical conclusions from facts. It uses the facts to increase the number of truths derived from both within and without. But it does not stop here. The combining of truths to form new truths is as legitimate a process of the mind as the combining of facts to form truths. Truths derived from the combination of other truths become truths of a higher order. The fundamental method of creative nature, as explained in Chapter VI, applies to the operations of mind as well as to those of matter. This, as we saw, is the method of creating units of higher out of those of lower order and then using the latter as new units for still higher creations. This process of recompounding, or compound aggregation, which underlies all creative synthesis, when it reaches the intellectual plane is called *generalization*. This may be carried as far as the quality of the mind will permit, and the power of generalization constitutes the best measure of intellectual power.

Such is the constructive quality of the intellect, the most important of all the faculties, and probably, when comprehended in all its length and breadth, the one that has achieved the most, and contributed the largest additions to the general fact which is commonly understood as civilization.

184. (3) IMPARTATION OF INFORMATION.

We have now dealt with the receptive or acquisitive interest or appetite of the mind, and with its creative or constructive interest. It remains to consider what may be called its transitive or reproductive aspect, viz., the interest it has in conveying its acquisitions and constructions to other minds. It might be supposed that this would be very slight, but such is not the case. The developed human intellect is essentially altruistic. It delights in sharing its possessions with others. This is largely the case with simple knowledge, but it is still more true of ideas, or what it considers to be truth. At the end of a certain period, usually continuing some time after puberty, sometimes till the age of twenty or later, during which the mind becomes stored with a large amount of information, a desire gradually springs up to communicate a portion of this information to others, who, from their youth or from defective opportunities, are clearly seen to be wanting in most of it. This desire takes various forms. All that can be done by converse with others is accomplished in this way. Systematic instruction is often volunteered and offered gratuitously. The teacher's profession may be chosen, or a professional chair in some institution may be sought and obtained. More rarely public lecturing is resorted to. But when all these means fail, there always remains one other, viz., authorship. The history of ideas, of science, and of human achievement in general, shows that the greatest sacrifices have been continually made in order to propagate thought, to diffuse knowledge, to promulgate truth, and to advance science. Such employments are rarely remunerative, they are often made avocations in the enforced leisure of busy professional life. They are sometimes pursued in the face of poverty and want. This intellectual altruism is thus preeminently social, and the results are socializing and sociogenetic.

185. THE SAVAGE MIND.

The intellectual forces constitute the latest manifestation of the dynamic agent. No one of the three forms of interest that we have considered exists in the mind of the savage. He has no appetite for knowledge. The earliest aspect of this is curiosity or wonder, and it has been repeatedly observed by travellers that savages evince no curiosity even at what must be to them the strangest phenomena. The true explanation of the absence of curiosity, wonder, and all interest in or desire for knowledge among savages and inferior races generally, is that their brains have not developed to the receptive or acquisitive point. Its cells are comparatively coarse. If the neurons could be examined and compared with those of a highly civilized person, there is no doubt that great differences would be found.

186. THE LEISURE CLASS.

This brings us to the question of the genesis of the higher attributes of the mind. That the brain has been developing throughout all the early stages of man's history is altogether probable, since it must have developed during the prehuman stage until that particular creature ceased to be an animal confined to a definite area like other animals, and acquired sufficient control over his environment to adapt it to his needs. What may be called social differentiation began here. Various phases were passed through, the patriarchate was established, and finally the era of social integration was reached. There were probably gains all through, but an entirely new impulse was given to brain development with the advent of social amalgamation through conquest, subjugation, and the prolonged equilibration that followed. Of all the social structures wrought by this process the one that counted most effectively in accelerating brain development and intellectual refinement was the establishment of a system of caste. For with caste came the leisure class, and without a leisure class it would seem next to impossible at that stage of human history for any considerable intellectual advance to have been made. In the leisure class the struggle for existence is eliminated. The so-called physical wants are supplied, and there remains necessarily a large surplus of psychic energy demanding an opportunity to expend itself. With each successive assimilation fresh vigor is infused into society; the qualities acquired through leisure are diffused at least through the privileged classes, and filter down into the less favored ranks, and leaven the whole. The ruling class, the priesthood, the nobility, and a growing bourgeoisie, all free themselves from the thralls of want and join the forces of civilization. At the expense, it is true, of the "toiling millions" these favored ones develop physically and mentally. But, other things being equal, not only will a sound body contain a sane mind, but under these circumstances, the mind will develop more rapidly than the body, and there will ultimately be much greater mental than physical difference between the upper and the lower classes.

187. DEMOCRACY.

Unjust and almost diabolical as this method seems, it is the method of nature the world over, in the organic as well as in the social world. We have only to recognize the fact and endeavor through it to explain the results attained. With the rise of industrialism and in the multitudinous vicissitudes of human history, but chiefly, after all, in consequence of the enlightenment brought about through the intellectual activities of the favored classes, a great levelling up of mankind began in historic races some eight centuries ago which has continued to the present time, greatly accelerated during the last two centuries and especially during the last half of the nineteenth century, whereby class distinctions have been in great part broken down and the qualities, both physical and mental, of the higher types of men have been transfused throughout all classes. It is costing the world something to assimilate such a mass, and to some there may seem to be a lowering of the tone of former days; but what is lost in diffusion is more than made up in the wider field offered for selection, so that it is even doubtful whether the maximum result has suffered any reduction.

188. PLACE OF RELIGION IN INTELLECTUAL DEVELOPMENT.

A few words may now be said in regard to the place of religion in any study of the development of human thought. Primitive man is not troubled about the causes of the facts of everyday experience, but unbeknown to himself, he reaches the scientific conception of uniformity and invariability in this restricted field. As soon as he begins to reason about phenomena, *i.e.,* to draw inferences from the facts of observation, his data being insufficient to enable him to draw the correct conclusion, he consequently draws an erroneous one. When we reflect that it has required ages of exhaustive scientific investigation to enable us to reason correctly about the causes of such everyday phenomena as an echo, a shadow, or a reflection in a Pool of water, we can readily see how impossible it must be for primitive man to reach the solution of the recondite problems that nature constantly thrusts upon him. But the fact that he *tries* to solve these problems, is just what stamps him as a superior being. This act of his is the beginning of Philosophy, and the study of the philosophy of primitive man constitutes legitimate data for sociology. Primitive philosophy is always anthropomorphic. A phenomenon, from its very name, is a change, a transformation, an activity. But the only being the primitive man knows to possess the power of spontaneous activity is himself, and he naturally imputes to every other change the same power. It is not necessary to trace the steps from this primordial stage to a full-fledged mythology, but mythology constitutes the philosophy of all undeveloped races. Out of mythology grows religion, which is essentially a product of man's rational faculties applied to transcendental questions. It is primarily and fundamentally rational. It had its origin in an effort of the reason. No being without a well-developed reason is capable of conceiving of a religious idea. It is, in fact, one of the great branches of philosophy, and the history of religion is in great part the history of human thought. At every stage it constitutes most important data for the science of sociology.

189. KIDD'S *SOCIAL EVOLUTION*.

Religion in other words is reason applied to life. Those who flippantly contend that a religious condition argues feeble intellectual powers make an immense mistake. But this view is by no means confined to the opponents of religion. It is clearly implied or openly expressed by many who strongly defend it. The latest of this class of philosophers is perhaps Mr. Benjamin Kidd. In his *Social evolution* he makes religion the mainspring of human progress and charges the reason with antisocial and antiprogressive tendencies. Whatever there may be true in his book, and its tone is generally healthy, it is not true, as he maintains, that religion and reason are opposed, or that religion proceeds from an unreasoning, or as he expresses it, an "ultra-rational" sanction. Religion is rational through and through. It is not to be compared to an instinct, such as both animals and men possess, adapted to produce such automatic activities as result in the safety and healthy development of races. On the contrary, it often and usually impels man to do just those things which his instincts and his natural propensities would never dictate. It counteracts the animal nature of man, and is one of those things which distinctively mark him off from the animal world. It could be easily shown that this is precisely the rôle that reason plays everywhere, and it is the failure to perceive this that has led many political economists and others into the gravest of errors in philosophizing about man.

190. RELIGION AND SCIENCE.

Religion has its very origin in reason. No animal has developed even the rudiments of a religion. It is an exclusively human institution, much more so than society. It is the product of thought; an attempt to explain the universe. In this, its primary quality, it does not differ in the least from science, and no true philosopher can doubt that these two great human movements, starting out from the same base, will eventually arrive at the same goal.*

REFERENCES TO WARD'S OTHER WORKS

- *Dynamic sociology*. Topics in Index, volume II: Advantage; Aesthetic; Altruism; Art; Code; Cosmopolitan; Christianity;

---

* Balfour, *The foundations of belief;* White, *Warfare of science with theology.*

Intellect; Intellectual; Intelligence; Monism; Moral-Morals; Music; Non-producers; Religion; Religious systems; Sympathy; Theology; Truth.
- *Psychic factors*. Chapter XVII. Index: Art; Character; Esthetic; Ethical; Ethics; Moral; Truth.
- *Pure sociology*. Chapter XV.
- *Articles*. The essential nature of religion; Ethical aspects of social science.

PART III

ACTION OF THE SOCIAL FORCES IN THE SPONTANEOUS DEVELOPMENT OF SOCIETY

SOCIAL STATICS

- 191. Social mechanics.
- 192. Classification.
- 193. The dynamic agent.

- I. The principle of Synergy.—
- 194. Definition.
- 195. Cosmic dualism.
- 196. Effects of cosmic dualism in the social world.
- 197. True nature of synergy.
- 198. Illustrated by artificial structures.
- 199. Synergy in the formation of organic structures.
- 200. Structure and function contrasted.
- 201. Structure and function statical.
- 202. Social structures.
- 203. Struggle for structure.

- II. The Social Order.—
- 204. Definition.
- 205. Human institutions.
- 206. Primary and secondary institution.
- 207. Marriage.
- 208. Religion.
- 209. Law.

- 210. Morality.
- 211. Political institutions.
- 212. Language.
- 213. The nature of social structures.

191. SOCIAL MECHANICS.

Mechanics is that branch of mathematics which treats of the effects of forces as exhibited in the production of motion or rest. In text-books the production of rest is treated before the production of motion, the state of rest being due to an equilibrium of forces. This department is called *statics*, and the department which treats of forces not in equilibrium, and therefore producing motion, is called *dynamics*. The principles of mechanics are in their fundamental aspects very simple, and the science is one of the most fascinating in the whole range of mathematics. Is there a science of social mechanics? The essential condition of such a science is the existence of true natural forces in society that can be depended upon to produce effects with the same certainty and exactness as do physical forces. The dynamic agent already explained furnishes the sociologist with all that he requires from this point of view. It is true that the complex phenomena of society make it necessary as yet to confine the attempt to treat sociology as an exact science to its most general aspects, but so long as this limitation is rigidly respected it is possible so to treat it, and the result becomes of the highest value. It is essential therefore to insist from the outset and throughout, that sociology is a domain of forces and susceptible of such treatment as fast as, and to the extent that, the action of those forces is thoroughly understood. It must be understood, however, that social mechanics is not sociology as a whole, but is a subscience of the science of sociology. It is that branch of sociology which deals with the action of the social forces. It relates to the dynamic agent only, not to the directive agent, and belongs moreover exclusively to pure sociology.

192. CLASSIFICATION.

The fundamental classification of mechanics, as we saw, is into statics and dynamics. We thus perceive that the mechanics of society naturally falls under the two general groups of social statics and social dynamics, the one defined as social forces in equilibrium, and the other as social forces producing movement and change. It will now be in order for us in this and the three following chapters to consider carefully these two important divisions of sociology.

193. THE DYNAMIC AGENT.

The dynamic agent is a powerful agent. There is no lack of power for propelling the social machinery, for social energy surges through society in all directions. The innate interests of men work at cross purposes; they conflict, collide, and dash against one another, but in such an unorganized, haphazard, and chaotic way that they do not produce equilibrium, but mutual ruin. The dynamic agent, like any other cosmic force, is centrifugal, catabolic, destructive. If there was no way of curbing or harnessing the social energy, there would be nothing but destruction—no construction. We must, then, take up the general problem of restraining social energy. As, however, the actual process that has gone on in society has done so under the operation of a truly cosmic or universal *principle*, it cannot be adequately understood without first understanding its simpler manifestations in nature at large.

I. THE PRINCIPLE OF SYNERGY

194. DEFINITION.

There is a universal principle, operating in every department of nature and at every stage in evolution, which is conservative, creative, and constructive. The word *synergy* seems best adapted to express its twofold character of *energy* and *mutuality*, or the systematic and organic *working together* of the antithetical forces of nature. The third and equally essential and invariable quality of creation or construction is still lacking in the name chosen, unless we assume that work implies some product, to distinguish it from simple activity. Synergy is a synthesis of work, or synthetic work, and this is what is everywhere taking place.

195. COSMIC DUALISM.

The name *monism* has come into use as the short and economical designation of the great truth that there is a unitary principle running through all nature. Second Only in importance, if not of equal importance, to the truth of cosmic unity is the fact of universal polarity. The universe is polarized throughout. Every force meets with resistance, otherwise there could be no energy. Universal conflict reigns. But for this conflict evolution would be impossible. The forces of nature are being perpetually restrained. If centrifugal forces were not constrained by centripetal forces, the very orbs of space would fly from their orbits and follow tangents, *i.e.*, straight lines. Not only do the centrifugal and centripetal forces engage in this struggle, but we also see contending on a gigantic scale the gravitant and radiant forces. We see attraction and repulsion, concentration and dissipation, condensation and dissolution. Though these are all equally modes of manifestation of the universal force, they are nevertheless, by the force of circumstances, pitted against one another in ubiquitous conflict.*

196. EFFECTS OF COSMIC DUALISM IN THE SOCIAL WORLD.

We have now to consider some of the effects of this cosmic dualism. Collision produces deflection, constraint, and transfer of Motion, resulting in increased intensive activity at the expense of extensive activity. Everywhere we have heightened intensity, increased energy, and more work. It is a process of securing constantly greater and greater cosmic efficiency. In the social world the same principle is manifest. We shall find that it also is a theater of intense activity, and that competing and antagonistic agencies are fiercely contending for the mastery. The complete domination of any one set of these forces would prevent the formation of society. Here as everywhere any single force, acting without opposition or deflection, would be destructive of all the order attained. Only through the joint action of many forces, each striving for the mastery, but checked and constrained by the rest and forced to yield its share in conforming to the general principle, can any structure result.

197. TRUE NATURE OF SYNERGY.

The true nature of the universal principle of synergy pervading all nature and creating all the different kinds of structure that we observe to exist, must now be made clearer. Primarily and essentially it is a process of *equilibration, i.e.,* the several forces are first brought into a state of partial equilibrium. It begins in collision, conflict, antagonism, and opposition, and then we have the milder phases of antithesis, competition, and interaction, passing next into a *modus vivendi*, or compromise, and ending in collaboration and cooperation. Synergy is the principle that explains all

---

* Tarde, *L'opposition universelle.*

organization and creates all structures. The products of cosmic synergy are found in all fields of phenomena. Celestial structures are worlds and world systems; chemical structures are atoms, molecules, and substances; biotic structures are protoplasm, cells, tissues, organs, and organisms. There are also psychic structures—feelings, emotions, passions, volitions, perceptions, cognitions, memory, imagination, reason, thought, and all the acts of consciousness. And then there are social structures, the nature of which is shortly to be explained. These are the products of the social forces acting under the principle of social synergy.

198. ILLUSTRATED BY ARTIFICIAL STRUCTURES.

An illustration may throw additional light on the exact nature of the principle of synergy. For example, a mechanism is something constructed. It may therefore be called a structure. As it is artificial, it is an artificial structure. The inventor or constructor of any mechanism, no matter how simple, virtually recognizes the law of the conservation of energy. He assumes that the quantity of motion is unchangeable. He has no idea of the possibility of increasing or diminishing the sum total of force. But he also recognizes the further truth that the particular manner in which forces act is indefinitely variable, *i.e.*, that the direction, velocity, etc., are matters of indifference, and will depend upon the amount and kind of resistance with which bodies meet. In other words, while he realizes that the quantity of motion is constant, he perceives that the mode of motion is variable. This enables him artificially to modify natural phenomena, to direct and control them.

199. SYNERGY IN THE FORMATION OF ORGANIC STRUCTURES.

So likewise the principle of synergy may be seen in the formation of organic structures. These complex structures furnish more of the elements that the sociologist must use and show the true nature of organization. For here we have true organs, and all the structures are more or less fully integrated. In the organic world the primary contending forces are those of heredity and variation. Heredity may be regarded as that tendency in life to continue in existence whatever has been brought into existence. That is, it obeys the first law of motion and causes motion in a straight line unless deflected by another force. This, if allowed to go on uninfluenced, would simply result in perpetually increasing the quantity of life without affecting its quality. But in the domain of vital force, in consequence of the multiplicity of objects in nature, there is necessarily constant collision, constant opposition, constant contact with other forces from all conceivable directions. These constitute the resistance of the environment. Heredity pushes through all this as best it can, striving to pursue the straight path on which it started, but as it is only one of the many forces involved in the contest, it obeys all the other laws of motion and is checked, deflected, shunted, buffeted this way and that, and compelled to pursue a very irregular path.

The impinging forces of the environment cause constant deviation from the specific type, *i.e.*, variation. The organism must therefore conform to the mold established for it by its environment, which requires modification in the specific type. The process of compelling the organism to undergo these transformations and secure this conformity is what in modern biological language is called *adaptation*. But as the environment is infinitely varied and the number of possible conditions to which organisms may be adapted is infinite, the effect is to differentiate the one original hypothetical form which heredity would perpetuate unchanged into an unlimited number of different forms. The resistance of the environment, therefore, so far from offering an obstacle to life, is of the highest advantage, and has made the existing multiplicity of organic forms possible. All of which brings clearly to view the extraordinary creative and constructive character of organic synergy.

200. STRUCTURE AND FUNCTION CONTRASTED.

It is in the organic world that we can best on begin the study of function. But for the function, organic structures would be worthless. The structures are only means. Function is the end. All natural structures are developed along with their functions, which may be regarded in a sense as the cause of the structures. The effort of nature to accomplish its ends results in material means capable of accomplishing them, and such means are structures.

201. STRUCTURE AND FUNCTION STATICAL.

Such being the relations of structure and function, and as all considerations of structure are statical, it is evident that all considerations of function must also be statical. The functions of nutrition and reproduction go on during the entire life of an organism without producing any organic change of structure. Function simply as such has no effect whatever in modifying structure. Not only are nutrition, reproduction, and all the so-called vegetative functions statical, where they simply preserve the life of the individual and of the species, but they do not cease to be statical when by excess of function they increase the quantity of life through growth and multiplication of the same unaltered types of structure. Size and number do not alter the conditions in this respect. There are some animals whose size seems to depend mainly on age and environment. This is notably the case with certain fishes. We may even go further and maintain that simple perfectionment of structure is statical so long as it does not involve the least change in the nature of the structure. Here the distinction becomes fine, but it can be successfully maintained by noting in any given case whether the principle on which the structure works is or is not altered. To illustrate in the case of artificial structures or mechanisms, as, for example, inventions. If a man were to invent a machine and make a rough model, too imperfect to work, he might obtain a patent. In such a case if another man were to present a model of the same machine, but much more exactly made, so that the model itself would work, he could not obtain a patent for an improvement simply on the ground that his model was better made. There must be some change in the principle, however slight, to entitle him to a patent for an improvement. It is precisely this distinction that separates the dynamic from the statical, whether in artificial or natural structures.

202. SOCIAL STRUCTURES.

We now come to social structures, for the better understanding of which only, other structures have been considered. If one has grasped the general principle on which all structures whatever are formed, it is easy to pass from organic to social structures. The principle is the same, and the only difference is in the forces. Social structures are the products of social synergy, *i.e.*, of the interaction of different social forces, all of which, in and of themselves, are destructive, but whose combined effect, mutually checking, constraining, and equilibrating one another, is to produce structures. The entire drift is toward economy, conservatism, and the prevention of waste. Social structures are mechanisms for the production of results, and the results cannot be secured without them. They are reservoirs of power. A dynamo generates electricity from the electrical conditions that surround it. Those conditions were there before the dynamo was built, but they produced none of the effects that the dynamo produces. They may be described as so much power running to waste. The dynamo simply saves and husbands this power for man's use. It is exactly the same with every true natural structure.

203. STRUGGLE FOR STRUCTURE.

Social equilibration under the principle of social synergy, while it involves a perpetual and vigorous struggle among the antagonistic social forces, still works out social structures and conserves them, and these structures perform their prescribed functions. Upon the perfection of these structures and the consequent success with which they perform their functions depends the degree of social efficiency. In the organic world the struggle has the appearance of a struggle for existence. The weaker species go to the wall and the stronger persist. There is a constant elimination of the defective and survival of the fittest. On the social plane it is the same, and weak races succumb in the struggle while strong races persist. But in both cases it is the best structures that survive. The struggle is therefore raised above the question of individuals or even of species, races, and societies, and becomes a question of the fittest structures. We may therefore qualify Darwin's severe formula of the struggle for existence and look upon the whole panorama rather as a *struggle for structure*.

II. THE SOCIAL ORDER

204. DEFINITION.

The social mechanism taken as a whole constitutes the social order. Order is the product of organization. Social synergy, like all other forms of synergy, is essentially constructive. Social statics may therefore be called constructive sociology. Without structure, organization, order, no efficient work can be performed. Organization as it develops to higher and higher grades simply increases the working efficiency of society. To see how this takes place we have only to contrast the efficiency of an army with that of a mob, assuming that both are striving to accomplish the same object. Social statics is that subdivision of social mechanics, or that branch of sociology, which deals with the social order. The social order is made up of social structures, and is complete in proportion as those structures are integrated, while it is high in proportion as those structures are differentiated and multiplied and still perfectly integrated, or reduced to a completely subordinated and coordinated system. This branch of sociology will therefore deal chiefly with social structures and their functions, with their origin and nature, their relations of subordination and coordination, and with the final product of the entire process, which is society itself.

205. HUMAN INSTITUTIONS.

The most general and appropriate name for social structures is human institutions. It should be stated at the outset that structures are not necessarily material objects. None of the psychic structures are such, and social structures may or may not be material. Human institutions are all the means that have come into existence for the control and utilization of the social energy. Attention has already been called to *the group sentiment of safety*,* the most fundamental of all human institutions. Out of it have certainly emerged one after another, religion, law, morals (in its primitive and proper sense based on mos, or custom), and all ceremonial, ecclesiastical, juridical, and political institutions. But there are other human institutions almost as primitive and essential, such as language, art, and industry, that may have a different root, while the phylogeny of thousands of the later derivative institutions may still be difficult to trace.

206. PRIMARY AND SECONDARY INSTITUTIONS.

A closer examination of human institutions reveals the fact that they are not all quite alike even in their general character. We have already seen that some are material and others immaterial, but even this is not as fundamental or as essential a classification as another. This might be called the distinction between natural and artificial, or between spontaneous and factitious institutions, although really one class is as natural as the other, and both are partly spontaneous and partly factitious. In many cases, however, there are two cognate institutions, one of which belongs to one class and the other to the other. In such cases the natural or spontaneous one seems older or more primitive, and the artificial or factitious one is in a sense an outgrowth from the first. The one class might therefore be called primary and the other secondary. From still another point of view the secondary institutions may be regarded as products or functions of the primary ones. A few examples will show both the real distinction between

---

* See chapter VII, paragraph 82.

these classes and also the difficulty in finding terms capable of clearly characterizing the distinction.

207. MARRIAGE.

If, for example, we take the institution of marriage, giving the term all the breadth necessary to embrace all stages of human development,—the customary relations of the sexes,—we perceive that there grows out of it or depends upon it the institution called the family, by which we need not, any more than in the case of marriage, understand any of the developed forms, but simply the customary way of raising children and the relations among kindred generally.

208. RELIGION.

If we consider religion as an institution, even the simple form of it called the group sentiment of safety, we shall see that out of it there grew a system of enforcing conduct conducive to race safety and of punishing conduct opposed to race safety. This is the beginning of both ceremonial and ecclesiastical institutions as defined by Spencer. In its later aspects it becomes the church, and just as Spencer expands the term *ecclesiastical* to cover these early forms, so we may expand the word *church* still further until it becomes correct and intelligible to say that the church is that secondary or derivative institution which religion, as a primary and original institution, made necessary and virtually created.

209. LAW.

Let us next take law, which is closely allied to religion, or is at least a branch, coordinate with the latter, of the still earlier and as yet wholly undifferentiated group sentiment of safety. Law in its simplest expression is merely a sentiment like religion. It may be called the *sense of order* in society. But out of it grew or developed the whole system of jurisprudence, which is therefore a derivative institution, and law bears the same relation to the court that religion bears to the church.

210. MORALITY.

Morality in its earliest stages was also a branch of the group sentiment of safety, and was coordinate with religion and law. At their base all these three are perfectly blended and inseparable. There was very little altruism in primitive morality. There was the parental instinct that exists in animals, and there soon came to be an attachment to kindred generally, which can scarcely be detected below the human plane. This sentiment expanded *pari passu* with the expanding group until the end of the primitive peaceful stage of social development. But it was always a *blood bond*, and the sole basis of adhesion was that of real or fictitious kinship. In fact this "ethical dualism"* lasted much longer, and will not have entirely disappeared until all race prejudices and national animosities shall cease. But morality within these narrow bounds, the germ of all ethical conceptions, was one of the primordial human institutions. It was essentially social, and had sociability as its central idea. Now to what secondary institution, corresponding to the church and the court, did this primary institution give rise? Why, to the moral code, to be sure. The ethical code of all races, peoples, and nations, with the whole mass of rules, precepts, and customs that attend it, constitutes a derivative and factitious institution, growing primarily out of the blood bond.

211. POLITICAL INSTITUTIONS.

Political institutions have a later origin, but we may mention as a case in point the institution of government in the abstract, as the spontaneous condition which required and ultimately produced the state. As this will soon come up for fuller treatment it need not be more than noted here among the correlative institutions.

212. LANGUAGE.

Language is among the earliest of human institutions, and was certainly spontaneous. By language is meant the power of rational intercommunication, which is an exclusively human institution. It is much broader than oral speech, and includes sign and gesture language. Language was a product of intelligence and has nothing to do with the perfection of the vocal organs. For without a certain amount of intelligence man would be incapable of language. No animal, no matter how perfect its vocal organs, could possess language without this minimum of rational power. Conversely, any animal endowed with it would inevitably develop language, and this irrespective of its anatomical adaptation. Just as the

---

* Ross, *Social control*, p. 72.

grammar of animals consists wholly of interjections, so the earliest human speech consisted of interjections and nouns. The other parts of speech, all of which indicate relations, came later, and the verb was one of the latest to appear. Language is thus obviously a purely natural product, the result of a struggle on the part of men to understand one another. It is spontaneous and original. We have then to inquire what is the corresponding secondary, derivative, and more or less consciously developed institution to which language gave birth. It consists in any means for broadening the influence of language. Simple language, whether based on sound or sight, availed only between persons in close proximity with one another and only for present time. The next problem was to communicate at a distance and to make a record for future time. Both these ends were secured by the same general device. We cannot now go into the history of written language through the stages of pictography, hieroglyphics, alphabets, symbolic writing and printing. It has been written over and over again, and all that remains to do is to point out that literature, giving the term its fullest breadth, is the normal functional outgrowth of language, the institution that was naturally built upon it as its base.

213. THE NATURE OF SOCIAL STRUCTURES.

This rapid and imperfect sketch of human institutions, or rather of a few of the principal ones, will afford an idea of the nature of social structures. They are all the result of some form of struggle among the social forces, whereby the centrifugal and destructive character of each force acting alone is neutralized and each is made to contribute to the constructive work of society. The structures once created become reservoirs of power, and it is through them alone that all the work of society is performed. All these structures are interrelated, and the performance of their functions brings them into contact or even conflict with one another. This mild struggle among social structures has the same effect as other struggles, and leads to general social organization. The final result is the social order, or society itself as an organized whole—a vast magazine of social energy stored for use by human institutions.

REFERENCES TO WARD'S OTHER WORKS

- *Dynamic sociology*. Topics in Index, volume II: Dualism; Institutions; Order; Organization.

- *Psychic factors*. Index: Institutions.
- *Outlines of sociology*. Chapter VIII.
- *Pure sociology*. Chapters IX and X, pp. 169-193.
- *Articles*. Evolution of social structures. Static and dynamic sociology.

SOCIAL STATICS (CONTINUED)

- III. Social Assimilation.–
- 214. Original heterogeneity.
- 215. Causes of heterogeneity.
- 216. Imitation and invention.
- 217. Expansion.
- 218. Social differentiation.
- 219. The horde.
- 220. The golden age.
- 221. Its duration.
- 222. Social integration.
- 223. Process of integration.
- 224. The struggle of races.
- 225. Conquest and subjugation.

- IV. Social Karyokinesis.—
- 226. The stages in amalgamation.
- 227. (1) Caste.
- 228. (2) Inequality.
- 229. (3) Law.
- 230. (4) The juridical state.
- 231. (5) Formation of a people.
- 232. Interest unites.
- 233. Other influences.

- 234. Social chemistry.
- 235. (6) The nation.

- V. Compound Assimilation.—
- 236. Compound races.
- 237. The lower races.

- VI. 238. Pacific Assimilation.

III. SOCIAL ASSIMILATION.

214. ORIGINAL HETEROGENEITY.

*The expression *social assimilation* implies original heterogeneity. However similar primitive races may seem to civilized men, they themselves recognize the greatest dissimilarity. Each race looks upon all others as utterly unlike itself, and usually there exists among different races the most profound mutual contempt. Whenever two races are brought into contact, it usually means war. If we go back in thought to a time anterior to all historic records, to a time before any of the early civilizations existed, before the Chinese, Indian, Chaldean, Assyrian, Babylonian, or Egyptian periods, and attempt to picture to ourselves the condition of the world of that day, while we may admit that very little is known of it, no one will deny that great areas of the earth's surface were already occupied by men. There existed at that time a great number of entirely different races, tribes, groups, clans, and hordes, each striving to maintain an existence. Whatever differences of opinion may exist in respect of other matters, all agree as to this primitive multiplicity and heterogeneity of mankind.

215. CAUSES OF HETEROGENEITY.

It is with regard to the cause of this heterogeneity that opinions chiefly differ. The simplest and most naïve explanation is that all these different races of men represent so many separate and distinct creations, the so-called state of *polygenism*. As a matter of fact the question of polygenism or monogenism is simply a biological, not a sociological question. The

---

* See in Bibliography under the names Gumplowicz, Ratzenhofer, Simmel, Tarde, Simons, Novicow.

sociologist has nothing to do with the origin of man. The heterogeneous condition of the human race as far back as concerns him is easily accounted for without any such violent assumptions. It is fully explained on the simple assumption of the animal origin of man, which is now accepted by the great majority of both biologists and anthropologists.

216. IMITATION AND INVENTION.

In animal life the first manifestation of a growing brain is excessive mimicry, *i.e.*, the special faculty of *imitation*. The next step after this power of imitation is the simplest manifestations of the inventive faculty. The least manifestation of this power would be such an immense advantage in the struggle for existence that natural selection would bring about the rest. For the least power over the environment, such as a slight development of the inventive faculty would give, checks the eliminating influence of the environment, and permits the reproductive power to expand to another and much higher stage. The faunal barriers are broken over and the species expands territorially, and consequently increases in numbers proportionally to the area occupied. The difference would be fully as great between such a species and other species as is that between civilized and uncivilized races today. The power, to wield a club in battle, many times increasing the efficiency of the naked hands; the foresight to lay up stores for the future; the art of skinning animals and wrapping the skins around the body for protection; the wit to dig a hole in a bank of clay and crawl in and out; and from this on to the stage of building fire, of making tools and weapons, and of providing more adequate clothing and shelter, and the still higher stage of simplest tillage, and the domestication and use of animals—such are some of the early steps by which the inchoate, intuitive reason of the creature that was ultimately to dominate the earth must have won its first victories over nature.

217. EXPANSION.

These steps once taken, everything else would follow as a matter of course. The faunal boundaries once broken over, the expansion, due to diminished checks to reproduction, would be in all directions. In a very short time the geographical extremes would represent great distances, and all contact with the parent stock would cease. Differences in the environment would alone account for all the differences that exist among the races of men. After the different stocks had lost all trace or recollection of one another, an accidental encounter between two hordes would lead to conflict. While between a human horde and the wild animals among which it lived there would be only fear or perhaps affection, between one human horde and another there would be both fear and hatred. Hence collisions, conflicts, and wars would begin even thus early in the history of a race destined to people and transform the earth.

218. SOCIAL DIFFERENTIATION.

Assuming the animal origin of man as established by the labors of Darwin, Huxley, Haeckel, and many other biologists of the highest rank, the next problem is to explain the origin and genesis of human society. We have already seen how the one differential attribute—incipient reason—removed the chief barrier to indefinite expansion and enabled that most favored race to overspread the globe. But this transition was attended with a large number of other modifications, some of them physical, others social. It was during this period that the principal steps toward the erect posture were taken. It was also at this time that the transition took place from a purely herbivorous and frugivorous to a largely carnivorous life. These were profound anatomical and physiological modifications, but not difficult to account for as the necessary result of continued brain development. From the sociological point of view the origin of the family, which also occurred during this period, is even more significant. Among animals the mother, at least, often knows her young, and with apes there is probably a somewhat general recognition of the nearest kinship relations. With primitive man this was carried further, and the members of the kinship group came to be closely cemented together into what may be called the family. When the family or kinship group becomes so large that it cannot longer hold together, it breaks up in various ways and scatters, resulting in numerous families or kinship groups. As we have seen, there could be no special first family or first pair because it is one long and slow development out of the animal state, but a primitive family or kinship group, taken in the abstract, may be regarded as a homogeneous and as yet undifferentiated unit. The name *horde* is loosely applied by ethnologists to something similar to this, and Durkheim has not inappropriately called this "social protoplasm."*

---

* *De la division du travail social*, par Emile Durkheim, Paris, 1893, p. 189.

219. THE HORDE.

Complete separation into hordes represents the lowest and simplest form of group life, just above the animal stage, but differing from any form of gregariousness in animals in the more or less rational recognition of consanguineal relationship. It was during this long maternal, or matriarchal, period that language was formed; but as hordes scattered themselves over vast areas, and lost all memory of one another and of their ancestry, each group developed a different language. At the same time customs, ceremonies, and religious rites and practices grew up, and these, too, would differ widely for each group. The enlargement of the groups was a function of the developing intellect, but there was a limit beyond which it could not go. The sole basis of group adhesion was kinship, and for everything not recognized as akin, there was no attachment, but intense aversion. Such a state of things can scarcely be called society, and yet it contained all the germs of future society. This was the stage of differentiation. The primitive social protoplasm was beginning to work itself up into multiform shapes and to pervade all lands. It is easy to see that there was no lack of heterogeneity. Although the groups all had the same general pattern, they soon came to differ in all their details. Their languages were different, their customs varied within certain limits, their cults were all different, their fetishes, totems, gods, all bore different names. Only a philosopher looking at them from the highest standpoint could see any similarity among them. They themselves saw nothing common, and regarded one another with detestation.

220. THE GOLDEN AGE.

This period of social differentiation represents that idyllic stage of comparative peace and comfort to which ethnologists sometimes refer as preceding the era of strife and war between more developed races. In all probability the pre-human animal was a denizen of some tropical clime, and many facts point to southern Asia as the region which saw the dawn of the human race. Nothing more definite than this can be said with any confidence, and even this is not certain. But that it was somewhere in the tropics of the Old World seems a tolerably safe assumption. Here amid natural abundance and under friendly skies, living like animals, but with sufficient intelligence to outwit and evade the larger carnivores, capable of so far modifying the environment as to escape the fate of other species that overstep the habitat to which they have become adapted, inchoate man could reproduce with great rapidity, and a sufficient number of those born could live to the age of maturity to cause an increase of population in a geometrical progression. Collision could be avoided by migration, and peace prolonged during a great period.

221. ITS DURATION.

The duration of this idyllic period depended principally on position. Those who wandered far could maintain their independence of others much longer than those who clung to the immediate center of dispersion. Certain races that worked off farther and farther into remote regions or even islands, remained wholly unmolested and continued their simple, half-animal existence, unchanged by contact with other races. Some such exist today, and it is from their study that we gain an insight into this truly primitive life of man. But those who did not migrate far came sooner into contact with others on account of the rapidly increasing numbers of men in all the groups. It was therefore in these regions that social differentiation ceased first, and the succeeding stages of human history earliest supervened, upon the one describe.*

222. SOCIAL INTEGRATION.

Prolonged as may have been the era of social differentiation, with its halcyon days and wild, semi-animal freedom, it could not in the nature of things always last, and as already remarked, its close came much earlier in the general region from which the human race originally swarmed forth to people the whole earth. Here the different races, now fully formed, and having lost all trace or tradition of any common origin, and acquired different languages, customs, arts, cults, and religions, first began to encroach upon one another, and finally more or less to crowd and jostle together. Regarding one another as so many totally different orders of beings, every race became the bitter enemy of every other, and therefore on the approach of one race toward another there was no course open but that of war. The proximity of hostile races was a powerful spur to invention, attention being chiefly turned to the production of the means of offense and defense. Success in war depended then, as it does today, on the mechanical superiority of the instruments of warfare, far more than on

---

* Morgan, *Ancient society*.

personal prowess. A warlike spirit developed, and ambitious chiefs began to vie with each other for the mastery.

223. PROCESS OF INTEGRATION.

At first sight this might seem to have nothing to do with social integration. We are now to inquire by what process and according to what principle this was accomplished. At the very outset it is important to note that this principle is none other than that by which all organization takes place, viz., synergy. We have the antagonistic forces at work here as everywhere, and we shall see that the entire process is identical with that which formed star systems, chemical systems, and organic forms. Weshall see all the steps in this process, and in many respects social phenomena are not only more, clear and patent than are other classes of phenomena, but they actually illuminate the latter, and give us a firmer grasp of the exact workings of this principle on the lower planes.

224. THE STRUGGLE OF RACES.

Gumplowicz and Ratzenhofer have abundantly and admirably proved that the genesis of society, as we see it and know it, has been through the struggle of races. This masterly presentation is without any question the most important contribution thus far made to the science of sociology. We at last have a true key to the solution of the question of the origin of society. It is not all, but—it is the foundation of the whole, and is the only scientific explanation that has been offered of the facts and phenomena of human history. It proceeds from a true natural principle which is applicable to man everywhere, and which is in harmony with all the facts of ethnology and anthropology. Finally, this principle proves to be a universal one, and is the one on which are also explained all other natural phenomena; for the struggle of races is simple and typical social synergy and is the particular way in which synergy as a cosmic principle operates in the social world.

225. CONQUEST AND SUBJUGATION.

The first step in the struggle of races is that of the conquest of one race by another. If one race has devised superior weapons or has greater strategic abilities than the other, it will triumph and become a conquering race. The other race drops into the position of a conquered race. At the lowest stages of this process there was practical extermination of the conquered race. The lowest savages are mostly cannibals. After the carnivorous habit had been formed the eating of human flesh was a natural consequence of the struggle of races. The most primitive wars were scarcely more than hunts, in which man was the mutual game of both contending parties. But at a later and higher stage head-hunting, cannibalism, and the extermination of the conquered race, were gradually replaced by different forms of slavery. Success in conquering weaker races tended to develop predatory or military races, and the art of organizing armies received special attention. Such armies were at length used to make war on remote races, who were thus conquered and held under strong military power. Here the conquered would so greatly outnumber the conquering that extermination would be impracticable. The practice was then to preserve the conquered race and make it tributary to the wealth of the conquering race. Prisoners of war were enslaved, but the mass of the people was allowed to pay tribute.

IV. SOCIAL KARYOKINESIS

226. THE STAGES IN AMALGAMATION.

Ratzenhofer compares this race amalgamation to conjugation in biology, and says that hordes and clans multiply by division. There certainly is a remarkable "analogy" between the process called karyokinesis in biology and that which goes on in societies formed by the conquest of a weaker by a stronger race. This process has been fully described and illustrated by both Gumplowicz and Ratzenhofer, and they not only agree as to what the successive steps are, but also as to the order in which they uniformly take place. The following are these steps arranged in their natural order, after subjugation has taken place. 1. Origin of *caste*. 2. Gradual mitigation of this condition, leaving a state of great individual, social, and political *inequality*. 3. Substitution for purely military subjection of a form of *law*, and origin of the idea of legal *right*. 4. Origin of the *state*, under which all classes have both rights and duties. 5. Cementing of the mass of heterogeneous elements into a more or less homogeneous *people*. 6. Rise and development of a sentiment of patriotism and formation of a *nation*.

227. (1) CASTE.

By conquest two different races are brought into close contact, but they are so unlike that no assimilation is possible. None is desired or attempted.

The society, if it can be called such, is polarized. The conquering race looks down with contempt upon the conquered race and in various ways reduces its members to servitude. The conquered race maintains its race hatred, and while sullenly submitting to the inevitable, refuses to recognize anything but the superiority of brute force. This was the origin of caste, and the two mutually antagonistic and defiant races represent the opposite poles of the social spindle. History shows how difficult it is to eradicate completely the spirit of caste.

228. (2) INEQUALITY.

The inequality of the two races is, however, something more than an inequality of rank. The races were primarily (*i.e.*, before the conquest) thoroughly heterogeneous. They spoke different languages, worshiped different languages, worshiped different gods, practiced different rites, performed different ceremonies, possessed different customs, habits, and institutions, and the conquered race would die sooner than surrender any of these. The conquering race professed absolute contempt for all these qualities in their subjects, but were powerless to transform them into their own.

229. (3) LAW.

The difficulty, cost, and partial failure attending the constant and unremitting exercise of military power over all the acts of the conquered race becomes a serious charge upon the conquering race. For a while, flush with the pride of victory, this race persists in meting out punishments to all offenders against its authority, but sooner or later such personal government grows wearisome, and some change is demanded. It is found that authority may be generalized, and that rules can be adopted for the repression of certain classes of acts, such as are most frequently committed. When this is found to be economical, still larger groups of conduct are made the subject of general regulation. By the continued extension of this economical policy a general system of such rules is ultimately, though gradually, worked out, and the foundation is laid for a government by law. So long as the law is not violated a certain degree of liberty is conceded to the subordinate race, and the performance of acts not in violation of law comes to be recognized as a right.

230. (4) THE JURIDICAL STATE.

There are always great natural differences in men. In a conquered race such individual differences are likely to make themselves felt. The assumption all along is that the races considered are not primarily widely unlike. The issue of battle depends only to a small extent on real differences of mind or character. It may be merely accidental, or due to the neglect of the conquered race to cultivate the arts of war. In all other respects it may be even superior to the conquering race. The latter therefore often has to do with its social equals in everything pertaining to the life of either group. The difficulty of enforcing law in a community constituted as we have described must be apparent. With such an intense internal polarization of interests, the conquering race would find it difficult or impossible to frame laws to suit all cases. It could not understand the conquered race definitely enough to be successful even in securing its own interests. In a word, the conquering race needs the assistance of the conquered race in framing and carrying out measures of public policy. This it is never difficult to secure. A large number of the members of the subject race always sooner or later accept the situation and are willing to help in establishing and maintaining order. The only basis of such order is the creation of correlative rights and duties under the law. This can only be secured through concessions on the part of the master race to the subject race and the enlistment of the best elements of the latter in the work of social reorganization. This, in fact, is what is sooner or later always done. The conquering race may hold out doggedly for a long time in a harsh military policy of repression and oppression, but it is only a question of time when experience alone will dictate a milder policy in its own interest, and the basis of compromise will at last be reached. The two principles involved are both egoistic, but equilibrate each other and contribute jointly to the result. These are economy on the part of the governing class and resignation on the part of the governed class. These produce concessions from the former and assistance from the latter. The result is that form of social organization known as the juridical state.*

231. (5) FORMATION OF A PEOPLE.

A people is a synthetic creation. It is not a mechanical mixture. It is not either of the antagonistic races, and it is not both of them. The details may

---

* Bagehot, *Physics and politics*.

differ, but the process of formation is always the same. There are two antagonistic races of nearly equal social value, one of which has by some means succeeded in subjugating the other and is striving to secure the greatest return for the cost involved in so doing. After a long trial of the stern policy of repression the physically superior race tires of the strain and relaxes in the direction of general law. Concession and resignation, compromise and mutual assistance, proceed apace. Animosity abates, and toleration increases.

232. INTEREST UNITES.

A number of potent agencies combine to accelerate the process. The most important of these is *interest*. It is a truth of the deepest significance that *interest unites while principle divides*. What all the theory of race superiority backed by the military power could not accomplish, personal interest and individual advantage secure. The looker-on is apt to concentrate his attention upon the race struggle and the political principles involved, and forget that there are other forces at work.

The individuals of both races have before them the problem of maintaining their existence. If they are of a sufficiently high development, they are also interested in the accumulation of wealth. In all this, however bitter their animosities may have once been, each needs the help of the rest. In order for the society to flourish and the state to be solvent and strong, arts and industries must spring up everywhere and commercial activity must be fostered and encouraged. The division of labor takes place, ramifying in all directions regardless of race lines. Business organizations and combinations are formed, based on character and fitness and not on race distinctions. Propinquity in such matters is a far more potent influence than race. The influence of men upon one another, other things equal, is inversely as the distance. It is those immediately around that interest and assist.

233. OTHER INFLUENCES.

But interest is not the only cementing principle. There are many other operations which at a certain stage of development inspire intense activities and possess a powerful socializing influence. Such are many of the ways of pursuing pleasure, knowledge, art, science, and philanthropy, through voluntary organizations. As these are forms of association that are based exclusively on personal qualities—affability, zeal, skill, talent—and not on race differences, they tend to break down race barriers and unify mankind through the recognition of true personal excellence. Finally, the time usually comes sooner or later when the state needs the physical and moral support of the lower elements, when outside invaders threaten to overrun and destroy it and plant an alien race over even the race that boasts of its own conquests. At such times the more numerous subject class becomes the main dependence, and to it the new state usually owes its preservation. When this is the case, two other unifying sentiments arise —a dim sense of gratitude oil the part of the ruling classes and a lively sense of pride on the part of the subject race. These work together to the same general end as all the other influences named.

234. SOCIAL CHEMISTRY.

Passing over many other equating and assimilating influences, upon which, like some of those here enumerated, far too little stress has been laid by those who have worked out the law of the struggle of races, mention must be made of one other, which, though in fact perhaps the most vital of all, has, singularly enough, been almost totally overlooked. This is what may be called the *social chemistry* of the race struggle, which begins with the primary conquest itself and continues through the entire assimilative period. In a war of conquest between two savage or barbaric races the women of the conquered race are always appropriated by the conquerors. There is never any such race antipathy as to interfere with the free play of the reproductive forces. Aside from purposes of lust, there exists a certain intuitive sense that the mixture of blood conduces to race vigor. It is an extension of the rule of exogamy and a survival of one of the earliest of human race instincts. Historic examples are numerous, the most celebrated, perhaps, being that of the rape of the Sabines. That this practice was in full force among the Israelites is amply attested by Scriptural passages.* Race miscegenation therefore begins immediately, but it does not cease after the subjugation is complete. Throughout all the stages of social karyokinesis that we have been considering, it is constantly going on. All attempts to keep the superior race pure fail utterly, and by the time the state has been established the majority of the inhabitants have in their veins the blood of both races. The formation of a *people*, therefore, is not only a political, civil, and social process, but it is also largely a physiological process.

---

* See especially Numbers xxxi; Deuteronomy xxi.

It is not until after all these steps have been taken, occupying a long period varying in different cases, that a new race is created through the blending of the two, originally hostile and antagonistic races. Thus are introduced the elements that give rise to new processes, and, by a cross fertilization of cultures, there is created a new social structure. This new social structure is a *people*.

235. (6) THE NATION.

All past animosities are now forgotten, and the people thus created have acquired a sense of unity and solidarity. There begins to be formed a national sentiment. A deep-seated affection grows up for both the people and the territory, and individuals come to feel that they have what they call a country. This affection is filial from the sense that the country has given them birth, and in most languages the name by which it is known denotes paternity—*patria, patrie; Vaterland*. The sentiment that it inspires receives a name derived from the same root, and is called *patriotism*. This sentiment is popularly regarded as a very high one, but it is by the same logic that places maternal love on such an exalted throne, when it is only an animal instinct and common to all mammals at least, to birds also, and probably to many reptiles. Patriotism is in reality not a very exalted sentiment and belongs to the same class as that by which animals become "wonted" to the particular spot where they have been raised with no reference to its superiority over other places.

But whatever its rank as a human affection, patriotism plays an important rôle in the process of social assimilation. It is the basis of the national sentiment, or feeling of social solidarity, that is essential to this last step in the process of social karyokinesis. It marks the disappearance of the last vestige of the initial social dualism. It means the end of the prolonged race struggle. It is the final truce to the bitter animosities that had reigned in the group. The antagonistic forces have spent themselves, social equilibrium is restored, and one more finished product of social synergy is presented to the world.

V. COMPOUND ASSIMILATION

236. COMPOUND RACES.

In the above meager sketch has been described one isolated and typical case of the simplest form of social assimilation by conquest, struggle, compromise, and equilibration. But it should be noted that such a simple case is theoretical, and that in fact all the known historic examples are complex or compound. By this is meant that social assimilation is a process of social aggregation or recompounding, and thus conforms in this respect also to the universal process going on in nature. But it must be remembered that collisions and conjugations of races have been going on ever since man emerged from the animal stage. None of the groups of which we have any historical knowledge is thus simple. The earliest conjugations were doubtless peaceful. The struggle did not begin till the patriarchal system succeeded the age of mother-right. Doubtless there have been numberless cases of the clash of patriarchal tribes as simple as the one described. But the historic cases enumerated by Gumplowicz, Ratzenhofer, and others are all later and between compound races. The process has to be gone through with over and over again. A nation is fully developed according to this process, when another more vigorous nation that has been similarly formed sweeps down upon it and subdues it. A new state, a new people, a new nation, have to be created by the same synergetic principle. But while it was incubating, other states, peoples, nations, were also slowly coming into being, destined, by further conjuncture, to become the rivals of the other, and so on forever. Races, states, peoples, nations, are always forming, always aggressing, always clashing and clinching and struggling for the mastery, and the long, painful, wasteful, but always fruitful, gestation must be renewed and repeated again and again. Nor need the social units always be of the same order. Conjuncture is as likely to take place between races of different orders as between those of the same

order. For example, the conquering race may have resulted from a third or fourth assimilation, while the conquered race may only represent a second assimilation, and have therefore acquired an inferior degree of social efficiency. An extreme of this case is where a so-called enlightened nation occupies a region inhabited by savages. The former may have undergone twenty assimilations, while the latter may be still almost in their idyllic stage. In the case of the United Kingdom of Great Britain and Ireland, for example, it is easy to trace five or six assimilations almost within historic time, and yet the last assimilation is so complete that, except in parts of Ireland, loyalty and patriotism are at high-water mark. Nearly the same is true of France and Germany, but the case is very different in Austria, where the process of assimilation is incomplete.

237. THE LOWER RACES.

The objection may be raised that all that has been said does not apply to races so different that they will not mix, and one of which is so inferior to the other that subjugation is very easy. The so-called low races of men have very little social efficiency. Social efficiency is the result of achievement. We can now see that social achievement is only possible through human institutions, and all higher and more developed institutions are the outcome of social assimilation. Those social units called states, peoples, and nations are of all orders, depending upon the number of assimilations. Every assimilation is a fresh cross fertilization of cultures, and renders the resulting social unit more and more stable and solid. That is, it gives it more and more social efficiency, and it thereby becomes increasingly capable of achievement in the full sense of the definition. The most efficient of all races are those that lie directly in the track of civilization, and which have never had their connection with the past cut off or interrupted. Through this social continuity, accompanied by repeated crossing of the highest strains, the maximum social efficiency and the maximum achievement are secured. Races that have lived wholly off this line of historic development, that have been, as it were, side-tracked, that have been long undisturbed and never subjugated, have only slightly felt the power of social synergy, and have been left far behind in the race. It is not so much their mental inferiority, though mind obeys the Lamarckian law of exercise and is strengthened by every fresh effort put forth. These races possess all the elements of development, but have lacked the opportunity which comes only through the struggle of races and repeated social assimilations.

The only kind of social assimilation that is increasingly fertile is that between races which occupy substantially the same social position. The case is very similar to that of sexual reproduction. For successful crossing the individuals must belong to the same species and not be too different. With these limitations the more they differ the better. It must be true crossing of stocks, and not hybridization or the crossing of different species. The social groups must, so to speak, belong to the same species.

VI. 238. PACIFIC ASSIMILATION

A final question remains. Is this, then, the only possible kind of social assimilation? Is it only through war, conquest, and subjugation that social structures must be formed? The answer is yes and no, according to the point of view. But the only answer needed here is to say that the purpose of this chapter is to study the *genesis* of society. The object has not been here to show what man in the social state may and will do. The object has been to show how man entered the social state and what the social state is that he has entered. Whatever may happen in society after it is fully formed, the truth remains that thus far there has been only one way by which society has been formed, and that is through social assimilation by conquest, caste, inequality, compromise, equilibration, and final interaction, unification, and solidarization.

But it may as well be said that there are other forms of social assimilation, late derivative, pacific forms, such as immigration, that have already begun to operate in advanced societies, and that may ultimately supersede the original, spontaneous, natural method. It may well be that the one great historic line of social evolution has well-nigh reached its term in the direction of forcible consolidation, and that an era of peaceful rivalry and friendly emulation is about to be inaugurated, but the world has evidently not yet reached the point where war shall cease and where the millennium shall be ushered in.

REFERENCES TO WARD'S OTHER WORKS

- *Dynamic sociology*. Topics in Index, volume II: Language; Man; Migration; Savages; Speech.
- *Pure sociology*. Chapter X, pp. 193-220.
- *Article*. Social differentiation and social integration.

14

SOCIAL DYNAMICS.

- 239. Definition.
- 240. Dynamic movements.
- 241. Social progress.
- 242. Social stagnation.
- 243. Social degeneration.
- 244. Social instability.

- DYNAMIC PRINCIPLES
- 245. Definition of these principles.
- I. Difference of Potential.—
- 246. Definition.
- 247. The principle of Sex.
- 248. Asexual reproduction.
- 249. Crossing of strains.
- 250. Effect of uniform environment.
- 251. Mingling of cultures.
- 252. Progress as the result.
- 253. "Dynamic density."
- 254. Influence of war on human progress.
- 255. Western civilization.
- 256. Theory of dominant races.

239. DEFINITION.

As social statics has to do with the creation of an equilibrium among the forces of human society, so social dynamics must have to do with some manner of disturbance in the social equilibrium. As neither the growth, the multiplication, nor the perfectionment of social structures involves any dynamic principle, we have yet to learn wherein essentially consists the condition that is truly dynamic. This should be postulated at the outset, as the necessary starting-point in the treatment of social dynamics. This postulate may be stated in the following form: *In all departments of nature where the statical condition is represented by structures, the dynamic condition consists in some change in the type of such structures.* In order to constitute a dynamic condition, a structure, whether cosmic, organic, or social, must undergo some change in its type, whereby its relations to the environment become different from those previously sustained.

240. DYNAMIC MOVEMENTS.

The word *dynamic* implies a *movement*. It is in this sense that it will be used in this chapter. The process by which structures are produced is not a dynamic process. Structures represent a condition of equilibrium and are the normal result of the equilibration of conflicting forces. But no dynamic phenomena can take place until structures are formed. Dynamic movements are confined to structures already formed and, as stated, consist in changes in the type of these structures. But the important fact to be noted is that the change of type must be brought about without destroying or injuring the structure. It is a differential process and takes place by infinitesimal increments or changes. It may be compared to the process of petrifaction, in which every particle of the vegetable substance is replaced by an exactly equivalent particle of mineral substance, so that it is often impossible to distinguish the one from the other, the minutest structures and even the color being exactly reproduced. This differential process is what characterizes evolution, and the contrast so often popularly made between evolution and revolution is the contrast between a truly dynamic process and a process which breaks up and destroys existing structures in order to make new ones.

241. SOCIAL PROGRESS.

It is common to speak of order and progress as opposites, but that is not the true relation between them. Assuming that the differential changes that take place in the types of social structures are advantageous or in the direction of structural advance, a dynamic movement becomes synonymous with social progress. The structure represents equilibrium, and as it must remain intact and still constantly undergo change it represents a moving equilibrium. As change in the type of structure presupposes structure to be changed, it is clear that progress presupposes order. Order is therefore the necessary basis of progress, its essential condition. This shows more clearly than any other viewpoint could do, not only why social statics must be taken into the account, but also why in the treatment of social mechanics social statics must precede social dynamics. When their true relations are perceived, it becomes apparent that the latter cannot be understood until a clear conception of the former has been gained.

In fact, however, the movement of all transformations, social as well as organic, can only be seen with the eye of reason, so that human institutions are, for all purposes of investigation, virtually fixed. The simple knowledge that they are changing need not disturb their quiet study any more than the knowledge that the earth with all that is on it is swiftly flying through space need disturb the operations of men inhabiting its surface. Nevertheless, the dynamic condition exists and much of the change is in the direction of progress. In general, the movement is in the direction of higher types of structure, having greater differentiation and more complete integration of their parts. We have only to look back over the brief span of human history covered by the written records to see that this has been true of human institutions during the past two or three thousand years, but especially so far as regards the historical races. It is probably true only to a less degree of the rest of mankind.

242. SOCIAL STAGNATION.

Social progress, however, is subject to a sort of law of diminishing returns. The progressive forces are themselves subject to equilibration and a rhythmic swing, which gradually diminishes in amplitude and ultimately comes to rest unless some new force is introduced. Imitation preserves what has been gained, but after a change for the better has been adopted and its value recognized, it becomes sacred with time, and the older an institution is the more sacred and inviolate it is. The permanence of social structures from these causes thus becomes the chief obstacle to reform when this is demanded by a changing environment and internal growth. Society is constructed somewhat on the plan of a crustacean. This is especially true of the more backward and somewhat primitive societies, while the later and higher societies have been reconstructed more on the plan of the vertebrate. Mr. Spencer truly says: "The primitive man is conservative in an extreme degree. Even on contrasting higher races with one another, and even on contrasting different classes in the same society, it is observable that the least developed are the most averse to change."*

There is a prevalent idea in civilized nations that progress is the normal condition and always welcome. Says Bagehot: "Our habitual instructors, our ordinary conversation, our inevitable and ineradicable prejudices, tend to make us think that 'Progress' is the normal fact in human society, the fact which we should expect to see, the fact which we should be surprised if we did not see. But history refutes this. The ancients had no conception of progress; they did not so much as reject the idea; they did not even entertain the idea. Oriental nations are just the same now. Since history began they have always been what they are. Savages, again, do not improve; they hardly seem to have the basis on. Which to build, much less the material to put up anything worth having. Only a few nations, and those of European origin, advance; and yet these think—seem irresistibly compelled to think—such advance to be inevitable, natural, and eternal."†

Sir Henry Sumner Maine, speaking from a still wider range of observation, fully corroborates these statements when he says: "It is indisputable that much the greatest part of mankind has never shown a particle of desire that its civil institutions should be improved since the moment when external completeness was first given to them by embodiment in some permanent record." ‡ "Vast populations, some of them with a civilization considerable but peculiar, detest that which in the language of the West would be called reform. ... To the fact that the enthusiasm for change is comparatively rare must be added the fact that it is extremely modern. It is known but to a small part of mankind, and to that part but for a short period during a history of incalculable length."§

---

* *Principles of sociology*, volume I, p. 78 (§ 38).
† *Physics and politics*, pp. 41-42.
‡ *Ancient law, its connection with the early history of society, and its relation to modern ideas*, by Henry Sumner Maine, with an introduction by Theodore W. Dwight. Third American from fifth London edition, New York, 1883, pp. 21-22.
§ *Popular government*, by Henry Summer Maine, New York, 1886, pp. 132-134.

To all of which it may be added that even these few persons in the most enlightened countries desire change or "reform" only in certain institutions and by no means in all. As Dr. Ross fittingly puts it: "How few there are who honestly believe that improvement is possible anywhere and everywhere! Who expects change in worship or funerals, as he expects it in surgery? Who admits that the marriage institution or the court of justice is improvable as well as the dynamo? Who concedes the relativity of woman's sphere or private property, as he concedes that of the piano or the sky-scraper?"* All this may seem incompatible with the general law of progress, and may lead some to wonder how there can have been any progress at all. The purpose in introducing it is to clear the ground for the application of the real dynamic principles. But another even more serious fact must also be frankly avowed.

243. SOCIAL DEGENERATION.

The well-recognized fact that social degeneration sometimes occurs has led many to look upon it as the natural antithesis of social progress, and it is said that nations and races have their regular stages of youth, maturity, and decline as with old age. There is a basis of truth in all this, as was shown under the head of Sympodial Development.† There is no true opposite to any form of evolution, development never goes backward, retracing the steps it has taken; the loss of any structure that has been acquired can only take place through the crowding out or extinction of the organisms possessing such structure, which is always done by the rise of other more vigorous organisms competing successfully for the means of subsistence. Human races are no exception to this law. There is therefore little to be said here except to point out that social degeneration or decadence, if we make these terms synonymous, is not strictly dynamic, but quasi-pathologic.

If savage man has come out of an animal state, if barbaric man has come from savage man, if half-civilized man has come from barbaric man, if civilized man has come from half-civilized man, if enlightened man has come from early civilized man, then there has in the long run always been progress in spite of all the forms of degeneracy and all the rhythms to which this series of phenomena has been subjected. Ethnologists have described certain low races whom they suppose to have degenerated from

---

* *Social control*, p. 195.
† Chapter II, paragraph 20.

some higher state, as, for example, the Veddahs, the Akkas, the Fuegians, and even the Ainos and the Esquimaux. From this there are certain to be some who will "jump at the conclusion" that all savages are degenerates. This is but to revive the ancient doctrine of a "golden age" and the degeneracy of all mankind, or at least Aristotle's doctrine that all savages have degenerated from a civilized state. These doctrines have all been definitely set at rest by Lyell,[*] Tylor,[†] and others, and need not occupy us.

244. SOCIAL INSTABILITY.

Although everything points to social evolution as having always gone on and as still going on, and although there are no indications that there is now or ever has been any true social involution in the sense of retracing the steps that have been taken, still it must not be inferred that all the modern discussion of the problem of social decadence is based on vain imaginings. The real problem is how to secure social stability.

There is a constant tendency in society to *ossification*, growing out of the intense appreciation that all mankind displays for those social structures that have served a good purpose. Men perpetually praise the bridge that took them across the river of life, and continue to praise it and cling to it after its timbers have decayed and its abutments begin to crumble. This highly useful conservatism thus becomes a dangerous misoneism, and the very stability which men thus seek to secure becomes a source of weakness. Here we encounter the distinction between the *stable* and the *labile*, or rather the real connection between the two. For only the labile is truly stable, just as in the domain of living things, only the plastic is enduring. For lability is not an exact synonym of instability, as the dictionaries, teach, but embodies besides the idea of flexibility and susceptibility to change without destruction or loss. It is that quality in institutions which enables them to change and still persist, which converts their equilibrium into a moving equilibrium, and which makes possible their adaptation to both internal and external modification, to changes in both individual character and the environment.

As there is no such thing in physics as absolute rest, so there is no such thing in society as absolute stagnation, so that when a society makes for itself a Procrustean bed, it is simply preparing the way for its own destruction by the on-moving agencies of social dynamics. Structures once

---

[*] *Antiquity of man*, chapter XIX, London, 1863, p. 379.
[†] *Primitive culture*, London, 1871, volume II, pp. 52 ff.

formed must either change organically and move on to higher stages, or they must succumb to the pressure exerted by surrounding dynamic influences. It is this that is meant by the instability of society or of civilization. Social decadence is never universal. If it is going on in one place, a corresponding social progress is going on in others, and thus far the loss has always been more than made up by the gain. The causes of social decadence have been so widely discussed in recent times that they need not be dwelt on. They are personal, racial, and social. We may recognize the fact that in society and in the human race generally the series has thus far been and still remains an ascending one, and that social, organic, and cosmic evolution prevail and have prevailed to the limit of our powers of fathoming the universe. But, on the other hand this scientific optimism should not, and, properly interpreted, does not teach any *laissez faire* doctrine, and we cannot afford to close our eyes to the patent facts of social instability.

DYNAMIC PRINCIPLES

245. DEFINITION OF THESE PRINCIPLES.

By discussing social stagnation, social degeneration, and social instability, the way has been prepared for the clear and intelligent discussion of the true principles of social dynamics. In some respects social dynamics is a more complex branch of social mechanics than social statics. In the latter we found that all the phenomena were controlled by a single principle, that of social synergy, tinder which social energy is equilibrated and social structures are formed. In social dynamics, on the contrary, several quite distinct principles must be recognized. We shall endeavor to reduce these to three, or at least to confine ourselves chiefly to the three leading dynamic principles. These are, first, *difference of potential*, manifested chiefly in the crossing of cultures, by which the equilibrium of social structures is disturbed, and stability is converted into lability; second, *innovation*, due to psychic exuberance, through which the monotonous repetition of social heredity is interrupted, and new vistas are gained; and third, *conation*, or social effort, by which the social energy is applied to material things, resulting in poesis and achievement. All these principles are unconscious social agencies working for social progress.

I. DIFFERENCE OF POTENTIAL

246. DEFINITION.

This expression is of course borrowed from modern physics, and it will be assumed that the reader is familiar with the distinction between potential and kinetic energy. It is the broadest of all the dynamic principles, and is, in fact, a cosmic principle like that of synergy. It cannot be dealt with in all its bearings upon social science, but must be confined chiefly to its one great application, the crossing, or cross fertilization of cultures.

247. THE PRINCIPLE OF SEX.

Biologists, *e.g.*, have only recently discovered the principle of sex. It had always been supposed, and is still popularly supposed, that the purpose of sex is to insure reproduction. But, paradoxical as it may sound, sex has fundamentally nothing whatever to do with reproduction. The great number of organisms now known to science which possess no sex, and which, nevertheless, reproduce asexually in the most prolific manner, clearly shows that sex is not at all necessary to reproduction. What, then, is the purpose of sex? What office does it perform in organic economy? The answer that modern biology gives to this question is that *sex is a device for keeping up a difference of potential.*

248. ASEXUAL REPRODUCTION.

In asexual reproduction heredity is simple repetition. The structures in existence exactly reproduce themselves. The offspring is in all respects like the parent. Function is fully performed. Growth and multiplication go on at rapid rates. There may be even considerable perfectionment of these same structures. But there is a constant tendency in both the vegetable and the animal kingdoms to escape from asexual reproduction and resort to sexual reproduction, and in the latter to secure the greatest possible separation of the sexes and difference in the parents. Although all this is brought about by natural selection, or the principle of advantage, still it overwhelmingly demonstrates that there is an advantage in sexuality. This advantage is clear to be seen, since it is nothing less than that of setting up a difference of potential between organic beings. This sex primarily accomplishes, and it is accomplished in increasing degrees by the wider and wider crossing of strains. Thus the object of sex is not reproduction at all, but variation. It is organic differentiation, higher life, progress, evolution.

249. CROSSING OF STRAINS.

The crossing of strains is in the highest degree dynamic, and it applies to all living beings. It is well to note that this is the principle that underlies all the customs and laws of primitive as well as civilized men looking to the preservation of the vigor of races. The most conspicuous and widespread of such customs are those which, in varying forms and degrees, and with varying severity, enforce the practice of exogamy. Among higher races the same principle is embodied in laws against incest, and in codes defining the degrees of consanguinity within which marriage is forbidden. Everywhere it is and always has been realized either instinctively, intuitively, or rationally, and now it has been demonstrated experimentally, that close interbreeding is deteriorating and endangers the life of society. This is one of the clearest exemplifications of the universal principle of social dynamics for which the phrase *difference of potential* seems to be the clearest expression.

250. EFFECT OF UNIFORM ENVIRONMENT.

But difference of potential is a social as well as a physiological and a physical principle, and perhaps we shall find the easiest transition from the physiological to the social in viewing the deteriorating effects of close interbreeding from the standpoint of the environment instead of from that of the organism. A long-continued uniform environment is more deteriorating than similarity of blood. Persons who remain for their whole lives, and their descendants after them, in the same spot, surrounded by precisely the same conditions, and intermarry with others doing the same, and who continue this for a series of generations, deteriorate mentally at least, and probably also physically, although there may not be any mixing of blood. Their whole lives, physical, mental, and moral, become fixed and monotonous, and the result is socially the same as close consanguineal interbreeding. On the other hand, a case in which a man should, without knowing it, marry his own sister, after they had been long separated and living under widely different skies, would probably entail no special deterioration, and their different conditions of life would have produced practically the same effect as if they were not related.

251. MINGLING OF CULTURES.

The transition from this semi-physiological aspect of the subject to the wholly sociological one is easy. The cross fertilization of cultures is to sociology what the cross fertilization of germs is to biology. A culture is a social structure, a social organism, if anyone prefers, and ideas are its germs. These may be mixed or crossed, and the effect is the same as that of crossing hereditary strains. The process by which the greater part of this has been accomplished, at least in the early history of human society, is the struggle of races. In this struggle may be found the principle of the difference of potential. A race of men may be looked upon as a physical system possessing a large amount of potential energy, but often having reached such a complete state of equilibrium that it is incapable of performing any but the normal functions of growth and multiplication. It is reduced by the very principle that constructed it to the power of simple repetition. If it were left to the initiative of savage races, there never would be any social progress. We may go further and say that if it were left to the deliberate and conscious action of mankind, human progress would be impossible. Fortunately there are great cosmic, unconscious principles that work for progress against the eternal resistance of established social structures. By sheer force of circumstance, by the pushing out of boundaries to avoid overcrowding, different races, charged with potential energy locked up in varied cults and customs, meet in conflicts, whereby all these divergent idea-germs are first hurled promiscuously together and then blend in the manner described under the head of Social Karyokinesis. Without destroying the structures produced by social synergy, a differential change is constantly taking place whereby they are perpetually changing in type and evolving into new and higher types of structure. This is the dynamic movement caused by the change of potential, which is in turn the result of the cross fertilization of cultures.

252. PROGRESS AS THE RESULT.

Progress results from the fusion of unlike elements. This is creative, because from it there results a third something which is neither the one nor the other, but different from both, and something new and superior to either. But these elements, although they must be unlike, must possess a certain degree of similarity so as not to be incompatible and unassimilable. It must be cross fertilization and not hybridization. All cultures are supposed to be assimilable. Whatever is human must have some points of agreement. Still there are some races whose culture differs so widely from that of others that they seem to form an exception to this law. They are theoretically, but not practically, assimilable. The one has so little potential energy that it produces no appreciable effect on the other, while the higher civilization immediately overwhelms, engulfs, and absorbs, or destroys, the lower.

253. "DYNAMIC DENSITY"

*Again, anything that increases social activity, especially if it affects the intensity of this activity, is dynamic. Thus increase of population, in and of itself, is not dynamic, but there is such a thing as the "dynamic density" of population. By the friction of mind upon mind, especially in a mixed population of a certain density, there is produced a difference of potential among individuals which is in a high degree dynamic.

254. INFLUENCE OF WAR ON HUMAN PROGRESS.

It is impossible in dealing with this subject to avoid the bearing of war and peace on human progress. All civilized men realize the horrors of war, and if sociology has any utilitarian purposes, one of these certainly is to diminish or mitigate these horrors. But pure sociology is simply an inquiry into the social facts and conditions, and has nothing to do with utilitarian purposes. In making this objective inquiry it finds that, as a matter of fact, war has been the chief and leading condition of human progress. This is perfectly obvious to anyone who understands the meaning of the struggle of races. When races stop struggling, progress ceases. They want no progress, and they have none. For all primitive and early, undeveloped races, certainly, the condition of peace is a condition of social stagnation. We may enlarge to our soul's content on the blessings of peace, but the facts remain as stated, and cannot be successfully disproved.

255. WESTERN CIVILIZATION.

As regards the more civilized races, this much at least must be admitted. The inhabitants of southern, central, and western Europe have led the civilization of the world ever since there were any records. They are and have been throughout all this time the repository of the highest culture,

---

* Durkheim, *Les règles de la méthode sociologique*, pp. 139-140.

they have the largest amount of social efficiency, they have achieved the most, and they represent the longest uninterrupted inheritance and transmission of human achievement. The several nations into which this race is now divided are the products of compound assimilation of a higher order than that of other nations. As a consequence of all this this race has become the dominant race of the globe. As such it has undertaken the work of extending its dominion over other parts of the earth. It has already spread over the whole of South and North America, over Australia, and over southern Africa. It has gained a firm foothold on northern Africa, southern and eastern Asia, and most of the larger islands and archipelagos of the sea. It is only necessary to understand the modern history of the world and the changes in the map of the world to see this. Much of this has been peacefully accomplished, but whenever any of the races previously occupying this territory has raised any obstacle to the march of the dominant race the latter has never hesitated to employ force or resort to war. Certain tender-hearted persons have almost always uttered a faint protest against it, but it has been utterly powerless to stem the current. Indeed, the whole movement by which the master race of the planet has extended its dominion over inferior races differs not the least in principle from the primitive movement described in the last chapter. The effects are different only because of the great disparity in the races engaged, due in turn to the superior social efficiency of the dominant race.

256. THEORY OF DOMINANT RACES.

Under the operation of such a cosmical principle it seems a waste of breath to urge peace, justice, humanity, and yet there can be no doubt that these moral forces are gaining strength and slowly mitigating the severity of the law of nature. But mitigation is all that can be hoped for. The movement must go on, and there seems no place for it to stop until, just as man has gained dominion over the animal world, so the highest type of man shall gain dominion over the lower types of man. The greater part of the peace agitation is characterized by total blindness to all these broader cosmic facts and principles, and this explains its complete impotence. There is a certain kind of over-culture which instead of widening narrows the mental horizon. Far safer guides are the crude instincts of the general public in the same communities. If the peace missionaries could make their counsels prevail, there might be universal peace, nay, general contentment, but there would be no progress. Whatever may be best for the future when society shall become self-conscious and capable of devising its own means of keeping up the difference of potential, thus far war and struggle with all that they imply have been the blind unconscious means by which nature has secured this result, and by which a dynamic condition has been produced and kept up.

REFERENCES TO WARD'S OTHER WORKS

- *Dynamic sociology*. Chapter X, volume II. Topics in Index, volume II: Cycles in social progress; Degeneration; Dynamic; Parasites—Parasitism; War.
- *Psychic factors*. Index: Progress; War.
- *Pure sociology*. Chapter XI, pp. 221-240.

15

DYNAMIC PRINCIPLES
(CONTINUED)

- II. Innovation.—
- 257. Fortuitous variation.
- 258. Social innovation.
- 259. Innovation through the leisure class.
- 260. "Instinct of workmanship."
- 261. Final criterion of a dynamic action.

- III. Conation.—
- 262. Explanation of the term.
- 263. Transformation of the environment.
- 264. Social progress not desired.
- 265. Effort the dynamic principle.
- 266. Dynamic effects are social.
- 267. Matter dynamic.

Attention has thus far been confined to those primary social structures called races and nations, which constitute the forms of human association. There are other almost equally important aspects of the subject having their roots in other classes of facts, and to these we may now turn our attention.

II. INNOVATION

257. FORTUITOUS VARIATION.

The dynamic principle next in importance to that of difference of potential is innovation. In its broader aspect it takes the form of what may be called *fortuitous variation*, an expression used by Darwin, Spencer, Romanes, Cope, and others, but not always given its full significance. The chief cause of organic variation, as shown in the previous chapter, is sex. When treating of sex as a device of nature for producing a difference of potential, it was not necessary to go beyond the primary dualism of the parental strains. But it is evident that for any developed organism with a long phylogeny the number of atavistic stirps must be next to infinite, and as any of these are liable to lie latent during many generations and crop out at any time, the possibilities of fortuitous variation are enormous. This is the inner explanation of fortuitous variation, and is the *way* in which nature fills every crack, chink, and cranny into which it is possible for life to be thrust. Whenever the life force breaks over the bounds of simple heredity and goes beyond the process of merely repeating and multiplying the structures that have already been created, it becomes innovation and changes the type of structure. In biologic language this is variation, and all variation is dynamic. Variation due to mere exuberance of life is quite as much so as when due to other causes. These erratic sports, under the life-giving power of sunshine and shower, call back into life and activity all the myriad germ-plasms that have been pushed aside in the march of heredity and line the wayside of evolution. These constitute an inexhaustible source of fresh variations, combining and recombining in an endless series of ever changing forms. Such are the conditions and methods of organic innovation, with which utility, advantage, and fitness to survive have nothing to do.

258. SOCIAL INNOVATION.

Social innovation proceeds upon the same principle, and although the immediate conditions and accompanying circumstances may appear very different, we have only to abstract the details and generalize the phenomena to perceive the fundamental unity of process. The tendency in social, as in organic structures is simply to conserve and reproduce; it is to copy and repeat, grow and multiply, but always to retain the same structures. But in society as in organisms there is a surplus of energy that must be worked off. This is not, however, universally diffused. The great mass have no energy to spare beyond the bare needs of existence. But nature always produces irregularities and inequalities. Its method is utterly devoid of economy. It heaps up in one place and tears away in another. A state of equality, if it could be conceived to exist, would be ephemeral. A state of inequality would quickly replace it. While, then, all the social energy if equally distributed might leave a very small surplus to each member of society, the actual case is: vast numbers in whom the social energy is below the level of healthy activity, and small groups in whom it is far above the possibility of ever consuming it. Surplus social energy is confined to these favored groups, and all social innovation emanates from them.

259. INNOVATION THROUGH THE LEISURE CLASS.

Our present task is to point out that social innovation has been largely due to this form of social inequality. Not wholly, however, and it is only necessary that the primary wants be supplied without exhausting the social energy for it to crop out in the form of innovation. Physical wants must be supplied, and most of this energy is thus expended, but everything goes to show that the moment this is done this energy overflows in the direction, of doing something new. This overflow, too, takes all conceivable forms, and by far the greater part of it is utterly wasted, often more than wasted. One only needs to read Professor Veblen's book* to see that this is so. It only helps to emphasize two truths: the non-economical character of all of nature's processes, and the small amount of energy that really makes for evolution or social progress. The apparently large gains in this direction are due to the almost unlimited time that there has been in which to realize them.

260. "INSTINCT OF WORKMANSHIP".

It is now our task to show not what the leisure class has done for human progress, others have already done that, but more specifically how it has done it. Mr. Veblen himself has given us the key to the whole process. It is his "instinct of workman, ship," which is nothing more nor less than the dynamic principle of innovation. The odium of labor, as be has so ingeniously shown, is something conventional and artificial. If body or

---

* *The theory of the leisure class.*

mind is not fatigued with the effort required to satisfy the needs of existence, activity in either is pleasurable. The leisure class *must* work or suffer ennui. Normally they will follow the instinct of workmanship and do something useful. So long as work is respectable, *i.e.*, so long as there is entailed by it no loss of caste, it will be done. When we reflect how intimately skilled labor is connected with invention, who can estimate the loss that the world has suffered by that pure conventionality which relegates all skilled labor to the mentally least-developed and least-equipped classes of society? For labor in and of itself is not dynamic. Most of the labor done in the world is purely static. It simply reproduces after the set pattern. It multiplies exact copies of what has been invented. Such is nearly all unskilled labor in all departments of industry. Such is also most so-called skilled labor, for the laborer only learns to make or do one thing over and over again in exactly the same way. Outside of his "trade" he is utterly inefficient, and when a new machine robs him of his trade, he is thrown out of employment and has nothing that he can do. Such, too, is all menial service and routine work, most of the work of women in civilized countries, the eternal round of feeding and caring for mankind. Finally, most charity and philanthropic work is static, and philanthropists are content to alleviate present suffering by temporary action, when they know that it will have to be done again and again. Many such would disparage a reformer who should suggest a general policy that would if carried out prevent the recurrence of the conditions that call for charity. The usefulness of statical work, however, cannot be questioned, since through it alone can the *status quo* be maintained. It is the conservative force of society, preventing the loss of the progress attained, and it must always absorb by far the greater part of all the social energy.

261. FINAL CRITERION OF A DYNAMIC ACTION.

What, then, is dynamic action? It is that which goes beyond mere repetition. It discovers new ways. It is alteration, modification, variation. When applied to production, it produces according to a geometrical instead of an arithmetical progression. But it need not necessarily be invention. It may be impulse, exuberance and overflow of spirits, of emotion, of passion even, which will not brook constraint, and dashes forward to higher and greater results. Dynamic action is progressive, and, instead of leaving the world in the same condition as before, leaves it in a changed, *i.e.*, in an improved condition. The final criterion of a dynamic action is achievement, and every innovation, however slight, constitutes an increment to the world's achievement. It is so much permanently gained, it can never be lost, and does not have to be done again. It constitutes the means of producing something better than could have been produced before, and this product is rendered perpetual by its continual reproduction through imitation or social heredity.

III. CONATION

262. EXPLANATION OF THE TERM.

We may now consider somewhat briefly the third dynamic principle, or *conation*. For all practical purposes this may be considered as consisting of a modification of the surroundings. It is easy to conceive of an action which should have no such effect. If the desire is for something very easily attainable, something practically in contact with the individual, with no intervening obstacles, it would not be a dynamic action at all, which is contrary to our hypothesis. But if there are any obstacles or obstructions in the way of the satisfaction of desire, the first part of the action is to remove these, and this modifies the surroundings to that extent. It is obvious that while there may be very simple degrees of this condition, there may be and are also all conceivable degrees of difficulty and complexity in the interval between the desire and its satisfaction. When we, consider developed man with some capacity for "looking before and after," we can readily see that most of his actions are thus complex, and that very few of his desires can be satisfied without first making considerable modification in his surroundings. This quality increases with his general development and with the increasing number and growing complexity of his desires. When at last his desires, like those of most civilized men, become chiefly spiritual and intellectual, usually it is necessary both to work and to wait, and this involves prolonged and intense activity. All this activity is expended upon the surroundings, clearing away obstructions and preparing a smooth road to the predestined goal. The satisfaction of every such desire works extensive changes in the immediate environment, and a large part of these changes is permanent, contributing somewhat in each case to the sum total of civilizing influences in society. The principal form that all this takes is that of creating means to the end, and such means are permanent contributions to civilization. They do not merely serve the end of the individual who creates them, but remain after he is through with them to serve the ends of other individuals for all time.

263. TRANSFORMATION OF THE ENVIRONMENT.

The effect of a dynamic action is therefore chiefly *to transform the environment*. If we examine this principle closely, we shall see that, within a legitimate extension of the terms, all social progress consists in transforming the environment. This is true not only of simple material progress, where this is obvious, covering as it does all economic and industrial operations, but also of all aesthetic, moral, and intellectual operations. It is, indeed, difficult to separate these, because the latter are to so large a degree dependent upon the former; but even if we succeed in doing this, at least in thought, still these higher spiritual operations wholly abstracted from their material base, constitute transformations of the environment in a very proper sense. These furnish not only the most important of such transformations, but also the most enduring of them. For civilization consists in human achievement, and the great achievements of mankind are not material but spiritual; material things are fleeting and evanescent, while spiritual things are lasting and indestructible. Still it must not be forgotten that these permanent contributions to civilization are simply the means by which transformations in the material environment in the interest of man can be wrought, and their value consists in the quality of enabling man to work such transformations constantly and for all time. We may therefore say that the dynamic effect of an action consists in that permanent transformation of the environment which constitutes human achievement.

264. SOCIAL PROGRESS NOT DESIRED.

Looking still deeper into the nature of this dynamic effect of action, it is perceived that it is not the effect desired or intended by the agent. The furtherance of social progress is not only a matter of complete indifference to him, but it is for the most part undesired, unintended, and unknown by him. Except in the most highly developed and most advanced and enlightened of all men, progress, as we have seen, is not only undesirable, but odious and detestable, so that the greater part of all progress, both in the past and present, has taken place and is taking place in opposition to the desires of men and in spite of the universal conservatism and misoneism of mankind. This is true of all progress produced by the cross fertilization of cultures, it is true of progress through innovation, and it is true of progress through conation. It is the *natura naturans*, the mysterious power of nature working for ends beyond the reach of human wisdom. It is the mission of true science to lift the veil and peer behind it into the workings of this power, and so far as may be to discover the principles and formulate the laws of these unconscious and deep-lying dynamic agencies.

265. EFFORT THE DYNAMIC PRINCIPLE.

If now we look squarely at this dynamic effect of action, we shall see that the quantity of the result is measured by the amount of *effort* put forth, so that the essence of the principle is effort. The greater the obstacles to be removed the greater the effort required. The more difficult the end is of attainment the more elaborate will be the means necessary to secure the end. The more remote the end the longer is it necessary to work in order to reach it, and all the work done in this time consists in transforming the environment in the interest of progress. In every case it is effort that produces the effect, and the quantity of the effect will depend upon, and be roughly proportional to the quantity of effort. Of course the quality has also to be taken into the account, and if the effort is chiefly mental, especially if it is inventive, the dynamic effect is far greater, and seems out of proportion to the effort. Effort is therefore the *dynamic principle*, and the term *conation* means the same. Not that all efforts are necessarily dynamic, for the word is often loosely used. In such case, conation and effort would not be strictly synonymous, and the latter term would fall short of exactly defining the principle. This principle of effort is the same in biology as in sociology, but there is an exceedingly important difference in the way in which it works in the two fields. This difference is expressed by the formula already suggested, that *in biology the environment transforms the organism, while in sociology man transforms the environment*. The one is a physiological effect, the other a sociological effect.

266. DYNAMIC EFFORTS ARE SOCIAL.

Society is the beneficiary of all the dynamic principles of sociology. The dynamic effects are social effects, and the general result is achievement and social progress. But we may look still farther into the process. However much mind may enter into it, the effort is expended directly upon the material environment. Its success in causing social progress is conditioned upon the fundamental truth that *matter is dynamic*. In the whole history of mankind it is found that effort expended upon matter has yielded advantageous results. Other expenditures of energy have been either statical or fruitless. Expended in coercing men, social energy yields no progressive results. Directed to purely spiritual things, it results in a weak, stagnant civilization, like that of India. Matter alone possesses the "promise and potency" of progress, and this has been demonstrated by the enormous strides made by the western civilization after it had fairly commenced to concentrate its energies on the material environment.

267. MATTER DYNAMIC.

The dynamic property of matter resides in its susceptibility to change under the influence of external forces. The law of the conservation of energy does not affect this. That law simply predicates the indestructibility of matter and motion. The *quantity* of matter and motion is fixed, but the *form* of matter and the *mode* of motion are indefinitely variable. This establishes the indefinite modifiability of all material things and the possibility of directing all the forces of nature according to the will of the agent. Nature is thus easily "managed" to the extent that her laws are understood, and there is no limit to the extent to which the inexhaustible forces of nature may be brought into the service of man. This is why the material progress of man has so greatly outstripped his moral progress, and this is what is meant by the definition of civilization as "the utilization of the materials and forces of nature." Matter is for man, endowed with intelligence and inspired by science, a veritable lamp of Aladdin, which he need but rub, and, as if by magic, all things take on the forms of utility and cast themselves at his feet.

REFERENCES TO WARD'S OTHER WORKS

- *Dynamic sociology*. Topics in Index, volume II: Artificial; Circumstances; Conation; Effort; Ennui; Environment; Leisure; Matter; Method of conation; Reform.
- *Psychic factors*. Index: Artificial; Conation; Ennui; Environment. *Pure sociology*. Chapter XI, pp. 240-255.
- *Article*. Moral and material progress contrasted.

PART IV

ORIGIN AND NATURE OF THE TELIC AGENT

16

THE DIRECTIVE AGENT

- *Introduction.—*
- 268. Social progress.
- 269. The pessimistic attitude.
- 270. The error of pessimism.

- I. The Objective Faculties.—
- 271. Classification of sensations.
- 272. Indifferent sensation.
- 273. Sensation.
- 274. Steps in the mental process.

- II. Control of the Dynamic Agent.—
- 275. The two agencies of society.
- 276. The genetic and the telic methods contrasted.
- 277. The two classes of social phenomena.

- III. The Final Cause.—
- 278. The efficient cause.
- 279. The final cause.
- 280. Telesis.
- 281. Thought utilizing force.

- IV. The Method of Mind.—

- 282. Prodigality of nature.
- 283. Telic economy.
- 284. Importance of the directive agent.

INTRODUCTION

268. SOCIAL PROGRESS.

In considering what progress has heretofore been made by man, it may be willingly admitted that the most advanced state that has been reached, even by the highest social types, is still far from ideal, still low, compared with what liberal minds are capable of conceiving. Still it would everywhere be found that the conditions of human life have been in process of mitigation for a long period. Great progress has been made in art, invention, and in altruism; nor would anyone deny the broad movement of intellectual progress. It is the characteristic mark of all modern civilization, and even those who deny its influence in bettering mankind never question the enormous strides that knowledge, science, and the practical arts have made.

269. THE PESSIMISTIC ATTITUDE.

Yet, on the other hand, philosophic pessimism T has taught us to look the facts of life in the face, and to see and acknowledge the truth of man's condition and his relation to the universe. So long as we do not exaggerate, so long as these relations, however bad, are the true relations, no possible harm can come of knowing and realizing the truth. It is the only healthy attitude; while, on the other hand, the ignorance of this truth or the refusal to avow it is fatal to progress, seeing that there are as many things that retard as there are that advance the race, and human progress seems to be adjusted so as to defeat itself.

270. THE ERROR OF PESSIMISM.

But it will not do to stop here. It is not enough merely to learn that things are bad. In fact, the chief error of pessimism is its failure to teach the true lesson for human society. There is no room for social Micawbers. Whatever "turns up" must be turned up. The passive attitude is suicidal. This folding of the arms and resignation to fate is certain to meet its fate. Action is the true logic of science, and only by busy brains and busy hands can the recognized evils of the world be lessened or removed. We must enlarge our knowledge by an actual investigation of the facts that lie within our reach. We must study the tangible, visible, demonstrable world and find out what it contains. We know that in the process of evolution man has been evolved, the only being who is endowed with life, feeling, and intellect, the only being who is self-conscious, rational, and intelligent. If, then, humanity as a whole is ever to eliminate the evils of life and to accelerate the movement of social progress, it must be through the intellect of man, the directive agent, which guides and directs the dynamic agent centered in the feelings. This directive agent, therefore, must now be discussed.

I. THE OBJECTIVE FACULTIES

The dynamic agent resides entirely in the subjective faculties of mind, and thus far attention has been wholly concentrated on those faculties. The directive agent resides exclusively in the objective faculties, and we have now to concentrate our attention on these faculties and to search after their true nature.

271. CLASSIFICATION OF SENSATIONS.

The classification of sensations is the most fundamental of all considerations relative to mental phenomena. The duality of mind begins here, and the two great trunks that diverge from this point never again approach each other, but always remain distinct. The two kinds of sensation, distinguished as *intensive sensation* and *indifferent sensation*, form the two primary roots of the mind, the subjective root and the objective root, and from this origin the two trunks rise as if separate and independent trees. By intensive sensation we must understand that form of sensation which constitutes an *interest* for the organism, and which must therefore be, to however slight a degree, agreeable or the reverse, and thus calculated to prompt action. Out of this grew the whole affective and motor side of mind constituting the dynamic agent.

272. INDIFFERENT SENSATION.

We have now to do with the other kind of sensation called indifferent, and we shall find that out of this has grown the entire objective, intellectual, or noetic department of mind. For example, the sense of touch is so constituted that it is often possible to experience very distinct and vivid sensations that are neither pleasurable nor painful in the slightest degree. Probably every point on the surface of the body is capable of such sensations, but some parts are far more susceptible to them than others, as, for example, the ends or "balls" of the fingers as compared with the back of the hand or even the corresponding parts of the toes. It is through these sensations that are neither pleasurable nor painful that the mind is able to distinguish objects, *i.e.*, that it gains its notions of the different properties of bodies. This is the important fact. Intensive sensations do not convey such notions. In fact it is through indifferent sensations and through these alone that sentient beings acquire all their knowledge of the properties of bodies, and thus acquaint themselves with the nature of the external world. It is through them that we are enabled to gain a knowledge of the environment, and thereby to adapt ourselves to it. Indifferent sensation constitutes the primary source of all *knowledge*; *i.e.*, knowledge of properties as distinguished from qualities.

273. SENSATION.

An indifferent sensation then is a distinct awareness not attended by any intensive quality. It arouses no *interest*, and therefore prompts no action. In an intensive sensation the next step is a disposition to act. But in an indifferent sensation there is no such disposition. It is exactly here that the two great departments of mind diverge. Although indifferent in the sense of not arousing a subjective interest, the kind of sensation we are now considering does give rise to a series of psychologic steps, but they are objective, in that they all relate to the object that has impressed the sense.

274. STEPS IN THE MENTAL PROCESS.

The sensation conveys to the mind a *notion* of the subject. Some *property*, if it be only that of resistance, is made known to the mind. Every property that really causes a sensation is reported at once to the mind and recorded there. This fact we shall call *perception*. Perception, then, is the first objective step in the psychologic process, and from this fact it seems appropriate to call the objective faculties of the mind *perceptive*, and to use this term as the antithesis to the term *affective* applicable to the subjective faculties. The product of the act of perception may be called a *percept*. As there exist in the mind many percepts, the next step is to unite these percepts into one, so that there shall be a state of consciousness corresponding to the whole object. The process by which this is done is called *conception*, and the product is a conception of the object, or a *concept*. The next step in the psychologic process is to compare percepts and concepts and detect likenesses and differences. This process is sometimes called *judgment*, and the mental state corresponding to the act is a judgment. Judgment in this sense is the simplest form of mental exploration, and the more complex forms more properly receive the name of *ideation*, the products being ideas, which are creations of the mind in a very proper sense of the word *creation*. Reasoning is simply a more complex form of ideation. The highest form of reasoning is generalization, whereby the larger conceptions and the conclusions or deductions from the widest inductions are grouped into still higher laws and truths and the maximum unity is attained in the operations of mind.

Such is a brief sketch of the nature of the directive agent with a view solely to distinguishing it clearly from the dynamic agent.

II. CONTROL OF THE DYNAMIC AGENT

275. THE TWO AGENCIES OF SOCIETY.

The two great agents or agencies of society are the dynamic and the directive. In previous chapters we have dealt solely with the propelling force of society, comparable to the wind that fills the sails or the steam power that turns the screw of a vessel at sea. We have found an abundance of this power, and we have seen what results it has accomplished. But the social forces are natural forces and obey mechanical laws. They are blind impulses. This is as true of the spiritual as of the physical forces.

The directive agent is not a force, and yet it has immense influence. The dynamic agent seeks its end directly, but the essential characteristic of the directive agent is that it seeks its end through means. It is to be compared to the helm of a ship, or rather to the man at the helm, or to a pilot. Clearly to see that this is not a force we have only to imagine the ship becalmed. It matters not how skillful the helmsman, he is powerless without the propelling agent. And so society would instantly stop in its whole career should the dynamic agent—the wants and passions of men—fail for any cause, and cease to propel the social bark. Nevertheless, social evolution must always remain on a comparatively low plane unless raised to a higher level and guided to better things by the directive agent—the rational faculty of man.

276. THE GENETIC AND THE TELIC METHODS CONTRASTED.

The restraint and control of social energy is therefore the only condition to social evolution. All true forces are in themselves essentially centrifugal and destructive. There are two ways in which the social energy has been controlled; the one, an unconscious process, is that by which all social structures have been formed. The conscious method remains to be considered. It is the telic method or social telesis. Through the unconscious or genetic method—social genesis—all the fundamental social structures or human institutions were formed, and under the operations of the several dynamic principles considered in chapter XV, these structures were enabled to change, and social progress was made possible. Moreover, through the several sociogenetic forces, though still genetic, a certain degree of socialization was achieved and civilization was carried forward to a certain stage. It only required the addition of the telic or directive agent to make possible all the higher steps that have been taken practically in the same direction. Throughout all the earlier stages of man's prehistoric, and even of his early historic career, this telic faculty was so exclusively egoistic, and so completely an adjunct to and servant of the dynamic agent or human will, that it accomplished little more than to heighten and strengthen man's fierce passions; sometimes, as in the subjection of woman, its effect was positively retrogressive, at least for a time. All through man's early history, therefore, and to a large extent throughout his later history and in the most advanced stages of society, the group reason has been compelled to counteract these effects, and has constructed vast systems of religion and government to this end.

277. THE TWO CLASSES OF SOCIAL PHENOMENA.

If, then, we take a comprehensive view of all the phenomena of society, we will see that they fall under two radically distinct classes: (1) the purely spontaneous or natural phenomena of society produced by the dynamic agent, and (2) the phenomena that result from intention or design, which are the products of the directive agent in the sense that but for the directive agent they would not have taken place. The social forces left to themselves blindly impel or propel mankind, and the world drifts as aimlessly as an iceberg. The mission of the directive agent is to guide society through no matter how tortuous a channel to the safe harbor of social prosperity.

III. THE FINAL CAUSE

278. THE EFFICIENT CAUSE.

The directive agent is a final cause. Genetic phenomena are produced by efficient causes only. In an efficient cause a force acts upon a body and impels it in the direction in which the force acts. There may be a plurality of forces having different intensities and acting in different directions, but the principle is not affected, and the general effect will always be the exact resultant or algebraic sum of all the forces involved. All natural, spontaneous, or genetic phenomena conform to this law.

279. THE FINAL CAUSE.

In contradistinction to this definition of an efficient cause, a final cause is always more or less remote from its effect or end. This is implied in the term *final*. It has been repeatedly said that the directive agent is not a force. It may now be equally said that a final cause is not a force. It is not, however, a simple, but a complex conception. No less than three things are embraced in the idea of a final cause. (1) The end is *seen*, *i.e.*, known, by the mind. (2) Some natural property or force is also known to exist, and its action upon the material things to be moved is understood. (3) This force or property is a means to the end, and it is only necessary to adjust the body to be moved in such a manner that the known natural force will impel it to the perceived end. This adjustment is usually accomplished by the exercise of muscular force of the agent in obedience to his will. Both the natural force and the muscular force are efficient causes, and all the motion is the result of these two forces. The final cause therefore consists essentially in the *knowledge* by the telic agent of the nature of the natural force and the relations subsisting between the subject, the object, the force, and the end. This again is the simplest case, but no matter how complex the case may be, it may be reduced to this simple form.

280. TELESIS.

*The three steps are: knowledge, adjustment, natural force. The last is what "does the work." Without the knowledge the adjustment would be

---

* See note on this word, Ward's *Outlines of Sociology*, 2^d ed., 1899, pp. 180-182.

impossible, and without the adjustment the force would be ineffectual. It may then be said that a final cause is the rational employment of the means to an end; the means is always an efficient cause, so that final causes consist in the intelligent command or utilization of efficient causes or the forces of nature. This approaches very close to the formula used as a definition of civilization: "the utilization of the materials and forces of nature," and when closely viewed, it is seen that civilization chiefly consists in the exercise of the telic faculty. If we regard all the forces of nature, including even the social forces, as so many means to the ends of man and society, telesis becomes the adjustment of means to ends, and all human effort is expended upon the means.

281. THOUGHT UTILIZING FORCE.

A final cause may therefore represent any amount of natural force that the intellect of man can reduce to his service. It is practically unlimited. The intellect has it in its power to subjugate all nature and to reduce all the forces of nature to the condition of contributors to man's needs. How far this process can be carried it is certainly too early to predict, especially in the light of what has been accomplished in the last two centuries, chiefly in the last one century. When we consider how little was done in this direction in all the ages that preceded the era of science, how little all the races of the world, outside of the one race that leads the movement, have ever done, and compare this with the achievements of that one race during this brief space of time, we dare not attempt to peer into the future. And when we realize that all this is the result of thought set in the right direction and devoted to things, which are, as we have seen, essentially dynamic, we may truly say that thought is the sum of all forces.

IV. THE METHOD OF MIND

282. PRODIGALITY OF NATURE.

The method of mind is the precise opposite of the method of nature. The method of nature with unlimited resources is to produce an enormously redundant supply and trust the environment to select the best. This survival of the fittest involves a sacrifice of a great majority. It is therefore in a high degree wasteful. Nature aims only at success, and success is secured through the indefinite multiplication of chances. All genetic processes are characterized by this same prodigality. Everything accomplished by nature is uneconomical, irregular, and imperfect. Nature works out a few "favored" forms wrought at enormous expense and involving infinite sacrifice of life and energy. But it matters nothing, as the resources of nature are infinite. Such is the economy of nature, which is simply the absence of all economy.

283. TELIC ECONOMY.

The only true economy is telic. Mind only knows how to economize. Economy is possible only through prevision. Mind sees the end and pursues it. True economy harnesses the forces of nature and simply guides them to the foreseen end. Knowledge gives foresight, and foresight dictates the proper steps. In telic action there is no waste, or at least the waste is reduced to the minimum for the given state of any science, with the prospect of progressive reduction as the science and skill advance. Noetic phenomena are far more rapid than genetic. It requires millions of years to produce an organic structure. Social structures, even the purely genetic ones, grow, evolve, and change far more rapidly than organic structures. But telic structures are comparatively of mushroom growth. How brief is the life of the factory, the steamship, the railway, the telegraph, and the telephone! Yet most of these are giants, and if they do not stay, it will be because a superior substitute will take their places. The law of telic phenomena seems to be a geometrical progression, every new structure breeding a brood of younger and better ones.

284. IMPORTANCE OF THE DIRECTIVE AGENT.

Such is the method of mind, and in its upward reaches it attains enormous complexity. It is said that intellectual operations cannot be predicted. Still they are subject to a few of the most general laws. They have in the later stages of social evolution come to constitute so large a factor that they have wholly frustrated the plans of the political economists who refused to reckon with them. Sociology must not make this mistake, and all systems that ignore the directive agent are doomed to the same failure that has attended the political economy that was based on the "economic man." Both economics and sociology have a psychologic basis, but that basis is as broad as mind itself. Not only must all the interests of men, including their cerebral interests, be recognized, but the faculties upon which the highest types of men chiefly rely for the certain success of those interests—the

198 | A TEXT-BOOK OF SOCIOLOGY

objective faculties—must be equally recognized and thoroughly understood.

REFERENCES TO WARD'S OTHER WORKS

- *Dynamic sociology*. Chapters VIII to XI inclusive. Topics in Index, volume II: Causes; Instinct; Mind; Nature, economics of; Sensation—Senses; Teleological—Teleology.
- *Psychic factors*: Introduction. Chapters I to V inclusive, and XX, XXXIII. Index: Causation; Causes; Directive agent; Economics—Economy; Genetic; Instinct; judgment; Mind; Nature; Natural; Perception; Sensation; Subjective.
- *Pure sociology*. Chapter XVI.
- *Articles*. Status of the mind problem. Psychologic basis of social economics.

17

THE GENESIS OF MIND

- 285. The intellect.
- 286. (1) Indifferent Sensation.
- 287. (2) Tentation and Intuition.
- 288. (3) Intuitive Perception. (4) Intuitive Reason.
- 289. What is meant by animal reason.
- 290. Illustrations of intuitive reasoning. (5) Indirection.
- 291. Meaning of the term.
- 292. The ruse. (6) Moral Indirecton.
- 293. Principal forms of deception:
- 294. Against animals.
- 295. Against inferior human beings.
- 296. In various kinds of occupations.
- 297. In national and social life.
- 298. The intent and the end.

285. THE INTELLECT.

It is evident that until the objective faculties are accounted for on natural principles there is no such thing as a science of psychology. Those who fail thus to account for them and still talk of the "science of mind" are wholly inconsistent. There is no science of what is unaccountable. Now the subjective and objective faculties have frequently been spoken of as constituting the two great branches of mind in its full sense. It would have been better, and even more scientifically correct, to regard the objective faculties as a branch of the subjective considered as the main trunk. The objective faculties grew out of the subjective. The intellect was at first only a servant of the will, a means to the attainment of the end of the feeling being. Its purpose was not to restrain and curb desire but to lead it to success. It is, as it were, a sort of "accident," that came into the world at a late and comparatively modern date, and for the greater part of its career held the position of vassal to that feudal lord, the will, which it not only served in abject submission, but, as we shall see, did not hesitate to stoop to acts of the meanest class and do the henchman's work of dark deeds and sinister practices. Let us now trace the origin and development of this all-important agent.

286. (1) INDIFFERENT SENSATION

In the last chapter, the importance of the two kinds of sensation, intensive and indifferent, was pointed out. It now requires to be noted that this distinction constitutes an initial step in the genesis of the objective faculties. The lowest sentient beings are destitute of it and really have no need of any but intensive sensations, leading them to what is good for them and driving them away from what is injurious, *i.e.*, they only need to know the *qualities* of objects. But very early it becomes advantageous to a creature, independently of pleasure or pain, to gain a notion of the *properties* of certain leading constituents of its environment. This advantage is seized upon by the principle of natural, selection, and those forms that acquire the power of discrimination among the objects with which they come in contact have their chances of survival increased, and ultimately survive while the other class die, out.

287. (2) TENTATION AND INTUITION.

The simple power of beholding objects, not necessarily through an organ of sight, it may be only tactual, is intuition. Its importance is shown by the fact that organs for this purpose are developed in so many very low organisms. They are not eyes at first, but sensitized areas, or specialized ends of tentacles, both of which ultimately become eyes. With the initial development of objective feeling—feeling that is neither good nor evil, but simply acquaints—the creature begins to explore its environment. Life becomes a series of more or less random trials. It is the stage of exploration or tentative stage. This initial faculty might be called *tentation*. Throughout all geologic ages, and in the existing condition of the earth, there have always been humble aquatic creatures, both marine and fresh water, whose lives are spent practically in the groping, exploring, tentative stage of activity. The only rudiment of a rational faculty that they possess is this faculty of tentation, or the somewhat more developed power of intuition, by which they distinguish good from evil, food from enemies, and which at least guides their movements in the direction toward the former and from the latter. It is the simplest of all forms of awareness applied to the most practical of objects.

288. (3) INTUITIVE PERCEPTION (4) INTUITIVE REASON

We have already seen that objective feeling leads to perception. This is the only source of a knowledge of properties, while subjective feeling reveals only qualities. But the primordial mind used this faculty solely for practical purposes, and the properties possessed by the irregularities of the sea-bottom or of the surface of the land in case of terrestrial beings, only concerned such beings in so far as they facilitated or obstructed the pursuit of food and mates. Most of these properties are simply relations, but they are relations among material objects having permanence, hardness, resistance, impenetrability, and for such creatures immovability. They must be avoided, surmounted, circumnavigated, or got around in some way, and the action or movements necessary to accomplish this could not be performed without the power of perceiving these relations and adjusting activities accordingly. Hence the primitive advantageous form of perception was the *perception of relations*, and the faculty of perception was developed through the elimination of those that failed to "take in" their situation and the survival of those that succeeded in taking it in. This form of perception may be distinguished as intuitive perception. It is strictly egoistic, and, although an objective faculty, it is intimately connected with subjective needs. In fact, it exists only for its subjective value in better preparing its possessor to attain its subjective ends. It is a clear example both of the impossibility of any faculty coming into existence unless it be thus advantageous, and also of how the most exalted attributes may have a humble and a simple origin.

289. WHAT IS MEANT BY ANIMAL REASON.

Like every other faculty, reason began as an advantageous faculty. But the primordial reason was not the *Vernunft* of Kant. Animal reasoning is not an analysis, but is intuitive, *i.e.*, it is synthetic. It is, as it were, seeing or intuiting a conclusion. Its elements are simple. They are the perceptions that were last enumerated. Having perceived properties and relations, they now see, behold, or intuit what follows from a comparison or putting together of several of them. This they do when it concerns some interest, when it secures some end, when it leads to the satisfaction of desire or to the avoidance of danger. It is not deliberative. It is instantaneous. Of course it is only the higher animals that manifest this faculty in any marked degree. In most of them it is intimately connected with instinct, which for those that cannot reason at all serves the same purpose, but stops at a much lower point.

290. ILLUSTRATIONS OF INTUITIVE REASONING. (5) INDIRECTION.

Reasoning of this kind, in such animals, for example, as the fox, is often exceedingly acute. In matters of interest animals may be almost unerring in their conclusions. Even in men it has been universally observed that reasoning is much more accurate when interests are involved than in indifferent cases. Dealers rarely make mistakes against themselves. An illiterate person who knows nothing of arithmetic will know it if underpaid for work. This is intuitive reasoning sharpened by the spur of interest. All reasoning was originally of this kind, and the more developed forms and refinements of the rational faculty and reasoning process have grown out of this primordial trunk, ignored by the schools. It is essentially active and aggressive, and hence dynamic and progressive. It seeks change, improvement, and a state of things better and higher than the actual state.

291. MEANING OF THE TERM.

We have seen that the directive agent is a final cause and that a final cause is the utilization of means to an end. We have now to note that this always involves indirection. The intuitive reason goes out in all directions. Its earliest manifestations must have been in connection with the environment in overcoming obstacles to the accomplishment of the ends of nature, nutrition and reproduction. For all organisms that derive their subsistence wholly from vegetation, this practically holds throughout the series. As, however, many even very low animals are predatory and depend mainly or wholly on other animals for subsistence, a radical difference arises in the nature of the objects of pursuit and in the properties and forces that the directive agent must utilize in securing the ends of the organism. The animals preyed upon seek to escape from their natural enemies, and the difficulty in procuring subsistence on the part of the Predatory species is increased.

292. THE RUSE. (6) MORAL INDIRECTION

The form of action primarily relied upon by predatory animals is the *ruse*. The creatures preyed upon seek by every means in their power to escape. Having developed under these conditions they have acquired through natural selection the means of doing this in the majority of cases,—fleetness, powers of flight, burrowing instincts, various means of concealment,—and if their natural enemies had to depend upon direct pursuit, they would usually fail and could not maintain a predatory subsistence. But the means of attack have also kept pace with the means of escape, though the predatory species have not so much relied upon fleetness and strength as upon cunning, not so much upon physical as upon mental qualities. In the means of offense and defense there is a close analogy between animal species and nations. As weapons of war improve, so do the forms of armor. The victory is not to the strong, but to the inventive nation. Mind in every case is the chief element of strength, and this strength is always proportioned to the degree to which telic methods are employed and the power acquired to call nature to the aid of muscle and sinew. Notwithstanding the enormous difference between the two planes of telic activity here compared, there is absolutely no difference in the principle involved. The ruse is the simplest form of deception, and this brings out the vital truth that in so far as mind deals with sentient beings deception is its essential nature.

The ruse and deception in general do not call for specially high intellectual powers. It is therefore not surprising that predatory animals, depending for their very existence upon other simple-minded species with specialized means of escape in case of open attack, should soon develop the telic faculty in the particular direction and special form of deceiving and entrapping their prey. Instinct went a long way on this road, as in the spider's toils, and the cunning of the higher animals is so highly specialized and limited that it becomes half instinct.

293. PRINCIPAL FORMS OF DECEPTION:

Man, although not probably developed out of a predatory animal, found himself at his origin endowed with ample powers of deception to lay the animal world under tribute to him, and the two great primitive stages of his history, the venary and the pastoral stages, testify to the extent to which he made use of this simplest telic attribute. But he did not stop with the control and utilization of psychic forces as manifested in the animal world. The more cunning men and those more favorably situated early began the control and utilization of the less cunning and less favorably situated. Thus was begun the era of *exploitation.* Mr. Veblen, with remarkable penetration, applies the term "predatory"* to the leisure class and points out that the methods of the "pecuniary occupations" even today are at least "quasi-predatory." The universality of deception in all mankind has been so generally recognized and so often illustrated that it is not necessary to treat it in detail. It will be sufficient to make a rough analysis of its principal forms arranged as nearly as practicable in the ascending order of intellectual development.

294. AGAINST ANIMALS.

The cunning displayed by man in outwitting and circumventing animals is only a step higher than the ruse by which predatory animals deceive and catch their prey. The purpose is primarily the same, and hunting, fishing, etc., are simple forms of predation among animals of different powers of mind, man being in so far a predatory carnivorous animal. But when the idea arises, which does not always occur at the same relative historic stage of culture, of taking animals alive and compelling them to serve their captors in any of the various ways in which domestic animals are made useful to man, a slightly higher form of telic action is resorted to. The animals must be tamed. But a full-grown wild animal cannot be tamed. They must be taken while young, must be left unharmed and supplied with food. In this way, at least after a few generations, they become docile. They may then be induced to breed freely and be multiplied at will. All this requires considerable intelligence.

---

* *The theory of the leisure class,* pp. 209, 336.

295. AGAINST INFERIOR HUMAN BEINGS.

In exploiting men a still higher exercise of telic power is requisite. After the formation of caste, the inequalities among men were greatly increased, and it was easy for a few of the higher class to keep the mass of mankind in subjection. This was accomplished primarily of course by force, but forms of deception were also constantly resorted to. The idea of the essential inferiority of the subject class must be steadily kept in the minds of that class. The least suspicion that this was not true would greatly disturb the social state. It was therefore a settled policy to enforce this idea, and a great variety of subterfuges were adopted to this end. At later stages, and even at the present time, those artificial social inequalities which enable the prosperous classes to thrive at the expense of the proletariat, and of the less-favored classes where no true proletariat exists, are chiefly maintained through the systematic deception of the latter, and the inculcation through religious beliefs, when not otherwise possible, of the doctrine that the existing social condition is not only natural and necessary, but divinely ordained.

296. IN VARIOUS KINDS OF OCCUPATIONS.

Deception may almost be called the foundation of business. It is true that if all business men would altogether discard it, matters would probably be far better even for them than they are; but taking the human character as it is, it is frankly avowed by business men themselves that no business could succeed for a single year if it were to attempt single-handed and alone to adopt such an innovation. The particular form of deception characteristic of business is called *shrewdness*, and is universally considered proper and upright. There is a sort of code that fixes the limit beyond which this form of deception must not be carried, and those who exceed that limit are looked upon somewhat as is a pugilist who "hits below the belt." But within those limits everyone expects every other to suggest the false and suppress the true, while *caveat emptor* is lord of all, and "the devil take the hindmost." In politics the practice of deception does not differ as much as is generally supposed from that of business. While principle is loudly proclaimed from the stump, interest lies behind it all. Back of the politician and demagogue lie the "vested interests," and these it is that are "making public opinion." It is customary in these days to laud the newspaper; but, except for the little news that it contains, which is to its managers a secondary consideration, the newspaper is simply an organ of deception.

Every prominent newspaper is the defender of some interest, and everything it says is directly or indirectly (and most effective when indirect) in support of that interest. We might take up the legal and the medical professions and we would there find the same general fact—systematic deception.

297. IN NATIONAL AND SOCIAL LIFE.

The form of deception used in warfare is called *strategy*, and the kind that nations practice is known as *diplomacy*. There is collective deception as well as individual deception. There is deception in the home and deception in the church. Fashionable society consists largely in sham; quackery is found in the professions and charlatanism in scientific bodies; falsehood permeates business, and most advertisements are in the nature of intentional deceptions.

298. THE INTENT AND THE END.

It must not be supposed that there is any malicious intent in this universal deception and exploitation that characterize the application of telic methods to sentient things. Neither animals nor men cause others pain for the mere love of it. It is only that creatures susceptible to pain get in the way of irresistible natural forces and suffer accordingly. The lava that rolls down the sides of a Vesuvius or a Mont Pelée is not deterred by the presence at the base of a Pompeii or a St. Pierre. It is about the same with the vital and psychic forces that impel living beings. The end is the sole consideration. If that can be attained without causing pain, it is the same to the agent. There is no particular reason why the telic method should be applied to feeling beings rather than to insentient and inanimate things. If such an exercise of mind promises the same results, it will be adopted. But the exploitation of other living things is simple and about the first thing to suggest itself.

REFERENCES TO WARD'S OTHER WORKS

- *Dynamic sociology*. Chapter XII. Topics in Index, volume II: Deception; Ends; Indirect; Reason; Reasoning.
- *Psychic factors*. Chapters XXI to XXVI, and XXXII. Index: Common sense; Cunning; Deception; Ends; Indirect; Indirection; Intellect—Intelligence; Intuition; Intuitive; Object; Reason.

- *Pure sociology.* Chapter XVII, pp. 475-488.

18

THE GENESIS OF MIND (CONTINUED)

- (7) Material Indirection.
- 299. Ingenuity.
- 300. Invention. (8) Inventive Genius.
- 301. The characteristic of genius.
- 302. Instruction in invention.
- 303. (9) Creative Genius.
- (10) Philosophic Genius:
- 304. In origin advantageous.
- 305. The emancipation of the intellect.
- 306. Beginnings of philosophy.
- 307. Phenomena of mind.
- 308. The study of the cosmos.
- 309. Its results.
- 310. Observation.
- 311. The scientific spirit.
- 312. The philosophic spirit.
- 313. Scientific genius.
- 314. The non-advantageous faculties.

(7) MATERIAL INDIRECTION

The exploitation, we might almost say deception, of inanimate nature requires a higher development of the telic faculty. Material things do not move of themselves. Their properties are hidden and must be searched for. Physical forces are invisible and intangible, and their utilization is an exclusively human power. Animals do not attain to the stage of imagination which constitutes the common parent of both creation and invention. It is the basis of and condition to both the great institutions that we call art—fine art and useful art.

299. INGENUITY.

The exercise of the telic faculty upon material things and physical forces, though not psychologically different from its exercise upon living things, is no longer called deception, and none of the terms employed in describing the different forms of deception—ruse, cunning, sagacity, tact, shrewdness, strategy, diplomacy—are applicable to it. The identically same psychic process is now called *ingenuity*, and the more involved forms of ingenuity result in invention. Ingenuity is the faculty, while invention is the act, and the term is also used for the thing invented. Ingenuity and inventiveness are nearly synonymous. But ingenuity was not at its inception a disinterested faculty. Man was seeking to utilize everything whether animate or inanimate that could serve his ends. Some material objects were nutritious and he could appropriate them directly, others must be altered or modified and the nutrient elements extracted by processes varying in complication and calling forth greater or less exercise of the telic power. At a certain stage, it was discovered that material objects might be made serviceable as aids in the capture of animals and as a protection from the elements. Thus weapons of the chase, traps and snares of simple design, and various devices were contrived to render the quest for food more easy and certain. A dead animal becomes brute matter, and while its flesh serves for food, its skin is used as a means of protection. Even its bones and claws may serve some useful purpose. Reeds and bamboos, palm leaves and sticks from the jungle, finally contribute to comfort and safety, and from such beginnings clothing and shelter must have been evolved. When the art of making fire was discovered, another great step was taken, and thus little by little the human animal emancipated himself from the purely animal condition and assumed the rôle of man. The most important result of this early exercise of the directive agent upon the inanimate world was the control thereby gained of the environment, whereby that strictly animal characteristic was outgrown which restricts every species to its own particular habitat, to which it has become adapted, and beyond which it cannot range without encountering such hostile elements as to destroy it.

300. INVENTION. (8) INVENTIVE GENIUS

We are concerned here with material indirection only as a phase of the genesis of mind. We have seen that it was intuitive, synthetic, and egocentric. Throughout the earlier stages of society it doubtless chiefly remained so, and the end to be attained through any ingenious device was constantly before the mind of the inventor to the practical exclusion of all other sentiments. But a time at length arrived when the mental exercise involved in invention began to constitute a satisfaction of its own. The inventor is dealing with material objects and with physical forces manifesting themselves through such objects. He takes advantage of the principle that while matter can be neither created nor destroyed nor the sum total of its activities increased or diminished, its mode of motion may be varied in any desired way. Invention consists then essentially in varying the mode of motion of matter. But as this may be done at will, the particular way in which the inventor wills to vary it is that which will result in some advantage, primarily to the inventor, but ultimately to mankind in general. The inventive power consists therefore in the ability to see what variations in the mode of motion of the material objects under examination will result in advantage to man. This advantage to man constitutes utility, and therefore what the inventor is seeking is utility. Utility is a relation, and the perception of relations is one of the earliest manifestations of the telic faculty. But utilities are highly complex relations. Invention may then be defined as the *perception of utilities*. The complete oneness of the whole telic faculty from simple intuition to human invention is thus clearly brought out.

301. THE CHARACTERISTIC OF GENIUS.

Invention in its later stages becomes subjective and takes the form of genius. The distinguishing characteristic of genius is that it does not have preservation or reproduction for its end, but is, as we may say, an end in itself. This does not mean that it is devoid of motive, for if it were, it would be incapable of producing action. It only means that its motive is not an ontogenetic or a phylogenetic force, but is a sociogenetic force. It may be a moral force, and it is to some extent an aesthetic force, but it is chiefly an intellectual force. When we reach the stage of genius, the brain has become an emotional center, and the appetites, wants, and feelings of the intellect constitute motives of great strength. The perception of utilities, at first simply as means of attaining personal ends, often succeeded admirably in accomplishing this, and soon began to constitute an independent stimulus, so that the search for utilities became a pleasurable occupation. This double motive led to renewed application and heightened zeal, and there arose on the part of the inventor a tendency to lose sight, temporarily at least, of the practical end and to yield wholly to the spur of anticipated success residing in his own mind. When invention reaches this stage, it becomes genius, and henceforth it exists for its own sake. It becomes a passion and is pursued often at a sacrifice of other pleasures and satisfactions and even of positive wants.

302. INSTRUCTION IN INVENTION.

In modern times, there are many almost professional inventors employed for the most part by manufacturing establishments. The fact that such persons can always be found and that they have sufficient inventive ability to enable such establishments to keep abreast of the times and vie with one another in the constant production of improved appliances of all kinds, seems to prove that the inventive power of man is widely diffused and capable of being "developed," *i.e.*, stimulated into activity, by suitable opportunity. The surprising thing is that in all the best equipped universities and polytechnic institutes there seems to be no recognition of invention as a discipline apart from the regular professions of engineering, surveying, and manufacture. There is no text-book on invention in general, its fundamental principles and methods. It would seem that if invention could be recognized as a science or as a profession and thoroughly taught as such, the perception of utilities would be much more general among the educated public, and the awkward mechanical conditions under which society labors would be greatly improved. When we remember how vast have been the results that have been achieved through invention pursued in a purely spontaneous and unsystematized way, we naturally wonder what might be the effect of its reduction to scientific method and its inculcation through systematic courses of training and instruction.

303. (9) CREATIVE GENIUS

Although aesthetic art is one of the best recognized fields for the display of genius, it is perhaps more difficult to account for creative than for inventive genius, but it has been seen that the aesthetic faculty reaches far back into the animal world. By this is meant a certain pleasure in the sight, sound, or even the "feel" of certain things. Things that yield such pleasure are, to those who experience the pleasure, beautiful. In animals no higher stage is reached than that of appreciating beauty when it presents itself to their faculties, but man at a very early stage acquired the faculty of subjective creation at least, as imagination may be called, and of enjoying such subjective creations. The next step was to put together objects and parts of objects that imagination showed to be beautiful and thus to form ideals, *i.e.*, representations of things that did not exist, but of which only the parts or elements had objective reality. Such ideals are creations, and their production constitutes creative genius.

(10) PHILOSOPHIC GENIUS

304. IN ORIGIN ADVANTAGEOUS.

We come now to the faculty *par excellence* that has engaged the attention of the students of mind. The inventive faculty has been practically overlooked and the creative faculty has been taken as a matter of course, but the faculty or power of "abstract reasoning," as it is called, this is the great, the worthy, the noble attribute that exalts man above all nature and renders him divine. Briefly it may be said that an intellectual quality, talent, or faculty is a psychic structure based upon an organic structure of the brain. It must be advantageous at the start and common to all the members of a species to insure its original creation. But once in existence, any and all of these faculties may vary in any given direction and grow into wholly non-advantageous faculties, provided they do not become positively disadvantageous in the sense of endangering the existence of the race. In regard to the intellectual faculties, we find this same argument to hold true. For example, the relief from physical want which the system of caste and the formation of a leisure class, both sacerdotal and political, afforded, set free a large volume of intellectual energy hitherto expended in the struggle for existence, and it took a variety of directions. Its own innate interest constitutes its abundant motive power. The exercise of the intellectual faculties in the struggle for existence during countless ages had developed them to a very high degree, and, if the volume is present, the direction the impulse will take depends on circumstances. Freed now from egoistic exercise, this accumulated intellectual capital is liberally invested in disinterested, or non-advantageous projects. It is no longer held by the principle of advantage to any fixed course, and it goes off on strange lines and does unheard-of things.

305. THE EMANCIPATION OF THE INTELLECT.

Now the real élite of mankind, not the wealthy nor the influential, but those who use their reason most and who possess the largest stock of both knowledge and ideas, will not slavishly follow the herd, but are erratic. They rise above both gain and fashion, and persistently violate the code of social action and rules of propriety. This typifies the emancipated intellect everywhere, and although the leisure class was a ruling class and not under the influence of the rest of mankind, still it found itself emancipated from all forms of restraint, and those members, always of course relatively few in number, who took pleasure in intellectual exercise could freely follow the lines of least resistance and greatest attraction, and could follow these lines fully out to their extreme logical conclusions.

306. BEGINNINGS OF PHILOSOPHY.

Philosophy began as speculation. Facts or supposed facts of course lay at the bottom of it. Perceptions, conceptions, and ideas were in the minds of those early speculators, but they were little controlled, and imagination was scarcely differentiated from observation. Although thought took many directions, often wild and fantastic, the body of primitive speculation was confined to two great fields, which may be called respectively *cosmology* and *noology*. Neither of these can probably be said to have had priority over the other, but certainly the phenomena of mind claimed the attention of man as early as did those of the external world.

307. PHENOMENA OF MIND.

This extremely early study of mind is a sort, of anthropomorphism, just as primitive men understood life because they possessed it, and ascribed all movement to living beings like themselves, so the first thinkers understood mind because they possessed it, and not only projected their own intelligence into all nature, but proceeded to speculate upon mind before they did upon matter. This form of speculation was practically sterile, but it was fascinating, and bad the subjective advantage of cultivating and refining the thinking powers in a way that nothing else could do. Philosophers never abandoned this field and are still tilling it, almost as fruitlessly as at first. It never yielded any valuable results until it was cross fertilized by the germs of objective science, and metaphysics was transformed into psychology. Nevertheless an enormous amount of sublimated intellectual energy has been expended on mind, and few will deny that mind has been thereby exalted.

308. THE STUDY OF THE COSMOS.

The study of the Cosmos, on the other hand, was fertile from the start, and all that we know of the universe, including mind, has resulted from it. This is why it is beginning to be seen that the true Greek philosophers were not Socrates and Plato, but Thales and Pythagoras, and especially their talented contemporaries and followers, Anaximander, Anaximenes, Heraclitus, Empedocles, Anaxagoras, and Democritus. These may all be called cosmologists, although their theories differed greatly, and some of them combined the study of mind with that of nature. The form of speculation that seems to lie between thought and things and bind them together is mathematics, or, as the Greeks chiefly understood it, geometry. This presented a peculiarly attractive field, since it was free from the encumbrance of concrete objects, and dealt with relations, or, popularly speaking, abstract ideas. It harmonized well with speculations about mind, but it proved fruitful of results, and at the hands of Euclid it has come to constitute the basis of all knowledge of quantity.

309. ITS RESULTS.

At that date, when so little was known of the concrete facts of nature, mathematical study and abstract speculation were more profitable than reasoning about material facts, because all theories of the universe that could be formed from such imperfect data must be extremely vague and largely false. Yet when we remember that not only the true nature of the solar system, but also the atomic theory of chemistry and the doctrine of evolution were all formulated by the Greek cosmologists, so that they can be readily recognized by modern science, we are in position to form an estimate of the power of the thinking faculty to comprehend nature. These conclusions were reached not by "abstract reasoning," but by *generalization*. With any considerable number of concrete facts to reason from, generalization is a far more important process than abstraction. It leads to *truth* in the proper sense, *i.e.*, the relation of agreement or disagreement of conceptions, ideas, and groups or clusters of these. It classifies phenomena and coordinates facts, phenomena, and ideas, establishing comprehensive laws. This is true philosophy, and so long as error can be avoided every exercise of mind in this direction increases man's acquaintance with his environment and with the world at large.

310. OBSERVATION.

But observation as well as speculation has always gone on. Many minds are not specially constituted for abstraction and generalization, but take pleasure in observation, and when freed from want and exempted from the struggle for existence, such minds amuse themselves by exploring their surroundings, noting and perhaps recording rare and peculiar facts and phenomena, accumulating "curiosities" in private museums, and in many ways, perhaps unintentionally, increasing human knowledge. Many of the Greeks belonged to this class, especially during the later centuries, and Aristotle possessed the observational attribute in a high degree. The Alexandrian school supplied other observers, notably the Ptolemies, and the Romans furnished the Plinies. The spirit of both speculation and observation smoldered through the Middle Ages, but broke out anew at their close in a form that could not again be smothered.

311. THE SCIENTIFIC SPIRIT.

All know the history of science, and it is only necessary to point out the fact that scientific discovery, as it has gone on during the last five centuries, and especially the last two centuries, is nothing else than a revival of the philosophic genius of antiquity, this time applied to an enormously increased volume of facts. The spirit of observation and accumulation was never suppressed, and the world was in possession of a large supply of data for thinking, even in the time of Copernicus. It is often forgotten that science, which seems to have burst upon the world in the eighteenth century, had been incubating during the previous five hundred years, and could not have come forward in the manner it did but for that prolonged preparation. No matter what branch we study, we are always carried back at least to the fifteenth century, and if we look critically into it, we find that the chief reason why we cannot go back still farther is that it was in that century that printing was invented, and the greater part of the record prior to that event is lost from the inability to preserve manuscripts. So it was with all forms of knowledge, the materials for its scientific elaboration were accumulating during all these ages, and the solid character which the later study of nature took on was mainly due to the increased volume of facts.

312. THE PHILOSOPHIC SPIRIT.

The philosophic spirit also continued to exist, and with these enlarged resources it came forward in great force at about the same time as the scientific awakening. Mathematicians like Newton, Descartes, and Leibnitz did not hesitate to philosophize. Leonardo da Vinci and Sir Thomas More stand out conspicuously in the fifteenth century, Giordano Bruno and Francis Bacon in the sixteenth, Spinoza, Locke, and Leibnitz in the seventeenth. The early sociologists should also be mentioned, including Hobbes, Vico, and those of the eighteenth century.

313. SCIENTIFIC GENIUS.

Our present purpose is simply to show that the great scientific era was not suddenly inaugurated, but that it had a long and ample preparation in antecedent ages, without which it could not have begun. It would be possible to make another division of these faculties, and to call this application of thought to things *scientific genius*. But it is not generically distinct from philosophic genius, especially from that branch of it which took the direction of cosmology. The only difference is in the increased data involving a more exact and systematic method. Science proper consists in reasoning about facts and not in the accumulation of facts, but the ability to reason soundly depends upon the possession of the facts about which to reason. Neither the facts without the reasoning nor the reasoning without the facts can lead to scientific truth. Science is mainly interpretation, and interpretation is a special kind of reasoning. It is the method of all observational science, specially characteristic of geology, but true also of all the physical and biological sciences. In physics and chemistry the difference consists chiefly in the artificial production of many of the facts through experimentation, but after the phenomena are produced the method is the same.

314. THE NON-ADVANTAGEOUS FACULTIES.

We have thus rapidly passed in review the non-advantageous faculties of man. The term *non-advantageous* has been sufficiently defined so that no one need stumble over the obvious fact that these faculties are the most advantageous of all to mankind at large. The distinction may be characterized as that between *individual* and *social* advantage. In the social world the influence of the artificial emancipation of a part of mankind from the restraints of the environment, analogous to domestication, liberates the psychic energy and permits a large surplus to expend itself in biologically non-advantageous ways, some of which have proved sociologically advantageous.

REFERENCES TO WARD'S OTHER WORKS

- *Dynamic sociology*. Topics in Index, volume II: Philosophy; Scientific; Verification.
- *Psychic factors*. Index: Creation—Creative; Genius; Imagination; Invention; Inventors; Philosophy.
- *Pure sociology*. Chapters XVII, XVIII, pp. 489-510.
- *Articles*. Genius and woman's intuition. Weismann's concessions.

PART V

ACTION OF THE TELIC AGENT IN SOCIAL ACHIEVEMENT

19

SOCIAL ACHIEVEMENT THROUGH THE CONQUEST OF NATURE

- *Introduction.—*
- 315. Individual telesis.
- 316. The intermediate step.
- 317. Social or collective telesis.
- 318. The study of society made scientific.

- I. Human Invention.—
- 319. Empirical art.
- 320. Primitive invention.
- 321. Man's capacity for conquest.
- 322. Modification of the natural.
- 323. Pre-Hellenic and Greek art.
- 324. Westward movement of thought.
- 325. In mediæval period.
- 326. The modern era.
- 327. Eighteenth and nineteenth centuries.
- 328. Power of invention.

- II. Scientific Discovery.—
- 329. Invention and discovery.
- 330. The mission of science.
- 331. The stage of empiricism.
- 332. The Greek period.

- 333. Mediæval period.
- 334. Discoveries of the eighteenth century.
- 335. The problem of life.
- 336. The truths of biology.
- 337. Origin of species.
- 338. The law of evolution.

INTRODUCTION

315. INDIVIDUAL TELESIS.

Social progress is either genetic or telic. Progress below the human plane is altogether genetic and is called development. In the early human stages it is mainly genetic, but begins to be telic. In the later stages it is chiefly telic. The transition from genetic to telic progress is wholly due and exactly proportional to the development of the intellectual faculty. The intellectual method is essentially telic. Through it satisfactions are multiplied and life correspondingly enriched. There are two kinds of telic progress, or telesis, individual and collective. The former is the principal kind thus far employed. The latter is as yet so rare as to be almost theoretical. Society itself must be looked upon as mainly unconscious. Its operations are the result of the combined activities of its individual members. But the individual is conscious and seeks his ends by the aid of all the faculties he possesses. This is individual telesis. It constitutes almost the only social progress that has thus far taken place.

316. THE INTERMEDIATE STEP.

The intermediate step between individual telesis and social telesis is an organization of individuals into a limited body. Such organizations are always for some specific purpose, and the word purpose sufficiently indicates their telic character. It shows that there may be a thought common to a number of persons, and that several individuals can, as well as a single one, act teleologically toward a desired end. In modern society there is scarcely any limit to the variety in such organizations. If a small number of individuals may think and act for a common purpose, a larger number may, and there is no necessary limit until the totality of a people is embraced in the number. If such a universal organization has for its sole object the good of its members in general, it thereby virtually becomes the government.

317. SOCIAL OR COLLECTIVE TELESIS.

Individual teleology from the standpoint of society may be regarded as unconscious. The social benefits that it achieves are not thought of. They are as much accidental and unintended as are those that result from purely genetic or spontaneous activity. On the other hand, the social teleology now under consideration—the action of the central body or government which society creates to look after its interests—is conscious in the sense that, as a body, it always aims to benefit society. As government is an application of what society knows about the nature of the social forces, it is a true art; and collective telesis may therefore be called *the social art*. The science of society must produce the art of society. *True legislation is invention*. Government is the art that results from the science of society through the legislative application of sociological principles. In every domain of natural forces there are the four steps: First, the discovery of the laws governing phenomena; second, perception of the utilities (modes in which the phenomena can be modified to serve man); third, the necessary adjustments to secure the useful end; and, fourth, the application of all this in producing the result. The first of these steps is that of pure science; the second and third are involved in invention, and properly constitute applied science; the fourth is art in its proper sense.

318. THE STUDY OF SOCIETY MADE SCIENTIFIC.

Now, looking at society as a domain of natural forces, we may see how readily it admits of being subjected to this series of processes. Discovery of the laws of society is the natural province of the sociologist. He should also be looked to for the detection of utilities, but this work also belongs in a still higher degree to the legislator. Adjustment is the exclusive province of legislation, and laws, when framed according to these principles, would be such adjustments and nothing else. The execution of the laws is the resultant social art. It requires no great stretch of the imagination to see how widely this scheme would differ from the corresponding features of the present régime. It is still easier to see its immense superiority. The essence of telic action consists at bottom in making natural forces do the desired work instead of doing it ourselves. This is exactly what is needed in society. The desires, passions, and propensities of men are bad only in the sense that fire and lightning are bad. They are perennial natural forces, and, whether good or bad, they exist, cannot be removed, and must be reckoned with. But if society only knew how, it could utilize these forces, and their very strength would be the measure of their power for good. Society is now spending vast energies and incalculable treasure in trying to check and curb these forces without receiving any benefit from them in return. The greater part of this could be saved, and a much larger amount transferred to the other side of the account. In the following pages the influence of the telic agent in achievement, both individual and collective, will be illustrated and some attention given to the possibilities of socialization.

I. HUMAN INVENTION

319. EMPIRICAL ART.

*Empirical art consists chiefly in making useful things. It is what was characterized in chapter VI by the term *poesis*. The potter's art, which is very early and widespread, is a typical empirical art. But the making of tools and weapons contributed much more to the conquest of nature than did the culinary and domestic arts. Tools, first of rough, then of polished stone, then of copper (usually, but probably erroneously called bronze by archaeologists), and at last of iron, after the art of extracting iron from its ores had been acquired, have been the marks, and their quality the measures of culture in the progress of the race.

320. PRIMITIVE INVENTION.

That the keen imitative powers and sharp intuitive cunning of apes and other animals come very near to intelligence may be freely admitted, and it is only a step from this grade of cunning to that which could arrange a pitfall for an unwary animal or a rude snare for a fish. The earliest man, driven by the necessities of existence, took this step, and it was devices such as these that constituted the first inventions. Nothing could be more interesting than a list of the truly primitive inventions. This of course can never be drawn up, because there are no absolutely primitive races, and archaeology begins much too high in the series. But there have been some tolerably satisfactory approaches toward the preparation of such a list.

---

* Mason, *Woman's share in primitive culture*. Morrison, *The new epoch*.

321. MAN'S CAPACITY FOR CONQUEST.

Equipped with the directive agent as a guide to the dynamic agent, that "favored race" of beings called man set out on a career for the conquest of nature. Throughout his pre-human stage, like the rest of the animal world, this being had always been the slave of nature. His was a struggle for existence like the rest, but he proved himself the fittest to survive and he survived. Cephalization found in him its highest expression and brain became a factor in this struggle. *Facile princeps*, it soon gained the lead, and from that time on, this being, thus rendered human, distanced all competitors. He early saw the advantage of association and secured the added benefit of the law of the survival of the social. He passed through all the earlier stages, and emerged into the stage of compound social assimilation with a military régime of exploitation, a sacerdotal caste, an intermediate and independent free business element, and a subordinate slave population. The whole mass was rising, but parts rose with special rapidity, the business element through the exercise of its advantageous, and the leisure class of its non-advantageous, mental faculties.

322. MODIFICATION OF THE NATURAL.

No progressive race has ever been content with the natural. Everywhere and always the environment, although it embodies all the elements of existence, has obstructed human progress, has withheld the necessary supplies, has doled out its resources in a niggardly way, and has starved to death by far the greater number of all the creatures that have been born. But the human race, with its intuitive, egoistic reason, with its inventive faculty, with its intellectual prevision and telic power, began its struggle against the law of nature. The transformation of the environment in the direction of utility, *i.e.*, of human advantage, is no more difficult than in any other direction. It was therefore simply a question of knowing how to accomplish this, and knowledge of this kind is that which underlies invention. It was also discovered that nature is easily managed by intelligence. The earliest operations of this class were what are called *empirical*. The bow and arrow was a primitive weapon, being found in the hands of most of the lowest savages, and also among the relics of the lake dwellers. The arrow was probably a modification of the javelin and the bow the result of a series of steps in contriving means of hurling it with greater force and accuracy. Pottery, as already remarked, was a primitive art, but could not have antedated the art of making fire. Many think that the art is practically the invention of women, and Professor Mason* has shown that many of the most useful inventions have been made by women. It is nevertheless probably true and certainly quite natural, as Havelock Ellis maintains,† that the inventions and arts created by women are of a severely practical character and do not in their hands tend to become ornamental or aesthetic. The plow grew out of the digger, and the primitive plow had no mold-board, did not throw a furrow to one side, and merely scratched the ground. A wooden mold-board was introduced much later, but the iron plowshare was not invented until the end of the eighteenth century.

323. PRE-HELLENIC AND GREEK ART.

All the early pre-Chaldean arts are now known to have migrated northward from southern Asia, and the archaeology of middle and northern Asia, which has only recently been studied, is throwing great light upon the direction taken by the streams of primitive migration. If it can be completed, it will probably fill all the gaps between Asiatic and American civilizations. Most of the Greek art in the time of Homer was either Egyptian or Chaldean, both being introduced by the Phœnicians. Such were the arts of metal working (chiefly bronze and iron), weaving, the construction of boats and war chariots, also of tripods, which constituted their chairs, and of such houses as they had. Espinas‡ says that they "were acquainted with the spindle and distaff, the sail-boat, the bit, the bellows, the plow, the war chariot, the carriage, the hinge, the lock, the auger, the bow, the turning-lathe, the potters' wheel, the balance." From the Phœnicians they imported "prepared fabrics, wines, oil, and intoxicants; papyrus articles, linen (an exceedingly important product), ointments, prepared spices, incense, embalming-mixtures, perfumes, dyes, and drugs from Egypt, and the various products of metal work, ornaments and weapons of a superior quality."§ But prior to the Trojan war the Greeks were an almost exclusively pastoral people, consisting of nomads from the East who had conquered the original less aggressive inhabitants and reduced them to slavery, becoming themselves partially fixed, and subsisting chiefly upon their oxen and sheep and a rude agriculture.

---

* *Woman's share in primitive culture.*
† *Man and woman,* pp. 316-317.
‡ *Les origines de la technologie,* par Alfred Espinas, Paris, 1897, p. 45 (chiefly on the authority of Hultsch and Blümner).
§ *Homeric society,* by A. G. Keller, p. 19.

Nevertheless they did not know the use of cows' milk and had not learned to make butter or cheese. Eggs are not mentioned in the *Iliad* or *Odyssey*, and only the inhabitants of the maritime districts used salt. They reckoned by the decimal system, counting their fingers like other barbarians. They had no alphabet, but received later that of the Phoenicians derived chiefly from Egypt, so that until that time those great epics must have been simply traditions whose preservation was intrusted to priests or other specially appointed guardians to hold in memory and transmit to their successors. An alphabet and the art of writing on papyrus, or something more manageable than stone, glass, and metal, must therefore be set down as one of the great steps in civilization. Down to the time when Ctesibius of Alexandria invented the clepsydra, time was kept by the sun-dial, invented by the Babylonians and mentioned in the Bible (Isaiah xxxviii. 8). The power of steam was known and the principle embodied in Hero's engine, but no practical use was made by the ancients of so important a discovery. The extensive public works of the Romans prove that some of the most important principles of engineering, including those of the arch and the catenary, had been worked out and applied.

324. WESTWARD MOVEMENT OF THOUGHT.

It thus appears that the stream of human thought, intelligence, and inventive power moved westward from southern Asia to Chaldea, Egypt, and Asia Minor, thence to Greece and Italy, and that from the Mediterranean shores it slowly spread to western and northern Europe.* In these regions had been formed all the most highly assimilated races.

325. IN MEDIÆVAL PERIOD.

The aggressive attempts of the Romans to conquer the northern "barbarians" and add them to the empire, followed by the nemesis of barbarian invasion of Rome, resulted in the necessity of assimilating the entire mass, which caused an apparent retrograde movement and seemed to lower the status of civilization in the Mediterranean region. This was further complicated by the vast religious revolution attendant upon the substitution of Christianity not only for the pagan cults, but also for all the barbaric cults. The consequence was nearly fifteen hundred years of apparent intellectual stagnation. Yet even this long period was not wholly

---

* Bagehot, *Physics and politics*, p. 52.

fruitless. Here and there a flicker of inventive genius flashed up, as when the Saracen, Ebn Junis, at the end of the tenth century, invented the pendulum; when the compass, perhaps invented by the Chinese, and certainly used by them in traveling overland, found its way to Europe and was applied to water navigation; when gunpowder, likewise of Asiatic origin, but hitherto only used for pyrotechnic display, was applied to projectiles and became an engine of war; or when the Saracens invented a process of making paper from linen rags and cotton. Even the great art of printing, whose invention broke the spell, had been independently invented in China and was actually brought to Europe by Venetian navigators.

326. THE MODERN ERA.

The middle of the fifteenth century marks the beginning of the modern era. The invention and practical application of the art of printing was the turning-point, but a long train of other, often apparently independent, inventions and discoveries quickly followed. It would require pages merely to enumerate them all. Indeed there are always many the date of which cannot be ascertained, and still more that are so completely the products of natural evolution by minute accretions that they can scarcely be said to have had an origin. The steam-engine in the modern sense was preeminently the child of the seventeenth century, although it required the entire century to invent it. There can be no doubt that the invention of the steam-engine constitutes the most important economic and industrial step the world has thus far taken, and it can only be compared to the invention of printing, the greatest intellectual step in the history of civilization. With the latter began the era of thought, with the former, the era of machinery.

327. EIGHTEENTH AND NINETEENTH CENTURIES.

As following upon the maturing of the steam-engine it seems natural that the great inventions of the eighteenth century should be the loom and the spinning-jenny, as it is these three that practically constitute the factory, and although a great many other industries, each the result of a series of preparatory inventions, sprang up in response to the new demand, still it was the factory, and the extensive production of spun and woven goods by machinery, that characterized this age. It was the beginning of what by a contradiction of terms is known as manufacture by machinery, and which M. Tarde so happily and also so correctly renamed *machinofacture*. When we come to the nineteenth century, we find the inventions simply innumerable. It is difficult to characterize it by any single one, and it seems necessary to name at least two, but better still, three or four. If we mention the telegraph, there at once arise in the mind the colossal figures of the railway and the steamship. There also arise the other great applications of electricity. It may be called the age of electricity. But if we look to function rather than structure, it may be called the age of communication, for all these structures serve that end. The eighteenth century may then be called the age of production and the nineteenth that of distribution in the economic sense. In analogy to organic functions, the eighteenth may be regarded as an age of social alimentation or digestion, while the nineteenth was one of circulation. This circulation, however, includes both nutritive and neural, the telegraph and telephone constituting an internuncial system. But in all this it is not meant to imply that the organs of production developed during the eighteenth century were not active during the nineteenth. The productivity of man has steadily increased throughout all this time. It is only that to this great alimentary system there was added the system of circulation both of things, including men, and of ideas.

328. POWER OF INVENTION.

In the conquest of nature by man unquestionably the first place must be given to invention, to the perception of utilities and the utilization of properties and forces locked up except to the key of intelligence in the apparently dead and lifeless material objects, or invisible and intangible in the subtle forces of nature. Still, as has already been said, the principle does not essentially differ from that employed in utilizing the psychic properties of animals, either through the ruse in capturing them for food, or through those higher powers of cunning and calculation by which animals are domesticated and made to serve man. Thus invention has not only satisfied a thousand wants, but it has created many thousand more; and not only has it satisfied old wants and created new ones, but it has also satisfied these latter and thereby contributed in an incalculable degree to the fullness of life or volume of existence, which alone constitutes social progress.

II. SCIENTIFIC DISCOVERY

329. INVENTION AND DISCOVERY.

Invention and discovery are reciprocal. Invention leads to discovery and discovery leads to invention. Without the arts necessary in the construction of a seaworthy ship and the invention of the compass, the discovery of remote parts of the earth, including the New World, would have been impossible. Without the discovery of the power of steam and the nature of electricity, the invention of the steam-engine and the telegraph would have been equally impossible.

330. THE MISSION OF SCIENCE.

Just as the chief mission of invention in its broadest sense is to counteract and so far as possible nullify the uneconomical and wasteful genetic method of nature and substitute for it the economical and fruitful telic method of mind, so it was the chief mission of science in its broadest sense to dispel the illusions of nature and the errors of the primitive reason based on these illusions, and to substitute for them the truths that lie hidden beneath the superficial appearances and the laws of nature, that only reveal themselves to prolonged observation, experimentation, and reflection. The most fundamental of all nature's laws is the law of causation, and this is precisely the one that the primitive mind least understands.

331. THE STAGE OF EMPIRICISM.

The stage of empiricism overlapped far upon the scientific stage and cannot be said even now to have wholly passed away; but after social amalgamation had reached a certain point and social cleavage had become complete, the leisure class, freed from the goad of want, began to employ its surplus energies in the greater and greater exercise of its non-advantageous faculties. *Primum vivere, deinde philosophari.* The non-advantageous faculties had no reason for searching for utilities, and they expended themselves chiefly in the search for things that had no apparent utility whatever. Much of this early research, if it can be dignified by that name, had in fact no utility beyond that of exercising and thus developing the faculties themselves. The earliest scientific study consisted chiefly in observation. The considerable advances which it is known that the

Chaldeans, the Chinese, and the Egyptians made in astronomy were reached by this method. That these ancient astronomers were priests, and that this early study of nature was due to the establishment of a priesthood wholly exempt from the struggle for existence is evident from the fact that the results were regularly used in religious ceremonies. India, which is perhaps theoretically nearer to the primordial center of dispersion, does not show the same antiquity in observational science as Chaldea. In China astronomical records go back quite as far as in Chaldea. There was in the charge of the priesthood a tribunal of mathematics which prepared a calendar of eclipses (announced in advance) and of other celestial phenomena. The ancient Egyptians must have cultivated astronomy, but about the only records they have left are to be found in the construction of the pyramids, the exactness of which presupposes considerable advance in mathematics, engineering, and mechanical skill. All over Europe are to be found the remains of structures in stone erected by the prehistoric races that lived there ages before the present peoples invaded Europe from the East. The most remarkable of these is Stonehenge in Wiltshire, England.

332. THE GREEK PERIOD.

The want of a written language and the general character of sacerdotal observation and thought have kept the world in general ignorance of who the men were that performed these intellectual achievements, and we can only vaguely ascribe them to the races that inhabited the areas on which their monuments are found. But when at last we approach the new, and at first comparatively backward, civilization of Greece and the regions that surround it, we are near enough to the date of the invention of a symbolic alphabet and to records made on papyrus sheets or parchment to begin to learn what was transpiring in the world of thought. Beginning with Thales, Anaximander, Pythagoras, and Anaximenes, in the seventh and sixth centuries, and ending with the third and second centuries before our era, we have a great mass of cosmological ideas, which, seen thus in perspective, towers up into gigantic proportions. These men were not priests, but all belonged to the privileged class who possessed leisure and opportunity for observation and meditation; and while the earlier of them could only teach their doctrines to their disciples, these latter found ways at last of preserving and transmitting these thoughts, until they could ultimately be recorded and handed down as imperishable achievements of the human mind. Nothing has been said of the wonderful development of art, especially of sculpture, but almost equally of poetry and drama, although these too are imperishable achievements, because we are here dealing with the progress of the human intellect in compassing the conquest of nature.

333. MEDIÆVAL PERIOD.

As in the case of invention, so in that of scientific discovery, and in fact of about everything but church history, scholasticism, and religious casuistry, the first fourteen centuries of the Christian era offer almost nothing worth recording. It is also a fact generally overlooked, that during practically this same period Asia was passing through a phase of its history similar to that through which Europe had to pass just as Christianity supplanted paganism in the West, so Buddhism first supplanted the older Indian cults, and then Mohammedanism swept over the whole eastern world from the Mediterranean to the Pacific. It also invaded Egypt and northern Africa and strove to penetrate the continent of Europe, which it might perhaps have accomplished had it not been stopped and turned back by the hammer of Charles Martel on the plains of Tours in the year 732. But in Asia there has been no renaissance, except the recent awakening of Japan. In Europe the Middle Ages were to some extent a period of gestation. The barbarian and Mohammedan invasions and the Crusades had a powerful awakening influence and repeatedly disturbed the social equilibrium, infusing fresh, but as yet coarse, unassimilated mental and physical elements, and requiring long periods for their refinement and complete readjustment. Only a few names are worth enumerating among those who contributed anything during the Middle Ages to the advancement of man's dominion over nature.

334. DISCOVERIES OF THE EIGHTEENTH CENTURY.

The greatest discoveries of the eighteenth century grew out of seventeenth-century conceptions of ether and gravitation. They relate to heat, light, and electricity. But in astronomy and in chemistry the century was scarcely less prolific. In biology the eighteenth century was chiefly an age of accumulation and classification. But the great principle of organic development through the struggle for existence, involving descent with modification, was distinctly enunciated by both Goethe and Erasmus Darwin before the close of that century. At the beginning of the nineteenth century all the great sciences were fairly established and the number of investigators was enormously increased. All the leading universities had long been in operation in Europe and several existed in America. These were turning their attention more and more to science and establishing well-equipped laboratories for original research. All the great scientific academies had long been in existence and celebrated men were associated with them. In astronomy, in physics, in chemistry, in geology, in all branches of biology, and to some extent in anthropology, observations and experiments were being made, and every field of nature was being explored. Learned memoirs were published, the transactions of academies and societies were filled with contributions of all kinds recording the results of scientific work, and an immense monument was in process of erection to the industry and zeal of an awakened world. Thus began that "Wonderful Century" whose achievements Dr. Wallace has so ably summed up that it seems superfluous to attempt even an abridged enumeration of them.*

335. THE PROBLEM OF LIFE.

If the greatest triumphs over nature in the interest of man took place in the domain of physics and chemistry, the deepest thought of the nineteenth century was concentrated upon the problem of life. In every science a philosophic period precedes the period of maximum utilization. The nineteenth century was the philosophic period of biology. For by philosophy we do not now mean speculation, or the propounding of theories based chiefly on meditation and reflection, such as were most of those, however exact, of the ancients. We now mean theories or hypotheses, it may be, but based on great accumulations of facts and worked out through the study and comparison of these facts. They are in reality generalizations, and each step is established by a compilation and coordination of the facts. Such was the heliocentric theory as revived by Copernicus, such were Kepler's laws, such was the law of gravitation, and such was the atomic theory of chemistry.

336. THE TRUTH OF BIOLOGY.

The Greeks had stated many of the now recognized truths of biology, but their theories were only speculations, wonderful glimpses into natural truth, but wholly unsupported by scientific evidence. It must not be forgotten either that along with these just glimpses there went the wildest

---

* Wallace, *The wonderful century*, and *Progress of the century*.

vagaries, and these latter greatly outnumbered the former. It is only after a great truth has been scientifically established that we go back and pick out the rare cases in which it had been as it were accidentally hit upon in the midst of a great mass of erroneous ideas. These we leave behind and forget, or excuse as due to the insufficiency of the data at the command of those ancient philosophers. And we glean the few grains that we now know to be golden, but which the finders may have considered of little importance while imputing great value to what we now know to have been dross. It is thus that the forerunners of most great discoveries, instead of being neglected, as is usually supposed, often receive far more credit than they really deserve. In biology, then known as natural history and divided into botany and zoology, also including mineralogy, vast accumulations were made during the four preceding centuries, and from the time of Linnaeus, indeed for a century before his time, everything was described and classified, so that with the beginning of the nineteenth century, the entire known vegetable and animal kingdoms were represented in herbaria and museums, and all the species that could be distinguished were described and figured in large illustrated works. This was the period of biological statics, and it was supposed by all these early naturalists that species were absolutely fixed. Lamarck overthrew this doctrine and inaugurated the period of biological dynamics. This new discovery of the mutability of species and the genealogical descent of organic forms, perceived by Goethe and Erasmus Darwin as a poetic idea, gave a wholly new impetus to biological science.

337. "ORIGIN OF SPECIES."

When at last Darwin, just half a century after the appearance of Lamarck's *Philosophie zoologique* (1809), came out with his *Origin of species* (1859), laden still heavier with the facts of observation, and announcing the additional principle of natural selection, which explains *how* the transmutation of species takes place, the whole world was electrified, and a vast army of investigators plunged into the field of biology, determined to verify or disprove this bold yet fascinating hypothesis. The result, while it raised the hypothesis to a law of nature, also filled the world with knowledge of organic life and placed biology in the front rank of the advancing sciences.

338. THE LAW OF EVOLUTION.

The law of evolution*, in large part biological, but also cosmological, nay, also anthropological, psychological, and sociological, has been almost wholly the product of nineteenth-century science. It is probably the most important of all the generalizations of the human intellect. Philosophy ever asks the questions: What? Whence? Whither? Not content with the conquest of nature and the subjection of its laws to human uses, man is resolved to find out what he was, whence he came, and what is to be his destiny. Evolution furnishes the first answer that science has ever made to these questions, and when its truths are fully known, will furnish the final answer.

REFERENCES TO WARD'S OTHER WORKS

- *Dynamic sociology*. Chapter XIII. Topics in Index, volume II: Evolution; Knowledge; Prevision.
- *Psychic factors*. Index: Cosmology; Knowledge.
- *Pure sociology*. Chapter XIX.

---

* Headley, *Problems of evolution*. Stuckenberg, *Sociology*, volume II. Spencer's *Synthetic philosophy*.

20

SOCIALIZATION OF ACHIEVEMENT

- 339. Human achievement.
- 340. Socialization.

- I. Social Regulation.–
- 341. Classification.
- 342. Development of social regulation.
- 343. Legal regulation.
- 344. The juridical state.
- 345. Importance of the state.

- II. Collective Achievement.—
- 346. Conquest of man by society.
- 347. Necessity of collective regulation.
- 348. Growth of collectivism.
- 349. Collectivism and individualism.

- III. Social Invention.—
- 350. Backwardness of social science.
- 351. Analysis of an invention.
- 352. Social invention defined.
- 353. "Attractive legislation."
- 354. Social distribution.
- 355. The social increment.

- IV. Social Appropriation.—
- 356. Knowledge as achievement.
- 357. Social heredity.
- 358. Duty of society.
- 359. The most useful knowledge.
- 360. Need of a scientific system.
- 361. The fundamental principle.
- 362. Hindrances to civilization.
- 363. Public education.
- 364. Socialization of education.

339. HUMAN ACHIEVEMENT.

It now becomes possible to show the full significance of human achievement as the practical conquest of nature and the subjection of all the materials and forces of nature to the control and service of man. If we look over the whole field of human achievement and social evolution, we shall see that by far the greater part of it has been accomplished through individual telesis. The initiative is almost exclusively individual, and the ends sought are egocentric in the widest sense, which must include the satisfaction of intellectual, moral, and even transcendental interests, as well as those so-called physical wants that have to do with the functions of nutrition and reproduction. The social consequences are unintended, and social evolution, however large the telic factor in it may be, is to all intents and purposes unconscious. In fact, the phrase "social evolution" should be restricted wholly to this aspect, and would exclude from it any and all effects that can be shown to have been consciously produced. Such effects do not belong to *evolution*. They are products of social or collective telesis.

340. SOCIALIZATION.

The word *socialization*, now much used by certain writers, is as yet undifferentiated and has been given various shades of meaning, though all more or less connected with the ideas conveyed by the word social. There has been, however, of late a tendency on the part of careful writers to give to the verb *socialize* and the noun *socialization* a special meaning susceptible to exact definition. Thus, to socialize an industry, for example, means that society takes it under its charge and conducts it for its benefit. Socialization in this sense is conscious, intentional, wished for, and welcomed telic action, not of the individual as such, but of those individuals into whose hands society, by whatever means, intrusts the conduct of its affairs. If we were to inquire what has actually been accomplished in this direction, at first glance it might seem that very little would be found to reward such a search. Society in its collective capacity makes few inventions or scientific discoveries, and it also, for the most part, leaves thepractical application of these to social ends, to private enterprise, and the keen business instincts of individuals, capitalists, and the various voluntary organizations devoted to the accumulation of wealth. For anything answering to our definition of socialization some preliminary explanation must first be made.

I. SOCIAL REGULATION

341. CLASSIFICATION.

The classification of the functions of society into regulative and operative* is fundamental. While human achievement constitutes one at least of the most important operative functions of society, social regulation is that which makes it possible, is in fact a *sine qua non* of it. The conception of achievement must therefore be widened, and made to include the regulative function itself. Furthermore we see that social regulation is no longer individual achievement but collective achievement, and thus the condition to all achievement is seen to be a product, not of individual, but of social, telesis. Let us look further into this.

342. DEVELOPMENT OF SOCIAL REGULATION.

It is generally recognized that many animals are only enabled to survive in the struggle for existence by dint of their gregarious or social habits. But none of these are able to migrate indefinitely and people the whole globe. This was the prerogative of man, but not until he had not only acquired the social habit, but had developed the regulative function. Whether this was matriarchal or patriarchal, royal or sacerdotal, it was regulative, and had the power to check all wayward tendencies inimical to the race. In fact, long before there was anything that deserves the name of government, there existed that group sentiment of the need of race preservation, which, call it religion, law, government, or whatever you

---

* Spencer, *The principles of sociology*, volume I, p. 459 (§ 210).

choose, actually regulated the horde, clan, or social group, and permitted the operative functions to go on. Not merely the sentiment, but also the corresponding social structure existed, capable of enforcing the requirements of the group and punishing all antisocial violations of the group will. This was chiefly in the nature of "ceremonial government," but it was effective and all that was needed at that stage of social development. This group sentiment was at least dimly conscious. It was certainly intentional, and the results accomplished were desired and welcomed. It was a product of the group mind and had all the essential qualities of a telic phenomenon. All this becomes increasingly true through all the early stages of society until we arrive at the later stage following upon the first race amalgamation due to conquest and subjugation.

343. LEGAL REGULATION.

The first step in the direction of the amalgamation of two races thus brought together was the gradual substitution of a form of general regulation for the crude special regulation of the military power, which ultimately became too onerous and annoying for the conquering race longer to tolerate. This took the form of primitive law and finally grew into a system of jurisprudence. It was the natural homologue at this stage of the primordial group regulation or ceremonial government, and no doubt many of the features of the former were retained as a basis for the latter. The power was still military, but the amount of energy that it was necessary to expend in enforcing general rules was far less than had been required to treat each case separately. Although primarily devoted to holding down the subject race, this system proved capable of being applied to other forms of regulation.

344. THE JURIDICAL STATE.

By far the most important consequence of this was the constitution of the state. By a perfectly natural evolutionary process society everywhere and always has worked out a regulative system. It was the necessity for general regulation to take the place of the wasteful and difficult special regulation incident to conquest that gave rise to a system of law, and it was because of the necessity for a social mechanism capable of enforcing law that the state grew up and took definite form.* It was shown that until the

---

* Bluntschli, *Theory of the state*. Willoughby, *Nature of the state*.

state was formed there could be no property. There is no such thing as right outside the state. If property cannot exist except under the protection of the state, there can of course be no such thing as capital. There can be no industry in the economic sense. There is no use accumulating; the surplus cannot be retained. Wealth is only possible under the state. The more we reflect upon it the clearer we see that while the state itself achieves little, it is the condition to nearly all achievement. The state was primarily the mediator between conflicting races. Immediately following the conquest the conquered race had no status. It was completely under the dominion of the conquering race. Under the state as soon as formed the conquered race acquired rights, and the members of the conquering race were assigned duties. The state thus becomes a powerful medium of social assimilation. The capable and meritorious of the subject race are given opportunity to exercise their faculties. The members of the community not belonging to the nobility or the priestly caste enter into business arrangements, become a mercantile or capitalist class, and control the finances of the people. These ultimately form the "third estate," which, on account of its activity and usefulness, is destined to increase in influence, as all history has shown. From it chiefly, too, are recruited all the inventors, artists, and finally the men of letters and of science. Even in Greece, the priesthood had ceased to supply the brain of the race. After the revival of learning in western Europe the nobility and the clergy fell almost entirely out of the ranks of those who were advancing the world. From that time social progress was intrusted to the middle class, the industrial and commercial class. Many eminent men of science, however, as De Candolle* shows, have been sons or descendants of Protestant clergymen. The Catholic clergy, having no descendants, contributed next to nothing.

345. IMPORTANCE OF THE STATE.

The state was therefore the most important step taken by man in the direction of controlling the social forces. The only possible object in doing this was the good of society as a whole. In part it was no doubt a sentiment of safety. The greatest good possible would be its salvation. But this ethical sentiment was something more than mere race ethics. There was mingled with it some idea of actual social benefit. This went still farther and embraced some vague conception of amelioration and of social progress. But nearly everybody, and especially the weaker, who also constitute

---

* *Histoire des sciences et des savants*, 2ᵉ éd., 1885.

much the larger classes of society, instinctively feel that the state means well for them and is always doing all that the influential classes will allow it to do for the benefit of society at large. The old maxim of the common law that "the king can do no wrong" merely reflects this truth. The state can only err. It cannot commit crime or do a wrong act. It has no malice or enmity, at least toward its own citizens. Their good is all it knows or aims at. We thus see that the state, though genetic in its origin, is telic in its method; that it has but one purpose, function, or mission, that of securing the welfare of society; that its mode of operation is that of preventing the antisocial actions of individuals; that in doing this it increases the freedom of human action so long as it is not antisocial; that the state is therefore essentially moral or ethical; that its own acts must necessarily be ethical; that being a natural product it must in a large sense be representative; that in point of fact it always is as good as society will permit it to be; that while thus far in the history of society the state has rarely performed acts that tend to advance mankind, it has been the condition to all achievement, making possible all the social, industrial, artistic, literary, and scientific activities that go on within the state and under its protection. There is no other human institution with which the state can be compared, and yet, in view of all this, it is the most important of all human institutions.

II. COLLECTIVE ACHIEVEMENT

346. CONQUEST OF MAN BY SOCIETY.

It has been said that the state achieves little. It would have been better to say that society in its collective capacity does not take a direct part in the operations that have been described under the head of achievement. The greater part of these belong to the general movement that has resulted in the conquest of nature. This was preeminently the work of the individual. In contradistinction to this, the achievements of society, if we can call them so, have related to a sort of conquest of man. This has consisted in gaining a greater and greater mastery of the social forces, primarily of the antisocial effects of the social forces in the interest of social safety. It has been maintained from the first that man is not by nature a social being in the full sense of that expression. He was from the beginning and has always remained an exceedingly quarrelsome and willful animal. It has been noted that predaceous animals are not usually gregarious. Man early became carnivorous, or rather omnivorous, and cannibalism is one of the phases through which he has everywhere passed. The enslavement of the captured, which gradually succeeded and ultimately supplanted cannibalism, was a matter of policy and the rational calculation of the greatest gain. Exploitation worked no diminution in the predatory and ferocious nature of man. His whole career has been marked by belligerency, internecine strife, and universal rapacity. The slow growth of sympathy and the moral sentiments somewhat mitigated this, but less than is commonly supposed, and but for the beneficent power of the state, seen by all to be in their interest, society would have been impossible. Wherever this is even temporarily and locally with drawn, a state of things invariably results which is not only intolerable, but utterly incompatible with any form of human achievement. It is well known that the state was very slow in taking the punishment of crime out of the hands of private individuals, and the great prevalence of family feuds was a consequence of this.*

347. NECESSITY OF COLLECTIVE REGULATION.

But for collective action in some form this would be the normal condition of human society, or rather of the human animal, for there could be no society. In other cases where collective regulation is weak and ineffective we have a general state of brigandage. Such has been the condition of southern Europe during long periods, and such is still the condition of parts of it. It was with such conditions as these that society had primarily to grapple, and no one can say that it has not upon the whole successfully accomplished its task. From the standpoint of achievement such action is to be compared to all that part of the conquest of nature which relates to the mastery of hostile forces. The averting of evil naturally precedes the extracting of good from the raw elements of nature, and we do not deny to the invention of clothing and shelter the title to be called achievements, while awarding that title to the invention of a mortar for grinding corn. Society has always been rent by conflicting interests, and the great problem that presented itself to collectivity was that, not of harmonizing, but of reconciling, such conflicting interests. The means were law and the state, and the result was the substitution of civil justice for natural justice. Society exists because the rational mind was capable of perceiving the mutual advantageousness of submitting to authority. The process is one of

---

* "The origin of criminal law," by William W. Billson, *Popular science monthly*, volume XVI, February, 1880, p. 438.

adaptation, and law, state, society, and civilization are products of creative synthesis.

348. GROWTH OF COLLECTIVISM.

The domain of purely social action was at first very limited. As all know, the punishment of crime against individuals was not made a duty of society until after the fall of the feudal régime. The only crimes considered by the state were crimes against the state. But this is by no means the only function now considered necessarily collective that was once not so considered. Revenues were extensively farmed out to private parties, and the finances of nations were largely in the hands of individual financiers. It is generally believed that collectivism at the present time is more pronounced on the Continent than it is in England, and in certain respects this is true, particularly with regard to railroads; but there seems to have been a greater amount of factory and other forms of moral legislation in England. In the United States there is no settled principle, and it is a question of majorities and political influence. But the less favored classes are beginning to learn the power of their ballots and are casting them in increasing numbers for collectivism. Australasian countries have taken the longest strides in this direction, but the movement is more marked in some parts than in others. New Zealand leads, but South Australia is not far behind.*

349. COLLECTIVISM AND INDIVIDUALISM.

The growth of collectivism has been from the first a struggle with the forces of individualism, which were unrestrained and supreme at the outset. It is making a gradual conquest of this field, just as the individual mind is conquering the field of physical nature, where the primitive forces were originally acting each for itself. The formation of the state supported by general laws was the first step taken by the collective mind. It checked rapacity, but furthered activity. It has never ceased to do so even in countries farthest advanced in collectivism. The freer the individual activity the more fully will this law act, and the whole movement may

---

* *Newest England. Notes of a democratic traveller in New Zealand, with some Australian comparisons*, by Henry Demarest Lloyd, New York, 1900. See also *Fabian tract*, No. 74, London, 1896. For illustrations in South Australia, see *Bulletin of the American academy of political and social science*, New Series, No. 10, Philadelphia, November 14, 1899; *Publications of the academy*, No. 264. pp. 7-10.

almost be described as the growth of individualism. Collectivism is not therefore the opposite of individualism. It is the failure to see this that makes English collectivism, and Anglo-Saxon collectivism in general, such a paradox. That it should prove that the great Anglo-Saxon race, the embodiment of the principle of free individual initiative, has made the longest strides in the direction of social initiative and social achievement, is the marvel of those who ascribe Anglo-Saxon supremacy to this individualistic attribute. These writers, among whom we find Frenchmen such as Demolins,* see only half of the truth. The whole truth is that Anglo-Saxon supremacy is due to the ability of that race to see and act upon the principle that while individual initiative can alone accomplish great results, it *must be free*, and that, under the influence of the normal and natural forces of society, and taking the whole of human nature into the account, it cannot be free unless the avenues for its activity be kept open by the power of society at large. Even the economists are beginning to see that "free competition" in business is a myth, unless it be protected from the universal tendency of all competition in nature speedily and surely to end in monopoly.

III. SOCIAL INVENTION.

350. BACKWARDNESS OF SOCIAL SCIENCE.

We have seen that society has already gone far beyond its primitive rôle of mere regulation, with a view to antagonizing the natural competitive influences that choke individual activity, exaggerate inequalities, and restrict liberty. It has achieved in much the same sense that the individual achieves, the chief difference being that it has had to deal with the far more complex and inscrutable social forces. We have now to note another parallel between individual achievement and social achievement. We saw in the last chapter that most individual achievement had been due to invention and scientific discovery in the domain of the physical forces. The parallel consists in the fact that social achievement consists in invention and discovery in the domain of the social forces. Until within a few years there has been no investigation in social science such as that which led to the scientific era in the other departments. The study of society is today where that of physics and chemistry was in the fifteenth century. There are

---

* *Anglo-Saxon superiority.* Translation, London, 1899.

still those in high seats of learning who deny that there are social laws in the scientific sense. Those whose business it is to deal practically and directly with the social forces, legislators, administrators, judges, have rarely ever opened a book on sociology. Is there, indeed, on sociology a book from which they could gather any useful principles to guide them in the performance of their duties? There certainly should be text-books plainly setting forth these practical principles, and the science should be taught to all who are at all likely ever to be called upon to perform any of these high functions.

351. ANALYSIS OF AN INVENTION.

If we carefully analyze an invention, we shall find that it consists first in recognizing a property or force, and secondly in making material adjustments calculated to cause that property or force to act in the manner desired by the inventor, presumably to his advantage. He recognizes the property or force as always operative. The only difference he makes in it is to cause it to act in a certain way different from the way in which it was acting before he made his adjustments. In dealing with animals, while they are often driven and compelled through fear to go where they are wanted, it is usually found easier and cheaper in energy expended to induce or attract them by appealing to some want that is easily satisfied, as by showing them a lump of salt.

352. SOCIAL INVENTION DEFINED.

Now the desires and wants of men constitute the forces of society. Social invention consists in making such adjustments as will induce men to act in the manner most advantageous to society. It is possible, as with animals, to drive them, to force them, to coerce and compel them; but it is far better, safer, and more economical, whenever possible, to secure the end through some form of persuasion or inducement. The law of parsimony, as has been pointed out, is a universal law, and can be implicitly relied upon. The social inventor has only to make sure what will constitute a greater gain or marginal advantage and to devise measures that will harmonize this with the social good, in order to secure with unerring certainty such a course of action on the part of all affected by the measures as will secure the end sought.

353. "ATTRACTIVE LEGISLATION."

If in the framing of human laws this principle were always carefully studied, it would soon be discovered that man is as easily managed by intelligence, as, in the last chapter, nature was shown to be. It would be found that mandatory and prohibitory, and indeed penal legislation generally is for the most part unnecessary. That form of legislation, always heretofore and still the predominant type, is very expensive in many ways, but chiefly in causing irritation and reaction, and thus weakening the authority of the state. The day will undoubtedly come when it will be held to be intolerable. It restricts human liberty, of course presumably by liberating other assumed innocent parties whose liberty had been abridged by the offender. But the contention is that only the most obdurate offenders require to have their liberty restricted, since they, too, have wants, and the social inventor should devise means by which such wants shall be spontaneously satisfied through wholly innocuous or even socially beneficial action. This is the principle called *attractive legislation*.* This principle has been acted upon by enlightened states, though only to a limited extent. Most of the examples relate to the collection of revenues, which, from its paramount necessity, is the field in which the keenest collective thinking has been done. Moral purposes are also sometimes secured through the application of this principle, as where commodities regarded as socially injurious are excluded by duties so high as to become prohibitive, or where businesses, such as lotteries, considered immoral, are forbidden to send advertisements through the mails.

354. SOCIAL DISTRIBUTION.

Special attention should be called to the fact that it is not so much production as distribution that calls for intelligent collective action. Science and invention under purely individual initiative have rendered production practically unlimited. It is limited only by the difficulties in the way of distribution. This is an exclusively social problem and can only be solved by social action. It is today the most important of all social problems, because its complete solution would accomplish nothing less than the abolition of poverty and want from society.

---

* See reference at end of chapter.

355. THE SOCIAL INCREMENT.

One by one are the great achievements of the individual intellect becoming socialized through collective action. The question is being seriously asked why society as a whole, and all mankind from the highest to the lowest, should not profit by the brilliant achievements of the élite of mankind. Inventors and scientific discoverers are generous, and if they could dictate the policy of the world, the results would be freely distributed and completely socialized. All they would ask would be a modest competency for themselves and their families and a decent legacy for their heirs. Many of them, however, never obtain even this. The results are taken up by the great economic world, as, indeed, they should be and must be, if they are ever realized, and society secures only so much as cannot be prevented from filtering through the economic sieve, which is often very fine. The great world movement of socialization is nothing else than the gradual recognition of this by society in its collective capacity, and the tardy, often fitful, inconsistent, and uneven, but yet sure and steady, determination ultimately to claim and to have its full share in the achievement of the human race.

IV. SOCIAL APPROPRIATION

356. KNOWLEDGE AS ACHIEVEMENT.

Human achievement, it will be remembered, consists essentially in knowledge—knowledge of what and of how, of things and of ways—which constitutes from the time of its acquisition a perpetual source of all material and spiritual blessings. The products perish, are consumed and enjoyed, but the knowledge insures their unlimited reproduction and multiplication. It is therefore of the utmost importance that this knowledge be preserved. What specially characterizes the historical races is that they have preserved the knowledge bequeathed to them by their predecessors and are constantly adding to it, making the result cumulative. But knowledge, the social germ-plasm, is incapable of hereditary transmission.

357. SOCIAL HEREDITARY.

Social heredity, or social continuity, consists in the social transmission of this plasm from generation to generation, and this is not a vital but a social process. It consists in planting knowledge into individual minds after they are born. No one is born with the least rudiment of it inherent in his mental constitution. Everyone must *acquire* every item of it during life. Cut off any portion of mankind from the main stream of thought and it loses at once all that has been bequeathed to the civilized world at such enormous cost. This knowledge, wrought by toil and struggle, by patience and thought, by genius and skill, and heaped up little by little through ages of time, is the Promethean fire that must never be allowed to go out.

358. DUTY OF SOCIETY.

The supreme duty of civilized man is therefore obviously to maintain the continuity of social knowledge. It is social self-preservation and is as imperative from the standpoint of society as is life from the standpoint of the individual. Density of population, the press, means of travel and intercommunication, and the needs of commerce and industry, suffice to insure the general economic and material results of achievement, and to make the knowledge of which it consists generally available in society. But this is not complete social appropriation. This cannot be attained until the mass of mankind shall possess not merely the benefits of achievement but the knowledge itself. This knowledge is confined to a mere handful. No one possesses it all, for it is so vast that the best informed can have only general acquaintance with it as a whole. But by a careful classification it is possible to reduce it to a scheme that shall practically place it within the power of the ordinary mind to grasp and hold it, if presented in the proper way.

359. THE MOST USEFUL KNOWLEDGE.

What knowledge is on the whole of most worth? In reply it may be said that knowledge should be both general and practical. A knowledge of generalized truth enables a person to grasp the principles that underlie natural phenomena, to exercise control over the forces of nature, and to expand the powers of his mind for still other and broader generalizations. Such truths moreover are easy of comprehension. They deal with phenomena and hence with the concrete. No higher intellectual Powers are required to grasp them than are regularly employed in ordinary life. Along practical lines, knowledge should primarily tend toward the preservation of life, the fulfillment of its duties, and the increase of happiness. All this involves a knowledge of the environment. It is a knowledge of things, not of the ways of doing things, which is technical knowledge. Such knowledge would enable a person more wisely to forefend his life and to satisfy higher standards of physical, intellectual, and social wants.

360. NEED OF A SCIENTIFIC SYSTEM.

Among the most highly civilized races the degree of intellectual capacity already possessed is ample for the establishment of an efficient social system. But, although the amount of useful knowledge in the possession of society is sufficient, if properly utilized, to elevate materially the standards of social life, yet the average person possesses so little of this knowledge that he is not able to develop himself to a high degree of efficiency. An essential condition for future social progress, therefore, is the perfectionment of a scientific system for the more thorough and equal distribution of the great mass of social knowledge already originated. In other words, the organization and distribution of knowledge should no longer be left to chance. Society should itself by a systematic and wise direction furnish all its members with that fund of social knowledge which will enable them to attain a far higher degree of individual advantage, and thereby to contribute to social progress and improvement. The general conduct of mankind is determined by the opinions men hold. If such opinions are based on progressive principles, progressive actions will surely result. Education, from the social standpoint, is a systematic process for the manufacture of correct opinions. If the knowledge imparted is of a high order of generality and practicality, the general intelligence of mankind would develop progressive ideas and show increased capacity. Intellect would be strengthened and views expanded. Nothing is so effective in developing brain capacity as constant contact with broad and practical truth.

361. THE FUNDAMENTAL PRINCIPLE.

In *Dynamic sociololgy** attention was called to the five kinds of education, viz., the education of experience, discipline, culture, research, and information, and this discussion need not be repeated. The fundamental principle involved in the system is that education should emphasize the contents of the mind, and should insist on the impartation of the most useful and important truths. The normal mind longs for such truth and readily grasps and appropriates it. Such studies never weary or tax the

---

* Vol. ii, pp. 559 *et seq.*

mind, which under the present system so often weakens under the pressure of meaningless puzzles and poorly coordinated information. The youthful mind easily comprehends scientific truth, and indeed craves it, but wearies of unnatural ideas presented by still more unnatural methods. The wise distribution of knowledge therefore should be, next to its regulative function, society's most important duty, the fulfillment of which should be intrusted to the state.

362. HINDRANCES TO CIVILIZATION.

Civilization is both collective and individual. It depends on knowledge. Very many inhabitants of civilized lands are still savage or barbarian, in that they have not assimilated the civilization about them. Most of our pauper and criminal classes are such. They have normal faculties and capacities, but have not felt the influence of higher civilization. Under present conditions they are a drag and a menace to social progress, but under a wiser theory of education the benefits of civilization would be extended to them also. In self-defense, if for no other reason, the state must ultimately recast its educational methods so as to extend the benefits of social knowledge to all classes alike. The great mass of humanity are fully capable of attaining a far higher degree of progress if afforded an opportunity, and much social capacity is not utilized because untrained. Greatness does not depend on intellectual power so much as on emotional force. Achievement is usually accomplished by persons of average intellectual capacity who have vigorous ambition, strong will, and perseverance. Men of greater intellect often lack aspiration and force. If society wisely educates the average intelligence, men of greater capacity will certainly not be neglected.*

363. PUBLIC EDUCATION.

The consciousness of the necessity for the social appropriation of human achievement has worked itself out into a variety of different systems of public *education*, but so defective have been the ideas of mankind as to what constitutes education, that the whole educational movement of the world is blindly working toward a confused ideal. While many individuals have founded institutions, and while the church has always conducted educational enterprises, it is after all the state, or society in its

---

* Crozier, *Civilization and progress.* Winship, *Jukes-Edwards.*

collective capacity, that has made the most important advances in this direction. Whatever it has done has been of a more practical character than the efforts of individuals or ecclesiastical bodies. While it cannot be said to have clearly seen that education should consist in the social appropriation of the knowledge that has civilized the world, it has taken long steps toward the realization of this truth. Above all it has acted more than any other interest on the assumption that education is for all, that it is a social need, that its benefits are proportional to its generality. It is now, in the leading countries of the world, extending it to the masses. In France, in Germany, and in the United States, it now reaches the great majority of the members of society. It is true that for the greater number of these the amount of instruction is very small. It does not include any knowledge at all except as incidentally acquired, but it usually puts into the hands of the learner the *tools* with which he may, if so disposed, obtain knowledge for himself. The so-called rudiments of an education are this and nothing more. Surely this must always be the first step, but unfortunately it is too often the only one. But in the great cities of the world many other steps are taken, such as the development of the American High School and the State University. These are freer and more democratic than endowed institutions, and, while a few are somewhat affected by political issues, they are never suspected of being organized for the purpose of creating public opinion on questions supposed to affect vested interests.

364. SOCIALIZATION OF EDUCATION.

In France and Germany nearly all higher education is now socialized, and the state regards public instruction as one of its great functions. England and other countries are slowly working up toward this ideal, and there can be little doubt that the twentieth century will see the complete socialization of education throughout the civilized world. This is as it should be, for it is society that is chiefly interested in the result. It is the recipient of the principal benefits. Moreover, education is the one kind of human enterprise that cannot be brought under the action of the "economic law of supply" and demand. It cannot be conducted on "business principles." There is no "demand" for education in the economic sense. The child knows nothing of its value, and the parent rarely desires it. Society is the only interest that can be said to demand it, and society must supply its own demand. Those who found educational institutions or promote educational enterprises, put themselves in the place of society and assume to speak and act for society, and not for any economic interest.

The action of society in inaugurating and carrying on a great educational system, however defective we may consider that system to be, is undoubtedly the most promising form thus far taken by collective achievement. It means much even now, but for the future it means nothing less than the complete social appropriation of that individual achievement which has civilized the world. It is the crowning act in the long list of acts that constitute the socialization of achievement.

REFERENCES TO WARD'S OTHER WORKS

- *Dynamic sociology*. Chapter XIV. Topics in Index, volume II. Attractive legislation; Crime; Dangerous classes; Education; Evil; Government; Inequality; Laws; Legislation; Society; Sociocracy; State.
- *Psychic factors*. Chapters XXXIV to XXXVIII. Topics in Index: Competition; Education; Evil; Government; Human; Legislation; Reform; Reformers; Society; Sociocracy.
- *Outlines of sociology*. Chapter XII.
- *Pure sociology*. Chapter XX.
- *Articles*. What shall the public schools teach? Broadening the way to success.

Copyright © 2024 by Alicia EDITIONS
Credits: www.canva.com; Alicia EDITIONS.
ISBN E-BOOK: 9782384553686
ISBN PAPERBACK: 9782384553693
ISBN HARDCOVER: 9782384553709
All rights reserved.
Some punctuation and typographical errors have been corrected.
No part of this book may be reproduced in any form or by any electronic or mechanical means, including information storage and retrieval systems, without written permission from the author, except for the use of brief quotations in a book review.

www.ingramcontent.com/pod-product-compliance
Lightning Source LLC
LaVergne TN
LVHW032008070526
838202LV00059B/6351